*Watford Forever*

or so Watford fans who caught a specially chartered coach to the game headed north in a mood of cautious optimism. 'Frankly, we'd become so used to losing, it had become par for the course,' one of them would recall nearly half a century later. 'We'd reached the stage where we went in spite of the football and not because of it. Even so, I can remember thinking, Christ, it's only Darlington; we've got to stand a chance against them.'

It had been like this for as long as any of them could remember. On the rare occasions when Watford FC was mentioned in the national press, it was invariably accompanied by the word 'languishing'. Six years earlier, Watford had caused a good deal of surprise, not least among their own fans, by winning promotion from Division Three to Division Two. But it wasn't long before they fell into their old languishing ways. Relegated back to Division Three in 1972, Watford only lasted three seasons before sinking into the depths of Division Four.

Recently, both the club's doctors had resigned, complaining that they hadn't been paid for several months. As a result, any Watford players who needed medical treatment now had to go to their local surgery and wait in line along with everyone else. Meanwhile the club's directors, kept in the dark about Watford's finances and increasingly alarmed by what little information they could unearth, came and went with bewildering speed.

One of them left saying simply, 'Things are a little odd here.'

As Watford fans took their places on the visitors' stand – a set of uncovered concrete steps overlooking a wind-blasted patch of open ground – they could at least console themselves with the fact that the facilities at Darlington were even more rundown than their own. On three occasions in the last eight years, Darlington's financial situation was so dire that they had had to apply to the Football League for readmission.

In the early 1970s, the club had set a Football League record by being beaten 7-0 in two successive games. Shortly afterwards, the broadcaster David Frost had come to the town to make a

# I.

On the last Saturday of August 1975, Watford Football Club travelled to County Durham for what their manager, Mike Keen, described as a 'must-win game' against their Fourth Division rivals, Darlington. Despite being relegated from the Third to the Fourth Division three months earlier, Watford had begun the new season in bullish mood. 'It is the firm resolve of this club to prolong our stay in Division Four no longer than necessary,' the Watford chairman had declared confidently. 'We can assure all our supporters that no effort will be too much towards the target of immediate promotion.'

To prepare them for the challenge ahead, the players had been put through an intense fitness regime. Mike Keen himself was brimming with optimism. 'The pre-season training has gone extremely well and our players are as fit as any in the league,' he told the club's supporters.

But this fighting talk had had little, if any, effect on the players. Their first game of the season, a friendly against Weymouth, had ended in a 3–1 defeat. 'We were caught with our trousers down,' admitted Keen afterwards. By way of an excuse, he cited the very bad traffic they had encountered on their journey to the South Coast. 'We had to do without lunch, so we all had a bar of chocolate and a bottle of pop before the game.'

Keen also sought to put as much of a gloss as he could on the result. 'It may even be a bit of a blessing in disguise, as it has given us a chance to put a few things right.'

Yet these hopes too had quickly crumbled: Watford lost their next three league games and failed to score a single goal. However disappointing their start to the season had been, the eighty

# PART ONE

an opportunity he grasped with both hands and ran as hard as he could, brushing aside extraordinary obstacles along the way. And in Elton's case, it not only sent him on what he described as the greatest adventure he had ever been on, it did something even more dramatic. As he said when Graham died at the beginning of 2017, it not only transformed his life, it saved it.

John Preston

triumphs and apparently insoluble social problems suddenly don't seem so insoluble after all. But in the case of Watford, there's rather more to it than that.

One of the things that most appealed to me when I began to research the book is that the story of Watford FC may be a fairy tale, but it's a fairy tale set against a starkly realistic backdrop. As Elton well remembers, England in the late 1970s was a grim and forbidding place. For a start, racism was endemic. Unusually, Watford had two black players – back then, there were very few black football players in the UK. Both of them were regularly subjected to racist taunts from opposition fans, often accompanied by monkey-noises and volleys of bananas.

It was also an extremely brutal place with football matches being particular crucibles of violence. In a bid to keep rival fans from tearing one another to pieces, a number of clubs – although never Watford – put them into what amounted to enormous cages where they would snarl and rage and bay for blood. And if all this wasn't bad enough, homophobia was rife. Not only was Elton a pop star, he was a gay pop star. As a result, he too was on the receiving end of all manner of chants to do with his sexual predilections – something he tolerated with remarkable good humour.

While this is a story about football, I hope that it's a story that goes far beyond football. In essence, it's a story about finding hope in the most unlikely places, and that, surely, is something that anyone can relate to. After all, there is no shortage of Watfords in the US – small towns that seem somehow to have fallen off the map, where unemployment has shot off the scale and people struggle to find something to live for.

At its heart is a very human story about a pair of polar opposites who grew to love and depend on one another – and what that love can achieve. In Graham's case his friendship with Elton gave him an opportunity he might never have had elsewhere –

lives, and with this unlikely pair at the helm, Watford did something that no one could have predicted: they began to rise out of the depths.

Once they'd started there was no stopping them. As Watford started their remarkable ascent, so something else happened – something equally unpredictable. The town began to get its heart back. Both Elton and Graham believed passionately that a town's morale was closely tied to the fortunes of its football team. If the team did badly, everyone drifted about in a gloomy haze, but if it did well their mood was transformed. Sure enough, for the first time in history people went around actually boasting of coming from Watford. In the past, they'd tended to look shifty and hurriedly change the subject.

Not so long ago, American audiences were unlikely to thrill to the drama of a lowly English football club battling insurmountable odds. But all that too has changed. It's not just *Welcome to Wrexham* that has transformed people's attitudes. Before Ryan Reynolds and Rob McElhenney had their own wacky idea of buying non-league Wrexham, Jason Sudeikis, the former *Saturday Night Live* comedian, had pitched an idea to Apple TV which must have seemed just as eccentric: a comedy/drama series about an American football coach being taken on by another lowly British club – the fictional AFC Richmond.

But Sudeikis too would soon prove the doubters wrong. The first series of *Ted Lasso*, which debuted during the pandemic in 2020, was nominated for twenty Emmys – it won eight – and became the most-watched series on Apple TV. So influential was it that President Biden invited the cast to the White House to promote mental health and well-being. By the time the third season went out, every other American you encountered seemed to be discussing the personalities of the *Ted Lasso* cast and speculating as to what would happen in the next episode.

What these three stories have in common is that they are all fairy tales – a throwback to a more innocent age in which virtue the ultimate rich man's folly. Even those few people who were inclined to be sympathetic conceded privately that it was bound to end in tears. Except it didn't quite work out that way. Just as Elton's first visit to Watford had transformed his childhood, so his time as the club's owner would come to transform his adult life.

Watford's location, Vicarage Road, may have been a tumble-down wreck where mushrooms were reputed to grow on the bathroom walls and where a large colony of rats had taken up residence beneath the main stand, but it proved to be the one place in the world where he could go and feel safe from the pressures of stardom. Inside Vicarage Road, no one made a fuss of him, or bowed and scraped; they just treated him like another member of staff. Simply being there was a link back to his child-hood, back to how life had been before Reggie Dwight turned into Elton John.

Looking back, it's easy to forget how quickly Elton became hugely, universally famous. In just two years he went from play-ing in pubs to doing massive stadium tours in the States. With fame – and success – came all manner of demons, principally a drink and drug habit that soon spiralled out of control. But however chaotic his life became, whenever Elton was on tour, in whichever far-flung corner of the world he found himself, he would make sure that a lifeline kept him tethered back to Wat-ford. In those long-ago, pre-internet days, this involved him sitting in his hotel suite with a phone pressed to his ear when-ever a match was going on.

One of the first things Elton did when he bought the club was to install Graham Taylor as manager. Roughly the same age as Elton – in his early thirties – with jug-ears, neatly parted hair and no interest whatsoever in rock music, Graham was Elton's polar opposite, a man as traditional as Elton was uncon-ventional. Yet the two of them soon formed an indissoluble bond. Both would have an enormous effect on each other's

# Introduction to the American Edition

Long before Ryan Reynolds and Rob McElhenney came to Wrexham, Elton John came to Watford. He was just six years old when his father, Stanley, first took him in 1953 to see Watford play and it was an afternoon that changed his life. Born and brought up in Pinner, six miles away, Watford were his local team and Stanley had long been an avid fan.

Time and time again when Elton and I started talking about the book, the conversation would swing back to that first visit – to how much it had meant and how it had changed him. How it was his first experience of being part of a live audience, of seeing how the crowd's mood ebbed and flowed with the passage of play and how normally buttoned-up, stiff-backed men like Stanley suddenly started roaring their heads off.

More than twenty years later, in 1976, Elton did something that no celebrity had ever done before – he bought the club. This was despite the fact that everyone from his manager on down begged him not to. Watford, they said, quite truthfully, were a bunch of complete no-hopers, forever anchored to the bottom of the Football League – a team made up of flops and has-beens, whose kit was full of holes and whose assistant scout was ninety-five years old. If the football club was in a wretched state, the town was equally run-down. Its workforce had been decimated by factory closures, its heart torn out by idiotic town-planning and its identity subsumed in London's never-ending sprawl.

In the past, English football clubs had tended to be owned by local businessmen who had as little to do with the club's supporters as possible. As far as the English press were concerned, for a rock star to buy a soccer club – or as we say, a football club – was

'But is this story believable? Ah, it all depends on whether you *want* to believe it.'

J. L. Carr, *How Steeple Sinderby Wanderers Won the FA Cup*

In memory of Oli Phillips and Eddie Plumley

First published in Great Britian in 2023 by Viking, an imprint of Penguin Random House

Copyright © 2023 by WAB Global Limited

For information about permission to reproduce selections from this book,
write to Permissions, Liveright Publishing Corporation, a division of
W. W. Norton & Company, Inc., 500 Fifth Avenue, New York, NY 10110

For information about special discounts for bulk purchases, please contact
W. W. Norton Special Sales at specialsales@wwnorton.com or 800-233-4830

Manufacturing by Lakeside Book Company
Production manager: Anna Oler

ISBN 978-1-324-09547-7

Liveright Publishing Corporation
500 Fifth Avenue, New York, N.Y. 10110
www.wwnorton.com

W. W. Norton & Company Ltd.
15 Carlisle Street, London W1D 3BS

1 2 3 4 5 6 7 8 9 0

# Watford Forever

How Graham Taylor and
Elton John Saved a Football Club,
a Town and Each Other

## JOHN PRESTON
## IN COLLABORATION
## WITH ELTON JOHN

**Liveright Publishing Corporation**

*A Division of W. W. Norton & Company*
*Independent Publishers Since 1923*

television programme about the club. What he found astonished him. Talking to Darlington's owner, Frost learned that there were only eight fully paid-up members of the supporters' club. That season alone, Darlington got through five different managers. Asked why he retained such a passionate allegiance to the club, one of their supporters cheerfully admitted to being 'totally blind'.

Although the 1975/76 football season had been going for only a month, it had already been marred by some of the worst outbreaks of hooliganism ever seen in the UK. In Wolverhampton, hundreds of Manchester United fans had gone on the rampage leaving fourteen people with stab wounds. On the same day that Watford played Darlington, Liverpool fans travelling back from a game at Leicester set fire to the train causing £70,000 worth of damage – an editorial in *The Times* referred to them as 'marauding fiends'. With unemployment exceeding the one million mark, there were fears that this upsurge in hooliganism might presage more widespread outbreaks of civic unrest.

Once, Watford had had a hooligan problem of its own. Supporters of the club's near neighbours and oldest rivals, Luton Town, were always assured of an especially robust welcome whenever they visited Watford's ground, Vicarage Road. But those days were long gone. Now the fans were in no mood to cause any trouble; they were far too dispirited for that.

On a hot muggy afternoon punctuated by rumbles of thunder, Watford's familiar failings soon revealed themselves. Among their players, the club's centre-forward, 22-year-old Ross Jenkins, was singled out for particular scorn. Six feet four inches tall, with legs that, as one commentator put it, looked as if they had started life on a baby giraffe, Jenkins had been hailed as an exciting new discovery when he'd joined Watford two years earlier.

Yet that too now seemed an age away. After a promising start, the goals had dried up, and so had the fans' patience. Now Jenkins was regularly referred to as one of the worst signings in the club's history. His ball control was so erratic that it was said that he couldn't trap a sack of wet cement if it landed at his feet. As for his heading, this was reckoned to be even worse – fans joked that he could be outjumped by any one of Snow White's seven dwarves.

On the few occasions when Jenkins managed to score, Watford supporters had taken to breaking into ironic applause. Before the start of the season, another Fourth Division club, Huddersfield, had offered Watford £12,000 for him. Fans implored him to accept the offer, but Jenkins had opted to stay put – a decision that prompted further gloom among the Watford faithful.

By half-time, Watford were already a goal down. During the break, Keen sent the substitute, Keith Mercer, over to the club's tiny band of supporters to try to whip up some enthusiasm. 'Mercer's request was successful, but only for a time,' noted the *Watford Observer*'s football correspondent in his match report: 'As one of the fans explained, "We kept on chanting for Watford until we were surrounded by Darlington fans. After that we had to stop or get our heads kicked in.'"

In the second half, Watford seldom ventured into Darlington's territory. Whenever they did so, a collective panic seemed to come over them, as if they felt they had no business being there. Hurriedly, they scuttled back into their own half. At full-time the score remained 1-0.

As they trudged off the pitch, the Watford players were jeered by both the Darlington supporters and their own. As far as the Darlington directors were concerned, the catcalls of the Watford fans had an oddly melodic ring to them. 'To be honest, it made a change to see someone else getting some stick,' one of them said.

For Ross Jenkins, the defeat confirmed all of his worst suspicions: 'I remember thinking that we were at the bottom of a deep, dark ditch and I couldn't see any way out.'

On the substitutes' bench that day was an eighteen-year-old

striker called Luther Blissett, who had joined Watford straight from school as an apprentice and had just turned professional. Blissett was feeling every bit as downcast as Jenkins. 'There was no doubt that morale was terrible, and that obviously affected players' confidence. I think the worst of it was that no one seemed to have a clue as to how we were ever going to get out of this situation.'

After the game was over, Mike Keen refused to comment. 'I don't really want to say anything as I might say the wrong thing,' he told waiting journalists. When one of them suggested that nothing could be 'the wrong thing' after a performance like that, Keen still refused to be drawn.

To save money, the Watford players would often travel to away games by train rather than by coach. The 200-mile journey back down south passed in sombre silence, with the players quietly playing cards, or gazing glumly out of the window.

Afterwards the club's directors made no attempt to gloss over the gravity of the situation: 'Let there be no doubt in anyone's mind that the board, manager and players feel as shattered as all our supporters over our dreadful start to this season's league programme,' they announced.

No one could argue with this. Then, as now, there were ninety-two clubs in the English Football League, spread across four divisions. Bottom on goal average, Watford were lying in ninety-second place.

# 2.

One Saturday afternoon in the autumn of 1953, a six-year-old boy from Pinner in Middlesex called Reginald Dwight accompanied his father to watch Watford FC play at Vicarage Road. From the semi-detached house at 55 Pinner Hill Road that they shared with the boy's maternal grandmother, the two of them walked the half-mile to the tube station at Northwood Hills, then caught a Metropolitan Line train to Watford four stops away.

It was one of the first outings they had ever been on together and Reginald – always known as Reggie – had no idea what to expect. An only child, he had been terrified of his father for as long as he could remember. He was frightened of his mother too, but that was different. Whereas Sheila Dwight could be warm and vivacious one moment, then erupt with volcanic intensity the next, Stanley Dwight was a remote, staid figure – as solemn as he was judgemental.

A squadron leader in the RAF, Stanley was often away from home – when Reggie was two, his father went to Iraq for two years. With Stanley's return, the atmosphere in the house changed. Previously, Reggie had had only his mother and grandmother for company. Now, there was an unfamiliar face sitting at the kitchen table. Any sense of family harmony disappeared overnight. As far as Reggie was concerned, it was as if the air was crackling with tension.

Constantly, Stanley and Sheila were tearing into one another. Meanwhile, Reggie remained stuck in the middle, trying to make himself as inconspicuous as possible and never managing to shake a nagging sense of guilt that in some way he was responsible for his parents' marital strife.

But on that afternoon, something unexpected happened. Emerging from the tube station, Stanley reached down and took his son's hand. As he did so, Reggie had a sensation that he'd hardly ever had before, a feeling of closeness to his father; a sense that perhaps he might not be such a disappointment to him after all. And it wasn't long before Reggie felt something else that he had never experienced before – a feeling of pride that Stanley was allowing him to share in one of his great passions: Watford Football Club.

Walking along, the two of them were surrounded by a growing band of people. Many of them had blue and white scarves wrapped round their necks. All were heading in the same direction. When they reached the ground, Stanley paid threepence for a programme for his son, then they took their places on a small asphalt-covered mound at the Rookery End of the ground known as 'The Bend'. Although Reggie had often been to the cinema with his mother, this was the first live entertainment he had ever seen. While the cinema was quiet, with everyone sitting silently in the darkness, this was completely different. The ground was pulsating with noise, with people chanting and whooping away.

At home, Reggie would never have dreamed of raising his voice – 'I was far too shy for that.' But here he could shout and boo and holler as much as he wanted. Never before had he felt a sense of being part of a crowd, of being swept up in a tide of emotion. Of just belonging.

Looking around, with his father standing beside him, he thought it was the most exciting, the most glamorous thing he had ever seen. Later on, he would come to realize that it wasn't really glamorous at all. In reality, Vicarage Road was a crumbling ruin with two rickety stands and men's toilets so dark and dingy that mushrooms were reputed to grow on the walls. There was no women's toilet in the entire ground. The seating consisted of rows of bare wooden benches, all polished to a dull sheen by generations of working-men's bottoms. Only one of the stands had a roof – not that it offered much in the way of shelter; the corrugated-iron roof was pitted with holes. Nor was the ground heaving with people; attendances had fallen to the point where only eight or nine thousand diehards bothered to turn up.

Yet somehow none of that mattered. The first impression was what counted – and this first impression was so strong that it never left him. The moment the players ran onto the pitch, Reggie was even more smitten. To him, these men were titans; awesome, majestic figures with their baggy shorts and their brilliantined hair. Gazing at them, he had the same sensation as he'd had when looking up at Hollywood stars on the big screen; a feeling that these were completely different creatures from anyone that he had ever met in Pinner. What's more, they seemed to live in a completely different dimension from his own – a dimension he could never hope to inhabit.

When the game got under way, another impression struck him just as forcefully. 'I was bowled over by how passionate, how determined, the players were. How they gave it their all. These guys may have been stuck in the lower reaches of Division Three (South) and earning just a few pounds more than they would have been getting on unemployment benefit, but that didn't make the slightest difference. They still played as if their lives depended on it.'

But what made the biggest impression of all was the change in his father. At home, Stanley seemed to be sunk in gloom and for-ever on the verge of issuing another reprimand. Yet here he was roaring and chanting away with everyone else. This was such an extraordinary transformation that Reggie wasn't sure what to make of it. For a moment, he even found himself wondering if this new roaring, chanting Stanley might be showing more of his true character than he ever did at home.

And this was not the only difference he witnessed that after-noon. He also saw another, equally unfamiliar, side to his father – a more demonstrative, tender side. As it was a cold afternoon,

Stanley wrapped his son in his RAF greatcoat to keep him warm and at half-time he bought him a mug of Bovril. 'I can remember that when I became confused by what was happening on the pitch, he patiently explained the offside rule.'

In years to come, Reggie would look back on that Saturday afternoon as the day when his life changed for ever. From that moment, he would be as passionate about football – and Watford Football Club – as his father. Throughout his boyhood, whenever there was a home fixture, the two of them would go off to Vicarage Road. And every time they went, Stanley would fish into his pocket for some pennies and buy his son a programme.

'We always stood in the same place – we didn't have enough money to sit down. But that was fine; I wanted to be right in the thick of things. And I don't think we ever talked to anyone all the times we went, but that didn't matter either; it was the 1950s – no one talked to anyone. After the game was over, I would just bounce all the way home, I felt so happy. It didn't even worry me that much if we lost.'

The moment they came back to Pinner Hills Road, Reggie would run up the stairs to his bedroom where his new programme would join his growing collection – all of them in pristine condition and meticulously filed away. No matter how badly Watford did, no matter how many disbelieving looks people gave him when he told them which team he supported, Reggie never questioned his loyalty. Ever since he could remember, he had always had a natural affinity with the underdog – for the no-hopers, the laughing stocks, the perennial underachievers.

Being a Watford fan may have involved swallowing an almost weekly dose of disappointment, but to switch allegiance would have been unthinkable. They were Reggie's team, just as they were his father's team. It was as simple as that.

# 3.

Shortly after the end of the Second World War, full-page advertisements started appearing in local newspapers across England. They showed a photograph of what looked like an enormous tin can surrounded by hollyhocks. Beneath it was a block of text randomly spattered with capital letters which read:

> The ideal house chosen exclusively by the government for RURAL housing has now been made AVAILABLE for EVERY TYPE OF HOUSING SCHEME. What does this mean? Simply that you sir – and yes, you madam – can have an Airey Prefabricated Home with all its spaciousness, its extra warmth, its attractive appearance and its convenience. To those thousands needing a home of their own, the Airey Prefabricated House provides EVERYTHING THEY DESIRE!

Graham Taylor's family home in Scunthorpe was a pre-fab, one of 150,000 rapidly constructed from sheets of corrugated steel – often panels from decommissioned aircraft factories – to tackle the country's post-war housing crisis. The Taylors had moved to Scunthorpe from Worksop in Nottinghamshire when the second of their three children, Graham, was three. His mother, Dorothy, was a postwoman who would wake at four o'clock every morning, set off on her round and be back in time to cook the family breakfast. His father, Tom, worked as the sports editor of the *Scunthorpe Evening Telegraph*, where he wrote a weekly column under the pseudonym 'The Poacher'.

As a child, Graham accompanied his father to all Scunthorpe United's home fixtures. The two of them would sit on the narrow benches in the press box. Before the game started, Graham's father always gave his son a stopwatch to hold. The moment the whistle blew, Graham pressed the button on top of the watch; he then made a note of what time anything significant happened.

On the other side of a plywood panel sat the football correspondent of the town's other paper, the *Scunthorpe Star*. Every so often, a little hatch in the panel flew open and the man from the *Star* would ask his father when a goal had been scored. After consulting his son, Tom Taylor passed on the information and then the hatch would slam shut again.

All his life, Graham would remember the sound the wooden hatch made as it slammed shut – a sharp thwack – and the smell in the Scunthorpe United dressing room – a liniment called Wintergreen, so strong it was used to treat arthritic horses. And he never forgot the pride he felt when he looked at his father's match reports in the *Scunthorpe Evening Telegraph* and saw the times of the goals that he had recorded.

There was something else that affected him just as deeply. As he grew older, Graham saw how closely the success of the local team influenced the mood of the town. If the team did well, everyone seemed to be brighter and more full of beans. But if it did badly, their spirits sank back down again.

From his father Graham inherited a love of Shakespeare and romantic poetry, from his mother a strict work ethic, and from both his parents a sense of the importance of being a fully fledged participant in life, not just an onlooker dawdling about on the sidelines. A clever boy, he passed his eleven-plus and went to Scunthorpe Grammar School. The school was near the Scunthorpe United ground, and sometimes during a lesson the players would run past, recognize him as the 'Poacher's Boy' and give a wave. This always sent his own spirits soaring.

As well as being clever, Graham Taylor was sporty, self-assured, hot-tempered, ferociously competitive and the possessor of a wide-open guileless grin. When he was thirteen, he asked out a fellow pupil at Scunthorpe Grammar called Rita Cowling despite the fact that she was three years older than him. While Rita may have made less of an immediate impression on people – she was as quiet as Graham was talkative – she was just as strong a personality: steady, practical and not remotely bothered by what anyone thought of her.

They met during a school play, 'The Life and Death of Tom Thumb', in which Graham was playing the role of Lord Grizzle, and Rita was doing the make-up. Turning round in his chair, Graham saw a slim brunette in a yellow cardigan applying blusher to the boy sitting next to him. The next evening, he made sure he turned up early and bagged the next-door chair. 'From that moment, I was convinced that Rita would be the girl I would marry.'

What struck Rita most about Graham was his confidence; it seemed to come off him in waves. So much so that she never even thought about the age gap between them. 'The more I got to know him, the more I saw he was a natural leader,' she remembered. 'He was very single-minded, very ambitious and although he was young he had this air of authority. I don't think he necessarily knew that he'd got it, not to begin with anyway, but he did. You could tell from the way people behaved around him.'

At school, Graham was made a prefect when he was only sixteen. By then, he'd already decided that he wanted to be a professional footballer. No one from Scunthorpe Grammar School had ever become one – something that was a source of considerable pride to the headmaster. As soon as he got wind of Graham's plans, the headmaster called him in. 'He didn't invite me to sit down, so I knew it was something serious, and I was trying to think what it was I had done wrong.'

What followed was the biggest dressing-down that Graham had ever had. 'It was the quiet anger and disappointment that rose and swelled as he spoke that sticks with me to this day,' he would recall.

If Graham persisted with such a half-witted idea, the headmaster told him, then he would bring disgrace on the school as well as shame on his family. But that wasn't all. He would also be joining a lumpen underclass of people whose chances of making anything of themselves, let alone earning a decent living, were so slim as to be almost non-existent.

# 4.

Although Stanley Dwight may have cast off his normal air of gloom whenever he and Reggie went to see Watford play, as soon as they came home the dark curtain descended once more. 'Immediately, we would be back to where we'd been before and it was as if our going to the football had never happened.'

Why did things have to be like this, Reggie would wonder. Why couldn't they go back to the way things used to be – before Stanley had come back and spoiled everything?

The older he grew, the more explosive the arguments became between his parents, and the more convinced he became that it was all his fault. If only he wasn't around, then his parents would be happy and contented. 'A lot of the arguments seemed to be about me and that made me feel that I was responsible. I also felt caught between the two of them like piggy-in-the-middle.'

The one place where Reggie could go and hide was his bedroom. At the back of the house in Pinner Hill Road, overlooking the garden where his grandmother kept a neatly tended vegetable patch, his bedroom became his sanctuary. In contrast to the discord and chaos in the rest of the house, here everything was immaculately ordered, everything had its place: his Watford programmes, his books, his Dinky cars that always looked as if they had emerged straight from the box and never had a scratch on them. All of them stood neatly ranged in rows on his bedroom shelves. 'Everything had its proper place. That felt very important to me; I found it very comforting.'

There, Reggie would lie on his bed and read his comics – kept in equally immaculate condition as everything else. His favourite strip of all was Roy of the Rovers which appeared in *The Tiger* and recounted the adventures of Roy Race, star striker of Melchester Rovers. For close on forty years, Roy Race terrorized defences with his lightning runs, once surviving an assassination attempt by a disgruntled rival – by an odd coincidence, his would-be assassin was called Elton – and only hobbled reluctantly into retirement after losing his left foot in a helicopter crash.

However much solace this brought him, Reggie couldn't keep the outside world completely at bay. Never sure of himself, he became increasingly timid, shrinking into his shell, above all wanting to be approved of. For hours on end, he would stay in his room, gazing at his Watford programmes, even investing them with emotions and different personalities. If he felt they had been upset by the shouting downstairs, he would talk to them and try to soothe their feelings.

One of the few things Sheila and Stanley had in common was a taste for music. As a young man, Stanley had played the trumpet in several local jazz bands, while Sheila was an avid record collector. The moment she got her wages on a Friday afternoon – she worked as a milkmaid for United Dairies – she would rush off to the nearest record shop and buy herself a new 78.

It soon became clear that Reggie too had music in his blood. At the age of just three, he sat at the family's upright piano and – according to family legend – his fingers had rippled across the keyboard with astonishing dexterity. Stanley took great satisfaction in his son's musical prowess. If he walked past when Reggie was playing the piano, he would always give him an encouraging pat on the back. The trouble was these seemed to be almost the only times when he did approve of him.

Sheila, like Stanley, was mostly fond of big band music. But one Friday in 1956, when Reggie was nine, she came home with a record that was unlike anything she had bought before. A record which she had heard on the radio and adored, but which Stanley thought was an excruciating racket.

The record was called 'Heartbreak Hotel' by Elvis Presley and the moment Reggie heard it, he felt that a door had been thrown open – a door into a future that he instinctively knew would be very different from the world he was growing up in. A less stuffy, less narrow-minded world in which conventions were no longer set in stone and where – just conceivably – all the things that held him back might loosen their grip.

Like his mother, Reggie began to collect records, saving up his pocket money each week then rushing down to the record shop. Every time he bought a new record, he would take it up to his bedroom and write down the details on the label in a spiral note-book. Not just the titles of the A and B sides, but also the names of the songwriter, the publisher and the producer. Then, as soon as he had finished, he would memorize everything he'd written, as if he was somehow frightened that it might all be taken away, leaving him more marooned than ever.

The two great passions of Reggie's life – football and music – had now taken root. As he would discover in years to come, they had a good deal in common. Both were mainly working-class professions, whose members had to come up through the ranks and whose fortunes rose or fell depending on how the public reacted to them. And together, they would provide the only two unshakeable pillars in Reggie's life. 'Sport and music kept me alive, no doubt about that.'

Although he now had a new obsession in his life, the old one burned just as brightly. While Stanley had never played football seriously, the game still featured prominently in the Dwight family: two of Stanley's nephews were professional footballers – Roy Dwight and John Ashen. At one stage, they both played for Fulham. Every so often, one or other of them used to drop round to 55 Pinner Hill Road.

Like the players Reggie saw at Watford, his cousins too were impossibly glamorous figures. Instantly, they became his heroes, their photographs pinned to the noticeboard on his bedroom wall. John Ashen, in particular, was very keen on American cars, and always liked to show off his latest purchase. Whenever this happened, a wildly excited Reggie would be taken out to the street where he would gaze awestruck at what looked just like a space rocket that had landed in Pinner Hill Road.

Yet such respites were few and far between. At home, Reggie lived increasingly in his own fantasy world. 'It was the 1950s. There was no television, at least not in our household. You had to make your own make-believe.'

Every night, after he had gone to bed, he listened to the latest releases on Radio Luxembourg. With the volume turned down low, he would twist his transistor radio about beneath the blankets, trying to improve the reception, catching snatches of melody between the gales of static. As he did so, Reggie would let his imagination run wild, rushing off to places it would never have dreamed of going during the day. 'Basically, my whole world was make-believe. In between the records, I would pretend to be a disc-jockey and then, as soon as a new song came on, I would pretend to be the singer. Pretence was a wonderful thing for me; in a lot of respects it saved me.'

Sometimes when he was lying in bed, Reggie would fantasize about Watford doing something gloriously unpredictable. Something that might have stepped straight from the pages of *The Tiger* – such as them coming from nowhere and thrashing one of the top teams in the country. Perhaps even reaching the FA Cup Final, as Roy Dwight would go on to do a few years later. But such moments never lasted long. Soon the fantasy faded, reality swept in and with a sharp bump he fell back down to earth.

# 5.

His headmaster's warning about what fate lay in store may have given Graham pause for thought, but it didn't deter him for long. Leaving school a year early, he joined Third Division Grimsby Town as an apprentice. The first time he walked into the Grimsby dressing room, he was deeply shocked by the players' language – far cruder than anything he had encountered before. Nor did he much care for the way the senior players waved their willies about with a proprietorial flourish in the communal bath.

Despite this, he was undeterred; if he had to make one or two adjustments to his behaviour in order to fit in, then so be it. Having started out as a centre-forward, after a few months Graham was moved – much to his annoyance – to full-back. Yet slowly he began to see that this might not be such a bad thing after all. 'Playing at the back gave me a completely different impression of the game,' he recalled. 'Although I didn't realize it at the time, I was learning not just about my own job in the team, but also about what everyone else should be doing.'

On 14 September 1963 – the day before his nineteenth birthday – Graham made his Football League debut. At the end of his first season, when he was offered a new contract, he was so relieved that he burst into tears. Three months later, he and Rita got married. At just twenty-two, he became captain of Grimsby.

While Graham may have been a natural leader, his appointment hardly marked a dramatic transformation in Grimsby's fortunes. After the team had lost one match 7-1, the manager called them in the next day – a Sunday – for a special training session. The fact that they had lost to perennial no-hopers Watford made the defeat even more galling.

The players were told to run round the pitch for forty-five minutes. They were then allowed a piece of orange each before running round the pitch, in the opposite direction, for the next forty-five minutes. When someone asked what was going on, the manager replied, 'If you bastards won't run for me for ninety minutes on a Saturday, then you'll fucking well do it on a Sunday instead.'

Afterwards, reflecting on what had happened, Graham felt that the incident had taught him a valuable lesson. There was no point punishing people if they played badly, he realized. You had to be constructive in your criticism, or else you'd just end up with a team full of demoralized players. 'I already knew enough to know that a word of praise could make someone stand up a little straighter, pull their shoulders back and lift their head up, altering their entire demeanour for the better.'

By now his own morale was in uncharacteristically bad shape. One morning, instead of leaping out of bed as he usually did, he lay there gazing up at the ceiling. 'If I'm ever a manager,' he thought, 'I don't want my players feeling the way I'm feeling now.'

In the three years Graham spent at Grimsby, they slid from the Second Division down to the Fourth. Meanwhile, his wages barely rose from the same lowly rung he had been on since he joined – £12 a week during the winter, dropping down to £10 in the summer, when most players took on other jobs to supplement their income.

At the end of the season Graham asked for a transfer, and in 1968 he joined Lincoln City for a fee of £4,000. Once again, he was made captain, but soon after he arrived, he picked up an injury. He had already qualified as an FA coach – the youngest man ever to do so – and now, with time on his hands, he started training a team of local government officers. They weren't much good – far from it – but in a way, that was the point. Watching them hoofing the ball about on their days off, Graham learned another valuable lesson: you could learn more from coaching enthusiastic amateurs than you could from coaching hardened professionals.

There was no point getting frustrated by what the players couldn't do, he saw. That way madness lay. Instead, you had to work within their limitations and boil everything down to its most basic level. But what counted for more than anything else was fostering a sense of common purpose, of camaraderie. If you succeeded in turning a bunch of untalented players into a properly drilled team, they could amount to far more than their individual parts. And if you filled them with enough self-belief, they just might find themselves doing things they never imagined they were capable of.

As well as coaching his local government officers, Graham read a book that had recently been published called *The Football Man* by Arthur Hopcraft. A collection of profiles of footballing heroes such as Stanley Matthews and Bobby Charlton, it made an enormous impression on him – especially one passage in which Hopcraft wrote about what football meant to him:

> The way we play the game, organise it and reward it reflects the kind of community we are ... What happens on the football field matters, not in the way that food matters but as poetry does to some people and alcohol does to others: it engages the personality. It has conflict and beauty and when those two qualities are present together in something offered for public approval, they represent much of what I understand to be art.

Then something happened that drove all other thoughts from Graham's mind. At an away game in Northampton, he was taking a free kick when his right foot clipped the ground and his leg gave way beneath him. The ball trickled forward about five yards and then came to a stop. Lying there in agony, clutching his side, Graham could hear the Northampton supporters roaring with laughter.

X-rays revealed that he had a build-up of calcium on his hip joint. Brusquely, the doctor told him he would be lucky if he ever played again. He had a wife, two young daughters, a crocked hip, few educational qualifications and – as far as he could see – next to no prospects.

# 6.

When Reggie was eleven, the Dwights moved house – to North-wood, a couple of miles away. But any hopes he may have had that the atmosphere would improve quickly came to nothing. While the battleground may have changed, the fighting went on as intensely as before. 'I realized pretty soon that nothing was going to change; all I could do was keep my head down as much as possible.'

After another three years of pitching into one another, Stanley and Sheila finally decided their marriage was never going to work. Sheila had already met a local builder called Fred Farebrother – a divorcee with three children of his own. As soon as the Dwights' own divorce came through, Sheila and Fred got married. Together with Reggie, they moved, first into a rented flat in Croxley Green, then into a two-bedroomed flat in Northwood Hills. Meanwhile, Fred's children stayed with their mother.

Stanley had also met someone else – a lab technician called Edna Clough. They too got married and settled in Essex where the two of them ran a newspaper shop. By this point Reggie, now a pupil at Pinner County Grammar School, had started attending Saturday morning classes at the Royal Academy of Music.

With his father gone, he had become used to going on his own to watch Watford play. Every time he went, he would stand in the same place on the Bend where he and Stanley had first stood eight years earlier. Once a month Reggie would catch a series of buses and go to see his father in Essex. He always dreaded these visits. It wasn't just that he had to miss a game if Watford were playing at home – although that was bad enough. It was what happened when he got there: the fear that gripped him whenever he was in Stanley's presence, the pall of silence that always seemed to sit between them, and, above all, the constant sense that he was a disappointment to his father. 'I could see that he was happy with his new wife, but somehow that only made it worse. The fact that he could be happy and relaxed with someone else. I never had any feeling that I belonged in his life. Always I felt that I was an interloper, as if I wasn't really his flesh and blood.'

Shortly after Stanley and Edna had got married, Reggie wrote him a letter thanking him for a birthday gift of ten shillings. He then ventured into what he knew was likely to be a minefield. 'I also know what I want to do when I leave school,' he added. 'Actually, I have known for a long time, but I have never said so before because I thought everyone would laugh at me. I want to entertain – that is, to sing and play the piano. I know that it is not easy being an entertainer and I appreciate it takes a lot of hard work and of course luck, but I know I would really enjoy doing it. I hope you don't think I'm foolish, but I thought I'd tell you anyway.'

As he had anticipated, this did not go down at all well. Stanley didn't even reply to the letter, not directly. However, a few weeks later, he wrote to Sheila telling her he thought there was a serious risk that Reggie was going off the rails. Instead of dreaming up such ridiculous ideas of becoming an entertainer, he should be setting his sights on a respectable career – like working in a bank, or, better still, joining the RAF. What's more, if he didn't pull himself together, then he was likely to end up as a 'wide boy' – a 1930s expression for someone who may not have plunged headlong into a life of crime, but was plainly heading in that direction.

While Reggie was more estranged than ever from his father, he had become very close to his new stepfather, Fred – he called him 'Derf'. 'He was always incredibly warm and supportive.'

Far from disapproving of his stepson's ambitions, Fred did

everything he could to encourage them. One evening in 1962, he went for a drink in a pub called the Northwood Hills Hotel, opposite Northwood Hills tube station – the same station where Reggie and Stanley had first caught a train to go and see Watford play.

Fred mentioned to the landlord, George Hill, that Reggie, now aged fifteen, was an accomplished pianist who had set his heart on becoming an entertainer. It so happened that the pub's regular pianist, a man known as Albino Bob, had just decided to leave as the job involved too much travelling. Why didn't Reggie have a go at playing in the Public Bar and see how he got on, the landlord suggested.

The next Friday, dressed in a brown tweed jacket and grey flannel trousers, a bespectacled Reggie Dwight turned up to entertain the regulars in the pub. However nervous he was feeling, he already knew that there were some key do's and don'ts to performing in public.

On several occasions, he'd gone with his mother and Fred to a pub in Harlesden called the Orange Tree, where every weekend a man would play the piano and people would come from miles around just to watch him. 'I could see how brilliant this guy was at winning an audience over; he didn't just sit there like a stuffed bird. I remember him playing a song called "Mockin' Bird Hill" which was a hit for the Migil 5, and everyone in the pub was singing along. He had them completely in the palm of his hand. One night he even invited me on stage to sing with him. I think that was what first put the idea in my head that entertainment is all about manipulation, about getting people on your side.'

Doing his best to look as inconspicuous as possible, Reggie sidled towards the piano and sat down. What the landlord had omitted to tell Fred was that his Public Bar regulars had a reputation for being rowdy when they'd had a few drinks, and unusually morose when they hadn't.

Glancing up from the keyboard, Reggie could see them all staring beadily at him. 'It was obvious they were thinking, "What can this nerdy kid with glasses possibly show us?" '

To begin with, he was given a less than appreciative reception. As he launched into Johnny Ray's 'Cry', there were shouts of 'Get off!' along with a volley of empty crisp packets. With no microphone, Reggie struggled to make himself heard over the catcalls and the buzz of conversation. Despite that, he kept going, belting out a selection of country numbers, rock 'n' roll stompers and music-hall standards. And as he went on, something strange happened. Gradually, the shouting died away. After a while, as if stirring themselves from a deep slumber, people began to clap along. Some of them even joined in the choruses. His version of Jim Reeves's ballad 'He'll Have To Go' was given a particularly rousing reception.

While Reggie was hardly a stranger to pretending, to imagining he was someone else, now he was no longer singing along to Radio Luxembourg under the blankets at Pinner Hill Road. Now he was doing it for real in front of an audience. 'I could see that these people basically just wanted to have a chat with their friends. In order to get them to listen, you had to win them over. Slowly I could feel them starting to enjoy themselves; it was an amazing sensation.'

As he pounded doggedly away at the keyboard, it was as if his whole being was changing. 'When I was sitting behind that piano, all my fears seemed to go away. Somehow it put steel into me. If anything, I should have been terrified, but instead I felt fantastically safe, as if no one could hurt me. And then, the moment I stopped playing, I was back to being a shy boy again. But for as long as it lasted, I felt free to do anything I wanted, and to be anyone I wanted. That was incredibly liberating. I can remember quite clearly thinking, I like this, I can do it.'

At the end of the evening, Fred went around the bar with a hat asking if people would like to show their appreciation of his stepson's efforts. He raised almost £10 – more cash than Reggie had seen before in his life. Despite the landlord's conviction that Albino Bob was the one with the real talent, he asked Reggie if he would like to come back the following weekend.

# 7.

On 3 June 1958, the then chairman of Watford, T. Rigby Taylor, wrote a letter to his fellow directors. He was, he told them, 'too old, tired and disillusioned' to carry on. His successor, a man called Jim Bonser, was a builder from Preston whose grumpy appearance – and manner – concealed some unexpectedly exotic tastes: he liked to smoke hand-made cigarettes with his name printed along the side.

At the time of Bonser's takeover, the Watford manager was Neil McBain. A former goalkeeper who had played his last game for the Merseyside club New Brighton aged fifty-one – making him the oldest player ever to appear in a Football League game – McBain was then in his second spell as Watford manager. During his first, the club had enjoyed its longest-ever period of success. But a lot had happened since then.

Now a chronic alcoholic, McBain lived almost exclusively on whisky and fish and chips – the floor of his office was carpeted with old fish and chip wrappers. Whenever the team travelled to an away fixture, he would insist that the coach driver stop at the first pub they came to. The players then had to wait while McBain went inside and sank several large Scotches to fortify him for the challenge ahead. Meanwhile, supporters noticed that his programme notes became shorter and shorter, yet increasingly hard to understand.

In 1958, Watford were relegated from Division Three (South) to the recently created national Division Four. 'Division Three as soon as possible is the target,' Bonser told shareholders when he took over. In the hope of gaining rapid promotion, several new players were signed. One of them noted that when he met

Neil McBain in a pub to discuss terms, the manager deviated from his usual diet of fish and chips and ordered vegetable soup. But much to the confusion of staff, he asked for it to be served in a pint mug.

Watford remained in Division Four.

As the years went by, there seemed something increasingly symbolic about Jim Bonser watching his own name go up in smoke whenever he lit a cigarette. Occasionally, Watford managed to gain promotion to Division Three, yet they never succeeded in staying there for long. Within a season or two, they would be relegated again.

From 1962, the Watford players would run out onto the pitch at the start of every game to the theme music from the popular TV police drama *Z-Cars*. Confusingly, Everton did too, but as the likelihood of the two clubs ever playing in the same division was so remote as to be inconceivable, no one considered this to be a problem. For a time, *Z-Cars* seemed to bring Watford luck – it heralded the start of a twenty-nine-match unbeaten run. But after the effects had worn off, normal service soon resumed.

To read the official history of the club during the 1960s and early 70s is to find yourself trudging through a seemingly endless vale of disappointment – 'A depressing 6-0 defeat at the hands of Millwall'; 'Watford limped on through another uninspiring campaign' – broken only by some desperate clutching at straws: 'Watford lost the next ten games before ending their incredible run with a nil-all draw against Rochdale.'

Fed up with the club's record, the Watford Football Supporters Club became increasingly vocal in its criticism. In 1965, infuriated by what he regarded as their incessant carping, Bonser took the unusual step of banning them from the ground. Evicted from the corrugated iron hut that served as their headquarters – reputedly, an RAF officers' sleeping quarters during the war – they learned that they had been replaced by a new

Bonser-friendly organization: the subtly different Watford Football Club Supporters Club.

Like many of its Fourth Division rivals, Watford remained firmly stuck in the 1950s. On match days, directors were reluctantly permitted to bring their wives along. However, women were never allowed into the boardroom – popularly known as 'The Kremlin' on account of all the backbiting and scheming that went on there. Instead, they had to go to the even drabber 'Ladies Room' next door. On the rare occasions when Watford won a game, Jim Bonser's wife, Pat, would unlock a drinks cabinet and, with an air of great ceremony, pour her guests the smallest glasses of sherry they had ever seen.

In an attempt to generate more income, a greyhound track was installed around the edge of the pitch. This, however, brought problems of its own. Whenever there was a race meeting, the players were unable to get onto the pitch. The club's seating capacity was also doubled. Otherwise, little had changed in twenty years. During the early part of the season, Watford fans still liked to go blackberrying at half-time – there were some blackberry bushes in an untamed patch of undergrowth between the two stands.

Every so often, Watford would do something that took everyone by surprise. In 1970, they even reached the FA Cup semi-final for the first time, before losing 5-1 to Chelsea. But financially, the club was staring into the abyss. That year, Watford announced a trading profit of £170. This, however, didn't take into account debts of more than £60,000 as well as another £30,000 worth of outstanding bills.

By now things had become so bad that if a cup tie went to extra-time, Jim Bonser would be in a particularly bad mood as the electricity bill would be larger than usual. And these weren't the only problems. After the club's leading scorer had dropped his shorts and bared his bottom at opposition fans, he was put on the transfer list.

It wasn't just the football club that appeared to be in terminal decline, so was Watford itself. Described as a 'dear, dull little place' by one nineteenth-century resident, it had gone on to become one of the most prosperous towns in the UK. But since its heyday back in the 1930s Watford's fortunes had plummeted; factories had closed and the local brewery – Benskins – was teetering on the verge of bankruptcy.

Hoping to attract new customers, Benskins had gambled everything on a new high-alcohol beer called Triple A – a beer capable, according to one description, 'of temporarily changing a person's whole personality'. But the gamble had failed and another 200 people lost their jobs.

There wasn't much for anyone to do in the town. The only dedicated music venue was in the Watford Mercury Motor Hotel, a gloomy concrete block beside one of Watford's ever increasing number of arterial roads. For reasons that may have had something to do with the calibre of artistes they attracted, it was called 'The Drone Room'.

Meanwhile, the printing industry, long one of Watford's main employers, had laid off hundreds more workers. Lapped by north London suburbs that crept a little closer every year, the town's heart was being torn out piece by piece. In the early 1960s Watford's borough engineer had predicted, 'Anyone coming here in ten years' time will not recognize it.'

Sure enough, by the end of the decade, the *Watford Observer* reported that 'Only 40 historic buildings are still standing in the town centre and nine of those will soon be demolished.' According to one local historian, 'There had been an appalling rate of destruction, and what is worse, indiscriminate destruction.'

Asked to justify what was happening, a puzzled council official said, 'Why would anyone want a historic building when you can have a brand-new multistorey car park instead?'

The Earl of Arran, who lived nearby with his wife, a champion powerboat racer, along with their large collection of pet badgers, saw the destruction in even more dramatic terms: 'Watford,' he declared starkly, 'is a living hell.'

# 8.

Just when things were looking desperate, Graham Taylor was invited to come into Lincoln's boardroom for a chat with the club's directors. There they asked him a number of apparently hypothetical questions. Say, for instance, the post of manager became vacant, did he have any ideas about how he might do the job?

Yes, Graham said, he did. Very much so, in fact. He had two principal aims, he told them. The first was to create a team that would score plenty of goals and give supporters something to get excited about. And the second was to take players out into the local community 'so that people could see that the club was representing them'. Thinking back to Arthur Hopcraft's book, *The Football Man*, he went on to say that while football should be first and foremost a form of entertainment, it should also be something that brought people together and gave them a sense of pride.

To that end, he wanted to create as strong a bond as possible between the club and town. If he took over at Lincoln, he would insist that every player lived within ten miles of the ground. What's more, they would be expected to visit schools, hospitals, social clubs and factories. This would enable people to get to know them personally, and, if everything went well, would encourage them to take a closer interest in the team's fortunes. It would also ensure that players kept their feet on the ground and never became too uppity.

Was that it, the directors asked.

Not entirely, Graham replied. He would much rather the club used the word 'supporters' instead of 'fans'. As far as he was concerned, a fan was a flighty will-o'-the-wisp sort of character whose loyalty could never be depended on. A supporter, though, was a much more solid citizen – one who would be more likely to stick with the club through thick and thin.

A few days later, in December 1972, Graham Taylor was appointed Lincoln FC's new manager. At twenty-eight, he was the youngest manager in the Football League. That morning, before he took training, he told the players he had an announcement to make. 'I like to think I've got on with most of you,' he said, 'and if any of you really dislike me, you've hidden it well, but I've got some news for you. For some of you it will be good news and for some of you it might not be so good news, but I am your new manager.'

While they were taking this in, there was something else they needed to know, he said. In future, the players were no longer to call him Graham. They could call him whatever they liked behind his back, but to his face they were to address him as 'Gaffer' or 'Boss'.

The message couldn't have been clearer. He was no longer one of them; now he was in charge.

# 9.

The term before he was due to take his A levels, Reggie left Pinner County Grammar School. Like Graham, he was giving up a grammar school education in favour of a life that was as uncertain as it was hazardous. But unlike Graham's headmaster, Reggie's couldn't have been more encouraging. He could see that he had a great talent for music, he told him, and advised him to pursue it as wholeheartedly as possible.

Now seventeen, Reggie went to work in a warehouse on Denmark Street in Soho, where a company called Mills Music kept its stock of sheet music – his footballing cousin Roy Dwight, who was friendly with Mills Music's general manager, had got him the job.

However unsure of himself he may have been, Reggie had become increasingly convinced that he wasn't cut out for a conventional life, that he was destined to follow a different path. 'I know it sounds a strange thing to say, but I did feel there was something magical inside me. I didn't know what it was; I just felt there was something there, waiting to come out.' While he had no desire to be famous, he did want to work in the music business in some capacity, no matter how lowly. 'I never set out to become a star, or anything like that. I only really wanted to write songs. But I did have this enormous desire to prove myself, most of all of course to my father.'

Naturally, Stanley was livid when he heard the news: the likelihood of Reggie turning into a wide boy now seemed greater than ever. He would have been even more appalled if he'd known that Reggie had also co-founded a group called Bluesology – they used to practise in the back room of the Northwood Hills Hotel.

In July 1965, the group released their first single, a song called 'Come Back Baby' which Reggie had written.

It sank without trace.

He then joined the backing band of a singer called Long John Baldry, a flamboyantly camp Anglo-Canadian whose repertoire consisted of a hitherto undreamed-of combination of lachry-mose ballads and raunchy blues numbers. It was while Reggie was with Long John Baldry that he replied to an advertisement in the *New Musical Express* inviting aspiring songwriters to contact the Liberty Talent Agency in Albemarle Street.

Asked to audition by the agency's boss, Ray Williams, Reggie ran through some old country standards before rounding off with a rendition of Al Jolson's 'Mammy'. However eccentric his choice of material, Williams was impressed, especially when he learned that Reggie also wrote his own songs.

But there was a problem. While Reggie was able to write music, he had no aptitude for writing lyrics. Suddenly, Williams remembered another letter he had been sent a few weeks earlier – a letter from someone who could write lyrics, but not music. Digging it out, he passed it to Reggie. The address at the top was Maltkin Farm, Owmby-by-Spital, Lincolnshire, Reggie saw, and it had been written by someone who signed himself Bernard Taupin.

A couple of weeks later, Reggie and Bernard – who preferred to be known as Bernie – met in a restaurant in Tottenham Court Road. Immediately, Reggie had a sense that he had found a kin-dred spirit. It wasn't so much that he was knocked out by Bernie's lyrics – he found them a bit airy-fairy for his tastes – it was more that the two of them seemed to be perfectly in tune with one another.

They turned out to work so well together that Bernie decided to move down to London. Soon they had enough songs to fill an album. Thanks to Ray Williams, Reggie also had a recording con-tract. But before he went into the studio, there was something he wanted to do, something he had been thinking about for some time.

By then he'd begun to suspect that nobody was ever going to buy a record by someone called Reggie Dwight, no matter how good it was. He therefore decided to change his name, to Elton John – the Elton came from Bluesology's saxophone player, Elton Dean, and the John from Long John Baldry. Later, he would add a second name 'Hercules', which as well as being the name of a Greek god, was the name of the horse owned by rag-and-bone men Albert and Harold Steptoe in the TV sitcom *Steptoe and Son*.

But there was more to it than just a change of name. In the process, Reggie had given himself another persona, one that he could slip in and out of at will. By becoming Elton John, he was able to leave behind all the anxieties, all the insecurities, that had dogged him throughout his childhood. And by giving himself another name, he was also, in a sense, severing himself from Stanley; leaving everything Dwight behind.

While shy Reggie was still in there somewhere, in future it would be flamboyant, extrovert Elton who faced the world. Yet no matter which name he was using, there was one issue he couldn't seem to resolve. Sex had never been talked about in the Dwight family, nor had he been given any sex education at school. It was only after meeting Bernie Taupin that Elton began to wonder if he might be gay. 'Before that, I'd genuinely never thought about it; it was as if music was my sexuality.'

While the two of them never had an affair – Taupin was staunchly heterosexual – Elton was aware that his feelings for Bernie were different from any feelings he'd ever had before. 'In a way Bernie was like my brother; I really loved him. But although there was never anything sexual between us, that's when it first occurred to me that I might prefer men to women.'

Elton John's first album, *Empty Sky*, consisting of nine songs the two of them had written in his bedroom in Northwood Hills, came out in June 1969. It sold fewer than 4,000 copies. While this wasn't a disaster – there were a few tepidly favourable reviews – it piled extra pressure on his shoulders. A lot, possibly everything, was going to hinge on his second album.

He could afford one flop. Two might well prove terminal.

# IO.

Before Graham took over at Lincoln, his best friend, Alan Morgan, told him he would be mad to accept the job. 'I remember saying he would be on the scrapheap within eighteen months.'

Undeterred, Graham announced his intentions to the club's supporters in disarmingly frank terms: 'I demand nothing from you,' he wrote in the programme notes for his first game in charge.

> I am not in a position to do that. You have that privilege. However, I would ask of you that before you make any demands you try to assess everything as fairly as possible. I have had 12 years in football and won nothing.
>
> I am fully aware of Lincoln City's decline over a similar period of time. In terms of lack of success, we are in the same boat . . . If things do not go as planned, that can lead to frustration, bitterness and irrational thinking, so that eventually one has little chance of achieving anything. Therefore, all that I and my players can do on your behalf is to try and work at our best at all times and to keep fingers crossed that this will bring its due rewards.

Lincoln lost that game 3-2. They also failed to win any of the next ten games that followed. The mutterings of disapproval soon grew into an angry chorus. For his part, Graham became increasingly convinced that he had made a dreadful mistake; if only he'd listened to his friend Alan's advice. All his grand plans, all his carefully thought-out strategies, had come to nothing. He was so despondent that he thought of walking away from football altogether. 'I wondered about selling the house, getting some qualifications and taking a teacher-training course.'

It didn't help that his methods were so unorthodox, so open to ridicule. Much to the players' surprise, he liked to use tiddly-winks to show them how to execute particular moves. He also proved to be a tough disciplinarian – far tougher than anything they had ever come across before. Players would be fined for being late for training, or for being sloppily dressed – jeans were banned. They were also fined for showing dissent and for being unshaven, or even partly shaven (he didn't care for moustaches).

On one occasion Graham took the unusual step of fining him-self for running onto the pitch during a game and remonstrating with the referee. 'If a player had shown a similar lack of discipline and responsibility as I did, then he would have been fined,' he said afterwards. 'There is no reason why I shouldn't be subject to the same rules as everyone else.'

In essence, Graham's tactics were simple – attack, attack, attack. They were the same tactics he'd drummed into the local government officers he had coached a year earlier. That involved getting the ball forward as quickly as possible, with the backs sending long passes up field. Graham had already worked out that in any level of football – professional or amateur – most goals were scored from the same place. 'If you draw an imagin-ary semi-circle from the goal-line, taking in the two corners of the six-yard box and the penalty spot, you will find that perhaps seventy-five per cent of all goals are scored in that area.' If Lin-coln could get the ball into the right place – and do so quickly enough to catch the opposition napping – then they'd be able to create chances and score goals.

That was the theory anyway. The trouble was that nothing he did seemed to make any difference. Still Lincoln kept on losing. Despite his injured hip, Graham even put himself in the team, in his old position at full-back. That didn't work either – they drew two of the next three games and lost one.

In training, he was as persistent as he was unsparing, once getting the Lincoln players to practise the same move seventy-six times in succession. Horrified by his new regime, they complained that he was working them far too hard.

'Hard?' Graham would say. '*Hard?* You could always be doing nine-to-five on an assembly line.'

To make the point, he took them into local factories where they were able to see – some more wistfully than he had intended – the life that in other circumstances they might have been leading.

All the while, attendances continued to drop: on a bad day, they were down to 2,500. At the same time, the muttering had become louder. Graham, fans complained, was hopelessly out of his depth. Worse than that; he was an embarrassment. Better that he should be sacked straightaway rather than cause any more damage.

Once, Graham had liked to think he was pretty good at coping with pressure. As soon as he came home, he could forget about the job and not think about it until the next morning. But now he found himself lying awake at night, wondering what had gone wrong, awash with frustration, bitterness and irrational thinking.

# II.

'Watched the Grand National', wrote Elton in his diary for 29
March 1969. 'Then went to see Owmby Utd win 2-1' – he was staying with Bernie Taupin's parents at the time. A month later came
a pleasant surprise: 'Got home tonight to find that Aunty Win and
Mum had bought me a car – Hillman Husky Estate – superb!'

May brought a further flurry of excitement. 'Pinner Fair. Went
to the fair with Mick and Pat. I now own a coconut and two goldfish!! – John and Yoko.' However, his delight didn't last long. The
following day's entry read, 'My goldfish died tonight. Very upset!!'

Throughout the spring and summer, Elton's life followed a
similarly undramatic course. Then, on 27 October, came a slightly
longer entry than usual: 'Session [at] De Lane Lea [studio] 9.00.
Stayed home today. Went to South Harrow market. The session
was hilarious. Didn't do anything in the end. Wrote Your Song.'

At the beginning of April 1970, a weekly newspaper called *Record
Retailer* recommended a new album to its readers. According
to the paper, the artist who had recorded the album, a young
pianist and songwriter, defied easy categorization: 'He neither
belongs to the "progressive" cult, nor does he belong in the light
brigade of popsters.'

Although there were a couple of songs that the reviewer didn't
think quite came off, the rest were as original as they were memorable. 'He clearly possesses an ability to write a rather complex
structured melody somewhat in the manner of modern classical
composers such as Bartók, Sibelius and Neilson.' All told, it was
'an extremely professional performance in which it is well worth
investing £2'.

While no one else drew comparisons with either Bartók or Sibelius, there were other favourable reviews – a lot of them. 'A big talent,' declared *New Musical Express*. As far as *Melody Maker* was concerned, it was 'a truly great record'. Entitled simply *Elton John*, the album consisted of ten songs, including 'Take Me to the Pilot', 'Border Song' and 'Your Song'.

Two months after the album came out, Elton headed north, to a small village called Krumlin near Halifax. Even by the chaotic standards of most 1960s and 70s rock festivals, the Yorkshire Folk, Blues and Jazz Festival was not a great success. Pink Floyd were believed to be topping the bill, but it emerged later that no one had actually asked them to appear.

To try to appease the crowd of around 8,000 people who had turned up, it was announced that the band had been unavoidably detained in transit. It worked – at least for a time. But there was worse to come. Instead of the hoped for sunshine, the festival site was lashed by torrential gales. Trying to protect themselves from the rain, festivalgoers took to wearing bin liners, but the wind was so strong that these were soon reduced to shreds of polythene.

By the end of the first day, a large section of the stage had blown away and one of the marquees had collapsed. Some 330 people had been treated for exposure and seventy of them taken to hospital. Several days afterwards, the festival's promoter was reported to have been found wandering the Yorkshire moors in a state of confusion, muttering incomprehensibly to himself.

Things were no better backstage. One of the main attractions, the folk-rock band Fairport Convention, helped themselves to so much of the free liquor that by the time they went on stage they were in no state to perform. Halfway through their set, the band's violinist, Dave Swarbrick, decided that he needed to relieve himself. As his fellow band member Dave Pegg would recall, 'There was a hole in the canvas on the stage. Dave went over and stuck his chopper through the hole and had a piss.'

Swarbrick was under the impression that there was nothing on the other side of the hole except for open moorland, but he turned out to be wrong. 'Unfortunately, the press area was directly on the other side of the hole.'

There was, however, one bright beacon among the mayhem. The second act to appear was Elton John and his band. After kicking off with three of his own songs, Elton launched into a version of the Rolling Stones' recent number one, 'Honky Tonk Women'.

'He is like a white, male Aretha Franklin,' a member of the audience was heard to exclaim. One of the watching journalists, Chris Charlesworth from the *Melody Maker*, was equally impressed. 'It was the first time I ever saw Elton perform. On he came, very flash and he pounded hell out of that piano for an hour or so. I had never heard his music before, but I thought he was absolutely fantastic.'

It wasn't just the music that made such an impression on Charlesworth. 'All those miserable people in that field . . . by the time he had finished his set, they were happy. He got out some bottles of brandy and loads of plastic cups and he handed out brandy to people in the crowd, saying, "Sorry about the weather. It's not my fault, but I'll do the best I can to keep you warm, so there you go, some brandy." '

This too had gone down extremely well, Charlesworth noted.

# 12.

With Graham on the brink of being sacked, Lincoln at last won a game – his twelfth in charge. Although they lost the one after that, they then proceeded to hit a lengthy purple patch, winning ten out of their next twelve games. By the end of the 1973/4 season, Lincoln had climbed from nineteenth place in the Fourth Division to twelfth. For the first time, Graham allowed himself to stop thinking about selling his house and retraining as a teacher.

A year later, he had a meeting with the chairman of Lincoln, a local pig farmer called Heneage Dove. Despite the team's recent record, Graham went along feeling apprehensive; an earlier meeting with Dove had not gone quite as he had planned. He'd arrived at Dove's farm intending to ask for a pay rise, but before he had a chance to do so Dove had asked him to lie down and milk one of his pigs. 'It was a ludicrous situation. I was lying down underneath the rear end of a pig, trying to aim the milk into the jug, thinking that if this pig needed a shit, I was going to get it all over my face.'

Yet even here there was a valuable lesson to be learned. In future, whenever Graham wanted to impose his authority on a player, especially if he thought they were after a pay rise, he would try to put them at a physical disadvantage – making them sit on a much lower chair was a particular favourite. As a result, they found themselves on the back foot before they had even got started.

By way of an incentive, Dove bet Graham that Lincoln wouldn't manage to score more than 100 goals in the coming season. If he was right, Graham would give him £100 – roughly half his monthly salary. But if he was wrong, Dove would pay for something that Graham had had his eye on for some time: a new garage to go on the side of his semi-detached house.

While Graham was slowly winning round the doubters at Lincoln, not everyone was convinced. Among the players he had signed was a 26-year-old from Ashton-under-Lyne called Sam Ellis. With a head that looked as if it had been carved none too expertly out of a block of granite and a similarly uncompromising manner, Ellis had played for Sheffield Wednesday in the 1966 FA Cup Final when he was aged just nineteen.

But thereafter, his career had headed sharply downhill, due in large part to his activities off the field. After spending the night in a police cell following a pub brawl, Ellis had been sacked from Sheffield Wednesday for bringing the club into disrepute. Nor had he fared much better at his next club, Mansfield. 'I knew one or two of the lads at Lincoln and they said, "Look, you can't go much lower. You'd better come here." '

Although Ellis didn't know it, Graham was looking for what he called a 'big ugly centre-half' – someone who, like him, possessed natural authority, was able to command the respect of other players and could control play on the pitch. Nothing in Sam Ellis's career so far had given much – indeed any – indication that he might be that person. However, Graham thought he had qualities that no one else had spotted, and offered him a contract.

Delighted to be given a job of any kind in football, Ellis signed straightaway. But as soon as he went to Lincoln, he found he disliked everything about it – and the manager most of all. 'We just didn't get on. I didn't like how Graham behaved towards me and I didn't think much of his approach either.'

Ellis stuck it out for a year, then decided he'd had enough. 'I went to see Taylor's secretary and told her I was off after the match on Saturday.' That weekend, Lincoln were playing Crewe Alexandra at home. Ellis's father came to watch the game and after it had ended, Ellis explained what he'd done and asked his father to take him home. 'The moment I'd finished, my dad grabbed hold of me by the lapels and said, "You'd better stop arsing about. You're not going anywhere, because if you walk out of here, you're finished."'

Greatly taken aback – 'my dad had never done anything like that before' – Ellis did as he was told. But by the end of the season, he was even more determined to leave. He still didn't like Lincoln and he especially didn't like Graham Taylor. 'Basically, I thought he was an upstart.'

Once again, he went to see Graham's secretary. 'I just said, "Scrap my contract. I'm off." That afternoon, Graham paid a visit to the house where Ellis still lived with his parents. 'I really didn't want to see him; I couldn't see any point. But my dad was there and he insisted.'

The two of them spent the next five hours talking. It was a conversation that would alter the course of Ellis's life. 'Normally, I'm a believer in first impressions, but as we talked I began to see that I might have been wrong about Graham. He told me what he wanted out of me and out of the players generally. And although he could be a bit raw and touchy, I realized he had thought more deeply about the game than anyone I'd ever come across before.'

What Graham had thought about most of all was how to get the best out of players who had courage and conviction – even if they didn't necessarily have vast reserves of talent. 'I remember him saying that if you have two players of equal ability, what separates them is attitude. Who will drop by the wayside when the going gets tough, and who will stick it out?'

Although Ellis had twice tried to throw in the towel, Graham had clearly decided that he had it in him to be a sticker. Someone who would keep on fighting right to the final whistle, no matter how desperate the cause.

'At the end of those five hours, we said goodbye, Graham went away and the two of us never had a problem again.'

The next season, with Sam Ellis as captain, Lincoln won thirty-two out of forty-six matches. They topped the Fourth Division with a record number of points and didn't lose a single home game. They also scored 111 goals.

Graham got his new garage.

# 13.

The *Elton John* album sold more than 10,000 copies and remained in the album charts for fourteen weeks. At the age of twenty-three, Elton suddenly found he was famous. To celebrate, he repaid his mother's generosity and bought her a car – a new Mini. Along with money, fame brought him the one thing that had always eluded him: confidence. For the first time, he no longer felt he had to apologize for who he was, to hide away in the shadows. Now he could wear whatever he wanted and do almost anything he wanted, unencumbered by guilt or self-consciousness.

Some things, though, stayed resolutely the same. By this point, he and Stanley scarcely ever saw one another. Whenever they did meet, the atmosphere was as bad as ever. 'Even after I became Elton John, I felt embarrassed to go and see him. He never once said "Well done", or anything like that. There was nothing, no acknowledgement of what had happened to me at all. The silence was deafening. And however successful I had become, I never lost that sense that he disapproved of me, that I'd done something wrong. In the end, it was just easier to stay away.'

In August 1970, shortly after he had returned from the Yorkshire Folk, Blues and Jazz Festival, Elton flew to Los Angeles to play the first of six concerts at the Troubadour in West Hollywood. After landing at LAX airport, he emerged to find a double-decker bus waiting outside with a banner on the top reading, 'Elton John Has Arrived!' He was so embarrassed that he spent the journey to Beverly Hills crouching below the window so that no one could see him.

The Troubadour concerts were to be Elton's introduction to

an American audience. Before the opening night, he was feeling more nervous than he'd ever felt before. 'It was like one of those terrible nightmares where you're back at school, sitting a test, then realize that you're not wearing any trousers or underpants.'

As had increasingly proved to be the case, flamboyant clothes provided a handy protective screen. Elton came on stage wearing a pair of bright yellow dungarees and matching yellow workman's boots adorned with large blue wings. Despite this, no one took much notice at first; they just stood around the bar chatting away loudly. By this point, his nerves had given way to something equally characteristic: a flash of temper.

Standing up, Elton kicked his piano stool away and said, 'Right, if you won't listen, perhaps you'll bloody well listen to this.' He then dropped to the floor, balancing on one hand while carrying on playing with the other. Then, hurling himself forward, he did a handstand on the keyboard.

The audience stopped talking.

The next morning the reviews appeared. The *Los Angeles Times* rock critic, Robert Hilburn, kicked off his review with the verbal equivalent of a blast of trumpets. 'Rejoice. Rock music, which has been going through a rather uneventful period recently, has a new star,' Hilburn wrote. 'He's Elton John, a 23-year-old Englishman, whose debut Tuesday night at the Troubadour was, in almost every way, magnificent . . . He's going to be one of rock's biggest and most important acts.'

Others were equally impressed. Shortly after the reviews were published, Elton went on a nationwide tour of the US. Right from the start, he was aware that something had changed – 'It was obvious, the moment I came on stage.' Much to his surprise, the audiences all seemed to know his songs. At one concert, they became so carried away that the promoter tried – unsuccessfully – to get Elton to stop playing, fearing that the floor was about to collapse.

When he reached San Francisco, Elton finally conquered his nerves and asked out a combustible Scotsman called John Reid, Tamla Motown's label manager in the UK. It was the start of a love affair that would last for four, increasingly bumpy years.

Initially, the tour had been conceived as a low-budget, whistlestop affair to introduce Elton to American audiences. But everywhere he went, his reputation preceded him. By the time the tour finished a month later, there was no longer any doubt about it; something really had changed.

To his own astonishment, the delight of his mother and, it seems safe to say, the disbelief of his father, Elton John, formerly Reggie Dwight of 55 Pinner Hill Road, was being hailed as the biggest thing to hit America since the Beatles.

# 14.

In November 1972, Watford offered Crystal Palace £30,000 for a young striker called Ross Jenkins. Never before had the club paid so much for a player, and Jenkins arrived at Vicarage Road carrying a huge weight of expectation on his shoulders: he was the man who would lead them out of the depths of despair towards the lush pastures they had dreamed of for so long.

Or so it was claimed.

Born and brought up in Richmond, Surrey, Jenkins had been obsessed with football ever since he was a child. He never supported a particular team, nor was he much of a one for hero worship; he just loved to play. Whenever he did, his father, a window-cleaner, would try to fit in his rounds so that he could come and watch. Worried that Ross might be put off if he saw him, he used to hide himself away in the bushes.

By the time Jenkins was eleven, he was close to six foot. He shot up at such a rate that in a single week he played for his school's Under 12, Under 13, Under 14, Under 15 and Under 16 teams. Because he was tall, he was always put up front – 'like the Lone Ranger'. At sixteen, Jenkins had already decided to try to become a professional footballer. Twice a week, after school, he would travel across London to Highbury and train with the Arsenal junior team.

But after he had been going there for a year, he received a letter from the club secretary.

'Dear Ross,' it began. 'I am sure you will realize that we have to make assessments on all the young players taking part in evening training sessions . . . In your particular case, we feel that you have not quite measured up to the required standards and we regret that we have to withdraw your training and coaching facilities at this club.'

However, the letter ended by offering a faint cheep of encouragement. 'That does not necessarily mean that you should give up altogether because you obviously have a fair amount of ability to have been invited in the first place.'

Not especially downcast to see the back of Arsenal – he'd never much liked it there – Jenkins joined Brentford's youth team. He then went, as an apprentice, to Crystal Palace. As well as being unusually tall for his age, Jenkins was unusually mature. Shortly after his eighteenth birthday, he got married – to one of the teachers at his school.

Two years later, he made his first-team debut against a Manchester United side that included George Best, Denis Law and Bobby Charlton. Although Palace lost – 3-1 – Jenkins was reckoned to have made a decent enough showing. But afterwards the pent-up nerves got to him and he threw up in the dressing-room toilets.

If Jenkins was anxious about being outplayed on the pitch, he wasn't shy about speaking his mind off it. At one post-match inquest, he became fed up with the endless attempts to work out why Palace had lost the game. Instead, he offered his own, more down-to-earth analysis. The main reason they had lost, Jenkins said, was because the other side had scored a goal and they hadn't.

As well as being a plain speaker, Jenkins was the possessor of an unusually penetrating stare. From his great height, he would focus his unblinking gaze on anyone who he disagreed with, and watch as they shrank before him. Neither of these things went down too well – either with the manager or the senior players.

For the next couple of seasons Jenkins bobbed about on the fringes of the Palace first team, scoring the occasional goal, but never quite cementing his place. And then Watford came calling. With little or no idea what he was letting himself in for, Jenkins agreed to the transfer. Like so many others before him, his first impressions of Vicarage Road made his heart sink. 'Christ, it was basic. I remember it as being a very dark, windy, inhospitable place. Everything about it seemed sparse, including the supporters.'

But to begin with everything looked promising. In his first appearance, Watford won their first away game for eighteen months – 'Tall, gazelle-like Ross Jenkins showcased many talents in a brilliant display to win the Man of the Match Award,' recorded the *Watford Observer*.

It proved to be yet another false dawn; they lost the next ten games on the trot. Even by Watford standards this was a disappointing run and Jenkins, inevitably, was singled out for blame. That season, he scored just two goals.

The next season – 1973/4 – he managed a total of four. 'Although I knew in my heart I wasn't such a bad player as everyone was making out, I came to feel like a sacrificial lamb. I can remember wishing I could just disappear for a while.'

It wasn't only the Watford supporters who turned against him; so did the directors. According to the club's manager, Mike Keen, 'As far as the board was concerned, he was a joke; an expensive failure.'

In the summer of 1975, Huddersfield Town offered to buy Jenkins for £12,000. Everyone – the board, the supporters, even some of his fellow players – begged him to accept. By then he had been at Watford for two and a half years, and he felt the least he could do was go up to Huddersfield and have a look.

Huddersfield too had recently been demoted to the Fourth Division, having finished bottom of Division Three the previous season. Jenkins duly met up with the club's manager and, to his surprise, was offered more money than he got at Watford. They agreed terms, Jenkins said he would call in the morning with his decision, and then he and his wife, Evie, went off to look at some houses where they might live.

But that night, he found he couldn't sleep. Lying in his hotel room, Jenkins stared at the ceiling as the hours ticked by. 'I stayed up all night, mulling everything over. Trying to decide what I should do. I knew that the sensible thing would be to cut my losses and move on. But in the back of my mind, I just had this feeling that I had a score to settle. That there was something unresolved – and that if I didn't sort it out then I might regret it for the rest of my life.'

In the morning, he phoned up the Huddersfield manager, thanked him for his offer and said that he'd decided to stay where he was. Later that day, Jenkins did something he hadn't done for a long time: he went and bought himself a new suit. 'It was a symbolic thing in a way. I was saying to myself that a line had been drawn under the past. That this was a new beginning and I wanted to be smartly dressed to face whatever lay ahead.'

*From the Headmaster's Letter, Pinner County*
*Grammar School, Winter 1972*

Mr and Mrs Pelzer and Miss Young took a party of 19 senior pupils on a skiing holiday to Macugnaga Staffa, Northern Italy, during the half term break . . . I have already reported to the appropriate committee through the Director of Education the theft on the night of November 3rd/4th of three transistor radios, a typewriter and 30 pence from the dinner float . . .

Meetings of Stag [the Sixth Form Society] have included talks on 'Forensic Science in Detection', 'The Soviet Union', 'Local History', 'On Being an Air Pilot' and a never-to-be-forgotten visit of ex-pupil Elton John who delighted the younger membership with his songs, and pleased the older members with the very real charm and common sense which lies behind the gimmickry of his profession.

# 15.

In early November 1973, a Mr P. R. Gurney from Bushey, representing Watford FC's Minority Shareholders Association, wrote a letter to the *Watford Observer*. It was headlined 'What's Wrong with Watford Football Club?'

It was a question more and more people were asking. In the 1971/72 season, Watford managed just two victories in their first sixteen games. Although they won their next two games, another nineteen would go by before their next victory. By this point the club's overdraft stood at £35,000 and there was a further £33,000 owing on the lease and a repair bill to one of the stands. A proposal to raise money by holding a monthly horse and pony auction at the ground was turned down by the council. If the club really wanted to make any money, one council member was quoted as saying, then they should close Vicarage Road and build houses on it.

'The bottomless pit has come to an end,' announced Jim Bonser. 'I would willingly take a back seat if benefactors came forward.' But whenever anyone showed any interest in buying the club, it took only one meeting with Bonser, every bit as obdurate as he was wary, to bring them to their senses.

The fans were now in open revolt against the chairman. Irrespective of the result of a game, there would be regular chants of 'Bonser Out!' And it wasn't just the fans; one of the Watford players, the striker Keith Mercer, had even named his dog 'Bonser out'. Mercer liked to bring his dog into Vicarage Road and walk it round the greyhound track, shouting out its name in as loud a voice as possible.

Like the Earl of Arran, Mr Gurney had also fallen into despair.

But what concerned him wasn't so much the near-total demolition of the town centre, as Watford Football Club's repeated inability to learn from their mistakes. 'It is no good selling stars and trying to replace them with has-beens,' he wrote in his letter. 'It is no longer any use expecting the supporters to pay hard-earned money to see rubbish. A complete shake-up is what is needed. A new Chairman with go-ahead ideas and the capital to see that we can survive.'

As Mr Gurney acknowledged, the chances of this happening were so unlikely as to be well-nigh impossible. 'In other words,' he concluded glumly, 'I am hoping for a miracle.'

# 16.

Around 18,000 people came to see Elton play at the Hollywood Bowl on the evening of 7 September 1973. Afterwards, all of them felt able to agree on one thing – they'd never seen anything like it before. Decked out from head to toe in white feathers, he made his entrance down an enormous glittery staircase while the lids of five grand pianos rose, one after the other, to reveal the letters E-L-T-O-N. At the same time, 400 white doves fluttered into the night sky.

Shortly after his new album, *Goodbye Yellow Brick Road*, had topped the charts on both sides of the Atlantic – his third successive US number one – he set off on a tour of Australia and New Zealand. By now Elton had become so successful that his record company provided him with a personalized Boeing 707 to fly him from one concert to another. As well as having a double bed with swagged velvet curtains, it also had a piano which doubled up as a bar.

Although this wasn't the last word in rock star excess – Led Zeppelin's private jet had its own fireplace – it was still a long way from the Public Bar at the Northwood Hills Hotel. Yet however far Elton may have shot into the stratosphere, he remained every bit as obsessed with Watford Football Club. Shortly before leaving for Australia, he was interviewed by a journalist, a fellow Watford supporter, who mentioned that the club was in financial trouble. If Elton was sad to hear of the club's plight, it hardly came as a big surprise: 'The main reason they didn't have any money was because no one was interested in coming to watch them lose each week.'

Among those travelling with him was his partner – and now

manager – John Reid, along with his agent, Vic Lewis. One evening after the show, Elton and Lewis had supper. 'During the meal our conversation came round to cricket,' Lewis recalled. 'While he was interested in the game, Elton confessed that his deepest passion was for football.' What he wanted most of all, he told Lewis, was to join Watford's board of directors. The problem was he had no idea how to go about it.

Soon after their supper, there had been an unfortunate incident. John Reid lost his temper with a barman when a particular drink he wanted was unavailable. Although it was explained that fresh supplies were on the way, Reid was in no mood to be mollified. In the ensuing scuffle a female journalist fell to the floor with blood dripping from her mouth. A male reporter was also punched.

The next morning while Reid was having his breakfast, he was arrested. Later he was sentenced to a month in prison. The whole incident left Elton feeling very upset.

Back in London, and hoping to lift his client's spirits, Vic Lewis had an idea. He called up the football correspondent of the *Watford Observer*, Oli Phillips.

'The phone rang in my office,' remembers Phillips, 'and this voice said, "My name is Vic Lewis. I'm Elton John's agent and the reason I'm calling is that Elton's rather keen to get involved with the club."'

Involved in what way, Phillips wondered.

Well, he was thinking of putting on a concert to raise some money, Lewis told him. And perhaps even joining the Watford board.

Phillips said he thought these were excellent ideas, but advised Lewis to tread carefully. Watford's chairman, Jim Bonser, was a very tricky man, he told him, and if he had any inkling that Elton wanted a seat on the board, he was likely to react badly.

What did Phillips suggest?

'I said that Elton could become a vice-president. Although the title sounded grand, all you had to do was pay fifty quid a year. In return, you could have as much as you could eat from the cold buffet, then watch the game from the Main Stand. Basically, it was for people who wanted to be directors, but couldn't afford the fees. That way, Elton would be able to get his feet under the table without putting Bonser's hackles up.'

Another few weeks went by before Oli Phillips received another phone call from Vic Lewis. 'Elton wanted to know what I'd done. I said, "If you really want to go ahead, please heed my warning: you are dealing with a dictator who has no intention of letting go."'

Phillips duly arranged a meeting between Jim Bonser and Elton John. Before the meeting, Elton was feeling more nervous than he had done since appearing at the Troubadour two years earlier. 'Just going into the board room at Watford was extraordinary for me. Although I could see the place was absolutely horrible, it still felt like a religious experience – like going into the place in Jerusalem where Christ is supposed to have been born. I can remember looking through the window and seeing the place where I used to stand as a boy. That was an incredibly romantic feeling. But there was also something very nourishing about it; a feeling that I was closing a circle in a way, going back to when I was a child.'

Braced for a chilly reception, he found that Bonser and his fellow directors couldn't have been friendlier. 'Although I had huge eight-inch platforms on and green hair, everyone was very warm and welcoming. That really took me aback.'

A watching Oli Phillips noted how polite Elton was – 'I think he might even have called Bonser "Sir"' – and also how polite Bonser was back to him. 'Given the state Watford were in, I think even Bonser could see that it made sense having a world-famous rock star on board.'

By the time the meeting ended, Elton John had been made a vice-president of Watford FC, with all the attendant benefits: a ticket to every home game and unrestricted access to the cold buffet.

On 5 May 1974, he played a concert in aid of Watford FC at Vicarage Road, topping a bill that included his friend and fellow football fanatic Rod Stewart. Elton had hoped to appear dressed as the club's mascot, Harry the Hornet – back in 1959 Watford had changed their colours from blue and white to gold and black – but unable to find a hornet costume, he arrived dressed as a giant bee instead. In the programme, he was described as 'an unashamed schizophrenic who is equally at home in his Watford colours cheerleading in the back of the coach, or on stage in a $500 feathered outfit'.

Not even a sudden cloudburst could dampen anyone's spirit. As the skies opened, Elton led a rapturous crowd in a chorus of 'Singin' in the Rain'. A few days later, Oli Phillips presented Jim Bonser with a cheque for £35,000. Not unreasonably, Phillips had expected some expression of gratitude. Bonser, however, was not impressed.

'I was hoping for £10,000 more,' he told him.

The money went towards much needed repairs to the Main Stand, as well as poisoning the large colony of rats that lived beneath it.

Now that Elton was on the board of Watford, his passion for the club was more intense than ever. In the spring of 1975, on the day that Watford were playing their last match of the season, he ran into a record shop in New York asking if he could use their phone to call home. Learning that Watford had just been beaten 3-2 by Walsall – a result that sent them back down to the Fourth Division once again – he immediately sat on the floor and burst into tears.

Six months later, following a unanimous vote by the directors, Elton John became the vice-chairman of Watford Football Club. Yet far from signalling a rapid about-turn in the club's fortunes, things limped on much as before. On 26 March 1976, Watford were beaten 5-1 at home by Lincoln. 'A particularly spineless performance,' declared another of Watford's directors, Muir Stratford.

But it wouldn't be a completely wasted afternoon as far as Stratford was concerned. In keeping with tradition, Lincoln's young manager, Graham Taylor, was invited for a drink in the Kremlin after the game. 'You get a certain feel for people and as soon as Graham came in, I took a liking to him,' Stratford recalls. 'He seemed to be a very nice chap and he also talked a lot of sense.'

Meanwhile, the world outside was lurching from one crisis to another. Unemployment in the UK had now soared to 1,250,000, while the annual rate of inflation had gone up to 24.2 per cent – its highest level since 1800. At the same time there had been further outbreaks of football hooliganism – or the 'English Disease', as foreign newspapers had taken to calling it.

In an interview Elton gave to *Playboy* magazine, he too bemoaned the state of the country: 'England is falling apart; inflation is incurable and the politicians are useless.'

His own life, he acknowledged, had become so strange that even he found it hard to believe what had happened. Recently, he had played a concert at Madison Square Garden in New York. During the show, he introduced a special guest, John Lennon – the man that just seven years earlier he had named one of his goldfish after. It would turn out to be the last time that Lennon played in public.

Elton was then asked if he had any unfulfilled ambitions.

Absolutely, he replied. 'My real ambition is to make enough money to retire and become chairman of my local football club, Watford.'

# 17.

Events finally came to a head in the spring of 1976. Like his predecessor, Jim Bonser decided that he was too old, tired and fed up to continue. He offered to sell Elton the club outright – or rather give it to him if Elton agreed to settle the club's debts of around £200,000. Perhaps Bonser was expecting a little humming and hawing; after all, £200,000 was still a lot of money – more than a million pounds in today's terms.

In the event, Elton practically bit his arm off. 'I didn't need to think about it, not for a moment. I was so keen to accept.'

Elton John was now twenty-nine years old. The year before, he had been responsible for 2 per cent of the world's album sales. To put it another way, one album in every fifty sold had been by him. In rapid succession, he had made three of the best-selling albums of all time. A couple of weeks before buying Watford, he played seven consecutive nights at Madison Square Garden in New York to a total of nearly 140,000 people.

What he'd never done, of course, was run a football club, or chair a board meeting. But for the time being, these seemed like trifling concerns. Watford may have been one of the worst teams in the Football League, yet far from being put off by the club's plight, it brought out Elton's competitive streak. 'I remember when I took over telling the board that I wanted to take Watford into the First Division. They all looked at me as if I was stark staring mad.'

Possibly there was another factor that made him so keen to buy Watford – though he didn't become aware of it until much later. 'Perhaps my father was at the back of it somewhere.

Perhaps I wanted to do something to mark all the great times I'd had there as a kid.'

Not that Elton had even told Stanley when he bought the club. By now they barely ever communicated, still less saw one another. Nor did Elton have any idea how his father felt when he heard the news. But then neither did Stanley's new family; once again, he kept his feelings to himself.

Yet it must have been an extraordinary moment for Stanley. His son had bought his beloved Vicarage Road – the place where for years he'd been happier than anywhere else. Did his thoughts drift back to their first trip there almost a quarter of a century earlier? However bottled up Stanley may have been, it would have been very odd if they hadn't. And perhaps he found himself reflecting on something else. That this was a symbolic moment too: the moment when their roles had been irrevocably reversed; when the son had effectively usurped the father.

Others were much less restrained in their reactions. John Reid was incandescent when he heard, suspecting – quite rightly – that Elton's involvement with Watford was going to take up time when he could have been touring or recording. And Reid was not the only one who thought the whole thing was a terrible idea.

Traditionally, football clubs were owned by elderly business-men who kept their heads below the parapet, and as much distance between themselves and the fans as possible. This was the first time a club had been bought by a pop star, and a number of football journalists saw it as further evidence that the country was going to the dogs.

Almost the only person who didn't have a tremor of doubt was Elton himself. He was not remotely bothered by what people thought. 'Everyone was saying, "It's a rich man's indulgence, a five-minute wonder", and all the rest of it. They also seemed to have this idea that if you were a rock star, you were somehow stupid. That everything must have fallen into your lap. But these people didn't have any idea how hard I'd worked.'

And there was another factor too. 'None of them actually knew me. When I set my heart on something, I commit to it 100 per cent. I never gave a monkey's about the press anyway; all I cared about was getting the fans and the community on side. As far as I was concerned, everyone else could go screw themselves.'

Just as Graham's arrival at Lincoln had had no immediate effect on the club's fortunes, so life at Watford trundled on much as before after Elton had bought the club. Now that the club was owned by a rock star, there were those who felt that it was time to ditch 'Z-Cars' as their theme tune and adopt one of their new chairman's songs instead. Elton, however, wouldn't consider it. 'I never wanted my music played at the club; that would have been far too egotistical.'

Every match day, there were certain rituals Elton liked to perform. First, he would go to the players' dressing room before the game to wish them luck, taking care never to hang around for too long in case he disrupted their preparations. 'The players knew that I respected them; that I was on their side. A lot of chairmen slag off their players, but not me.'

Too restless to sit down and too nervous to eat anything, he would pace around the Kremlin waiting impatiently for the teams to run out onto the pitch. Then, once the game was under way, he would chew through several packets of Orbit sugar-free chewing gum. 'I had a ritual about this too: if Watford lost, I would always throw my Orbit wrappers away. But if we won, I would keep the wrappers in my pockets.' To throw them away, he felt, might somehow jinx any luck they were enjoying and consign them to yet another defeat.

He also had a ritual for what he did after they lost a game. On his way home, Elton would fish in his pockets for his Orbit wrappers, chuck them disconsolately into a bin and wonder when, or if, Watford's fortunes were ever going to change.

\*

While there was no shortage of rumours about Elton's private life, in public he had discreetly sought to fan the flames of heterosexuality. When he went to a game at Vicarage Road, he often took a young woman along – partly for company and partly to dampen down any rumours.

Laura Croker was working as Elton's UK press officer at his recently formed record company, Rocket Records, when she was asked if she would accompany him to a game. 'What I remember most is that Elton was very shy and very solicitous. It was bitterly cold that afternoon. He could see I was shivering, so he sent someone to fetch me something warm to wear from his locker.'

To her surprise, the man came back with a mink coat.

Then, in October 1976, Elton gave another interview – this time to *Rolling Stone*. Before he started, the journalist, a man called Cliff Jahr, told his photographer, Ron Pownall, that he was planning to ask Elton about his sexuality. Jahr, who was gay himself, realized he might be venturing into awkward territory – up until this point, no one in showbusiness had ever claimed to be anything other than incorrigibly heterosexual.

Possibly the presence of a photographer might make Elton clam up, Jahr felt. He and Pownall therefore agreed they should have a code word that would be the photographer's cue to leave. If Jahr said the word 'privacy', then Pownall would make himself scarce.

They hadn't been talking for long when Jahr casually steered the conversation towards Elton's privacy – or lack of it. Pownall duly disappeared into the room next door. But it turned out there was no need for such subterfuge: Elton was quite happy to talk about his sexuality – and anything else that came up.

Having fulfilled his ambition of becoming chairman of Watford, there was something else he craved, he said: 'I desperately would like to have an affair. My life in the last six years has been a Disney film and now I have to have a person in my life. I'm going through a stage where any form of affection would be welcome on a sexual level. I'd rather fall in love with a woman because I think a woman probably lasts much longer than a man. But I really don't know . . . I haven't met anybody that I would like to settle down with of either sex.'

'You're bisexual?' Jahr asked with a quiver of excitement.

'There's nothing wrong with going to bed with somebody of your own sex,' Elton replied. 'I think everybody's bisexual to some degree . . .'

'You haven't said it in print before.'

'Nobody's had the balls to ask me about it before. I would have said something all along if someone had asked me.'

What did Elton think the reaction might be, Jahr wondered. 'There shouldn't be too much reaction, but you probably know these things better than me,' Elton replied. However, there was one place where it was sure to go down badly, he felt. 'It's going to be terrible with my football club; it's so hetero, it's unbelievable. But I mean who cares! I just think people should be very free with sex – although they should draw the line at goats.'

On the day that the *Rolling Stone* article was published, the American news anchor Walter Cronkite covered the story on his evening show. Elsewhere, there was speculation that it might damage Elton's record sales – as it turned out, it had no effect whatsoever.

But in the UK, the interview sent the tabloid press into a frenzy. 'Elton Swings Both Ways!' read one headline; 'Rocketman Draws Line at Goats!' read another. Yet it caused much less of a fuss in the place where Elton had expected the most. After the stories about his bisexuality appeared, the Watford manager, Mike Keen, asked to see him.

Once again Elton braced himself for trouble, and once again he was pleasantly surprised. 'The team and I have read what it says in the papers,' Keen told him, 'and we don't care. You are our chairman and we love you.'

Elton was deeply touched. But while there was no questioning Mike Keen's qualities as a man, his abilities as a manager were coming under increasing scrutiny. In February 1977, another letter appeared in the *Watford Observer,* this time from a Mr R. K. Verna: 'Sirs, I along with others greeted the departure of Jim Bonser with great relief. But after eight months of Elton John's chairmanship, I can only come to one conclusion. Either they have a small gas leak in the boardroom, or someone is drugging the scotch.'

After banging on about Watford's deficiencies for some time, Mr Verna loosed off one last salvo: 'So, Mr Elton and your board, turn off the gas, wake up and do something!'

Three months later, a single sentence appeared in the same paper: 'Mike Keen's 45-month reign came to an emotive end at Vicarage Road on Saturday.' Keen had been sacked just before a home game against Huddersfield, but had insisted on watching from the touchline. Much to everyone's amazement, possibly including Keen's, Watford won the game 2-0, despite having two players sent off.

Now all that remained to be decided was who would take his place.

To begin with, Elton's thoughts turned to Bobby Moore. The former captain of England's World Cup-winning side in 1966, Moore was a legendary figure – elegant, commanding and unflappable, the rock around which any side could cohere. However, he knew little about management and even less about life in the Fourth Division.

And as Elton began to suspect, there was another problem with Bobby Moore: he was too nice. 'You need to have a thick skin to be a manager, and you've also got to be a bastard. What I wanted above all was someone young and hungry and inspirational. Someone who wasn't just going to splash my money about. You can't just go out and buy a team – that's always a disaster. You have to build it from the ground upwards.'

When Elton talked to the Watford board, Muir Stratford remembered how impressed he had been with Graham Taylor when they had met a year earlier. Elton then called the England manager, Don Revie and asked him who was the best young manager in the lower divisions. Revie didn't even have to think about it.

'Graham Taylor,' he said immediately.

# 18.

That same week, in the early summer of 1977, Graham got home from work in Lincoln to learn from his wife, Rita, that Don Revie had phoned earlier. He would call back later, he had told her. Graham had always been a big admirer of Revie's and had dreamed of following in his footsteps – at Leeds United, Revie had won the Second Division title, the First Division title (twice) and the FA Cup.

Graham spent a restless afternoon wondering what on earth the England manager wanted to talk to him about. For a moment he even wondered if Revie might be calling up one of the Lincoln players to the England squad, before telling himself that he must be getting carried away. When the phone went, he let it ring a couple of times before he answered, not wanting to appear too eager.

Revie got straight to the point. Was he still under contract at Lincoln?

Very much so, Graham told him; in fact, he'd recently signed a new deal.

'Ah, that's a shame,' said Revie, 'because I've just recommended you to a chairman.'

As Graham recalled, 'I could feel my chest swell a bit and I stood up a little bit straighter. It felt good to know the England manager was vouching for me.'

'Who's that?' he asked as casually as he could.

'Elton John,' said Revie. 'At Watford.'

Immediately, Graham's chest deflated. Having spent three years guiding Lincoln to the top reaches of the Third Division, the last thing he wanted was to take over a bunch of Fourth Division losers like Watford. What little he knew about Elton John made Graham even less keen. On the few occasions he had heard his music, he hadn't cared for it at all. His own tastes were rather more traditional. While he was a great fan of Buddy Holly's, his devotion to Vera Lynn knew no bounds.

'I tried not to let the disappointment show in my voice, but I couldn't believe Don was doing this to me. Why would he think I would want to take a step backwards? Suddenly, my confidence dipped. If this is what the England manager thought of me, was it how others felt?'

A few days later, Graham had another call. This time it was Elton John. He too came straight to the point. How would he feel about becoming the new manager of Watford? Too tactful to say what he really felt, Graham asked about Elton's plans for the club. As they talked, he found himself increasingly surprised. 'I still didn't know much about him apart from the pop star image I'd seen on television, so his voice and calm understated manner on the phone were not quite what I expected. Our call was not that long, but his passion for Watford and his knowledge of the Fourth Division did impress me. I realized in that short call this wasn't just a daft pop star with too much money messing about until he got bored and moved onto something else.'

What's more, the salary Elton was offering – £20,000 a year – was far more than any other Fourth Division manager was getting. Even so, Graham wasn't tempted. Although he had begun to feel that he might be outgrowing Lincoln, his ambitions were set far higher than Watford. Besides, he had other things on his mind; he and his family were about to go on their first ever foreign holiday – a caravanning trip to France.

'I'm sorry, I'm not interested,' he said.

'Ah,' said Elton. 'Well, that's a shame.'

They said their goodbyes, and Graham put down the phone.

\*

A few days after Graham returned from his caravanning holiday, his phone rang again. Picking up the receiver, he heard Elton's voice on the other end of the line. 'Look, I know you said no,' he said, 'and I don't want to be a nuisance, but I won't feel I'm doing my job properly unless I meet you and explain to you what it is we want to do.'

At the time, Graham and Rita were about to go to London where he was attending a Football League dinner at the Café Royal – it wouldn't be that much of a detour to go over to Elton's house in Windsor the next day.

On their journey down to London, Graham decided to have a quiet look at Watford's ground. It was even grimmer than he had anticipated. Stuck out on the edge of town, amid a jumble of second-hand car showrooms, with some allotments on one side and a hospital on the other, it was as bleak as it was run-down. From what Graham could tell, there seemed to be more life in the allotments than there was in the ground itself.

Fortunately, Watford were not the only club who were after him. Before he left for London, Graham had heard that West Bromwich Albion had also expressed interest. This was more like it. Apart from anything else, West Bromwich Albion were in the First Division. What's more, they had finished in seventh place the previous season, and were plainly going places. The West Brom chairman, Bert Millichip, was also attending the Café Royal dinner, and so the two of them would have a chance to talk afterwards.

Once the meal was over, Graham was invited to sit at the West Brom table. Over port and cigars, Millichip proceeded to tell him how lucky he would be to join the club. 'Graham, you've never played in the First Division or managed in the First Division, but I like to think we know all about you, and we're prepared to take a risk.'

While Graham hadn't expected to be showered with compliments, he hadn't expected to be patronized either. Already, he could feel his hackles starting to rise. 'They assumed I would agree to join them just because they were West Bromwich Albion.' He was even more put out when he heard how much money West Brom were proposing to pay him: £9,000 a year –less than half Elton's offer. Wanting to keep everything above board, he thought he'd better tell Millichip that he had been approached by another club.

'Do you mind telling me who it is?' Millichip asked.

'It's Watford,' Graham told him.

Millichip practically fell off his chair.

'Watford?' he exclaimed. 'But they're in the Fourth Division. You'll have to go to places like Rochdale, Halifax and Workington!'

Graham felt obliged to point out that Millichip had made an elementary mistake. Workington were no longer in the Football League – earlier that same day, the League's Annual General Meeting had voted not to readmit them. 'Mr Millichip appeared not to even know the result of the vote he'd participated in that afternoon. Or, if he did, it hadn't registered with him and that really irritated me. I felt it was disrespectful to another professional football club.'

Quite unaware of the effect he was having, Millichip steamed blithely on. 'You should give your right arm to join this club,' he told him.

That did it as far as Graham was concerned. 'My right arm is staying exactly where it is,' he said coldly. 'Attached to my right shoulder.'

The next morning, still smarting from their encounter, Graham and Rita drove off to Windsor to see Elton. On their way there, it had occurred to Graham that it might strike Elton as being a bit odd that he should bring his wife along to what was effectively a job interview, but he had been determined that Rita should come too. 'I wanted Elton to know that I would commit everything to whichever club I worked for next, but that my family was important to me. I wanted him to meet Rita, and for Rita to meet him.'

Things did not get off to a promising start. After they managed to negotiate the intercom set into the gate post – they had never seen one before and couldn't understand where this disembodied voice was coming from – the gates swung open. At the end of a long drive sat what Graham described as 'a mansion, and a beautiful one at that'.

The door was answered by a woman with short brown hair who Graham assumed at first was a housekeeper – she turned out to be Elton's mother, Sheila.

While Sheila took Rita on a tour of the house, the two men sat down to talk. Graham was still stunned by the opulence of the surroundings: 'the beautiful furniture and vases, the artwork on the walls, the cars in the drive, the expansive grounds outside.'

What he didn't realize was that once again Elton was stricken with nerves: 'I was so intimidated that I felt sick. I wasn't even sure what to say. I knew I shouldn't talk about money because I was sure he would have told me to fuck off straightaway. Besides, that wasn't what it was about; it was about selling the club and selling my dreams for the club. I can remember thinking, how am I going to convince this guy to come to a rundown shithole like Watford? A club with a rock 'n' roll chairman who was six feet four in his platform soles and had green hair? What was he going to make of me? He was probably going to think I was a complete tosser.'

There was no doubt they made an unlikely pair. At the time Elton was one of the most flamboyant men on the planet, while Graham was quite possibly one of the most conventional: he lived conservatively, dressed conservatively and behaved conservatively. Just about the only thing he didn't do conservatively was think.

But right from the moment the two of them started talking, Elton became aware that something unusual was going on.

'There was something magical about it, something almost spiritual. It really was as if fate had brought us together.' The only time it had ever happened to him before was when he met Bernie Taupin. 'I had exactly the same sort of feeling with Graham as I'd done when I met Bernie – that it was somehow meant to be.'

Although Graham and Elton may have been poles apart in some respects, they soon realized they were both as passionate as they were driven. 'That was the thing above all that we had in common: passion. My philosophy about football was that above all it should be entertaining. It's just like going to a concert; the last thing people want is to be bored. Graham felt exactly the same way; that was why he wanted his teams to attack the whole time.'

It wasn't only football they felt the same way about. 'We talked for hours and hours, about his dad, about my family, all kinds of stuff. What I loved was that we were so similar in some ways, yet so different in others.'

Graham clearly didn't know Elton's music well – if at all – but that was fine too. 'The last thing I wanted was someone who was star-struck; I just wanted someone who was going to get on with the job.' To Graham's surprise, Elton had clearly done a lot of research on what he had achieved at Lincoln, particularly on the community work the club had engaged in. If he was going to come to Watford, he would want to do the same thing there, Graham told him.

Far from being put off, Elton was delighted. He too believed that it was important for a football club to connect with the people in the town, to give them something to be proud of. And it was all the more important in a town like Watford, which had seen its employers melt away, its inhabitants grow increasingly demoralized and its identity smashed to bits by a wrecking ball.

Elton repeated that for him becoming chairman of Watford wasn't some passing fancy; he intended to devote as much time as he could to the club. That said, he was happy to give the manager a free hand to do anything he thought necessary.

'I think that was the important thing for Graham,' Rita recalled later. 'He would have walked away immediately if he'd thought there was any chance of Elton interfering.'

The more Elton spoke, the more Graham found himself being won over. 'But I still wanted to know if he had any idea what he was letting himself in for. Watford was a medium-sized town, close enough to London that people would be attracted to bigger clubs like Arsenal and Tottenham Hotspur. Hertfordshire was not a footballing hotbed and the club itself had very little pedigree to speak of. They had spent three years in the Second Division about a decade earlier and played in one FA Cup semi-final and that was about it. I decided to ask him exactly what he expected to achieve.'

It turned out to be a question that Elton had given a good deal of thought to. He had already told the club's directors that he wanted to take Watford into the First Division. Now he went a step further. 'I'd like to get into Europe,' he told Graham.

Now it was Graham's turn to fall off his chair. At the time, only the top two clubs in the First Division qualified to play European football the following season. The likelihood of Watford – back once again in the lower reaches of the Fourth Division – ever being in a position to do so seemed about as remote as them flying to the moon.

He found himself in a tricky position. Either he could treat this as clear evidence of rockstar egomania – possibly derangement – or he could take it at face value. While all Graham's instincts told him to go for the first explanation, he still found himself feeling torn. 'I thought, "This fella is crazy." For the first time since we started talking, I thought my initial fears were founded. Perhaps Elton really was just a pop star with his head in the clouds. But there was something about the look in his eyes that told me he wasn't joking, and his ambition did excite me.'

'OK . . .' Graham said in as measured a voice as he could muster. 'Well, what do you think it will cost to do that?'

'Well, what do *you* think it will cost?' Elton wanted to know.

There was no point in being mealy-mouthed, Graham decided. Far better to scare him off with an enormous figure than try to pretend it could be done on the cheap. 'I don't think you'll get much change out of a million pounds,' he said.

Elton didn't hesitate. 'Right, we'll give it a go,' he said – and then he stretched out his hand.

With his head still reeling, Graham shook it.

# PART TWO

*From the* Watford Observer

## UNTIDY AND DIRTY – THAT'S WATFORD!

Watford has been named one of the dirtiest towns in the south of England, following an upsurge in complaints about the squalid nature of the town centre. At first, a shortage of street cleaners was thought to be to blame. However, a council official said that in fact the street cleaners did a very good job, but as fast as they swept up, litter was dropped behind them.

Some councillors described how they watched people drop receipts, paper bags and wrappings on to the High Street, tossing them away with no thought to the consequences. 'It was just like a ticker-tape welcome in New York,' said Councillor Jack Twyndle.

## NEW TOWN CENTRE DRIVES SICK WOMAN OUT

A woman handicapped by a chest complaint claims she has been driven out of Watford by all the redevelopment. Mrs Binks Mundy left her house in Essex Road last week after living in Watford for 32 years.

She and her husband are moving to Mansfield in Nottinghamshire where Mrs Mundy hopes the air will be more beneficial. In future, she will no longer have to face the network of subways and underpasses in order to reach the town centre. What had once been a five-minute stroll took her 30 minutes after the recent ring-road development.

'Every time I tried to cross a road, I felt as if I was taking my life in my hands,' Mrs Mundy complained.

# 19.

On Wednesday 22 June 1977, Graham Taylor paid a second visit to Watford. 'Fact-finding visit prior to signing contract on Friday,' he noted in his diary. 'Decided to arrive by train and took the Metropolitan Line from Euston. Pleasantly surprised on arrival to see parts of Watford I had not anticipated.'

It was a very residential area, Graham noted approvingly. But while he liked the look of the semi-detached houses with their neat front gardens and freshly mown strips of lawn, he wondered if their occupants might be a bit too sedate ever to get worked up about their football club.

Nor was this his only concern.

I am conscious that I am pre-judging the playing staff, but I don't think they are good enough. They come from all over and are not readily on call. Met with Ron Rollitt (general manager and secretary) and chairman (Elton) came down. First impression of the club was that organisation and discipline were sloppy.

On seeing the wage structure it was obvious there had been no real policy. There's a lack of lead from the board who are immature and don't really know how a football club should be run. All very nice people though and the chairman is very sincere in wanting the football club to be successful.

At the end of a two-hour meeting, Graham was more confused than ever. 'There's a great deal to find out about a lot of people,' he noted. Then he added an afterthought: 'I am going to upset quite a number to get this club on its feet.'

The next time Graham and Elton met was in the Kremlin

at Vicarage Road to sign his contract. Elton arrived in his chauffeur-driven Bentley, while Graham, just as he'd done on his previous visit, took the Metropolitan Line tube. However daunted he may have been by the enormity of the task ahead, he was already fired up by the challenge. Yet he wasn't the most excited person in the room, he realized. His new chairman was practically bouncing up and down in his seat.

'Do you know,' Elton said to him in half-gleeful, half-incredulous tones, 'this is the first big decision I've made on my own in years.'

At that moment, something that Graham had been thinking a good deal about lately fell abruptly into place. 'Elton had scores of people looking after his career. People at his management company, people at the record company, people who organized his tours . . . He couldn't necessarily make decisions about his own career any more. It suddenly dawned on me why Elton enjoyed owning Watford Football Club so much; it was his passion and his project.'

As the two of them sat in the Watford boardroom, Elton was deep in his own thoughts, recalling the first time he had ever been to Vicarage Road – that Saturday afternoon a quarter of a century earlier when he had stood on the Bend with his father. When they had both roared and chanted, united for once in a common cause.

What would his boyhood self make of what was happening now, he wondered. What on earth would he have thought if he could have peered into the future and seen that one day he would be the owner of Watford Football Club? 'Becoming chairman of Watford meant far more to me than being famous. I may have become Elton John, but I was fulfilling Reggie's dreams. And in a way being chairman of Watford meant I could go back to being Reggie again, at least for a while.'

After he and Graham signed the paperwork, posed for photographs, then helped themselves to a celebratory drink from Mrs

Bonser's drinks cabinet, Elton was aware of something he had never experienced before – despite all the success he'd enjoyed, all the praise that had been heaped upon him and all the wealth he had accumulated. A feeling so strong that it quite bowled him over.

'I felt like the greatest man on earth.'

# 20.

*Extract from Graham Taylor's diary*

Friday, 24 June 1977: Board Meeting.

Elton John – chairman. Thirty-year-old multi-millionaire pop star. Watford supporter all his life. Local boy made world star. Wants success, doesn't really know how to get it. No grip of board meetings and yet has a mind of his own and is no fool. A lot of advantages but also disadvantages and simply because of who he is there are people who want him to fail.

The board is not stable in thought or policy at the moment and very reliant on chairman from a financial point of view. But they are prepared to work and are interested.

Shortly after Graham started work at Watford, he asked about the scouting system at the club. He was met with blank looks – apparently they didn't have one. But this wasn't entirely true. The club turned out to have a scout, along with an assistant, a former Watford player called Bill McCracken. Together, they would go and check out young players who played for local teams. However, they didn't do so very often.

Why not, he asked.

Because of the age of Mr McCracken.

Graham was even more puzzled. How old was he, he asked.

He was ninety-five.

Hoping it might prove a safer subject, Graham asked about the training ground. Again he was met with blank looks; there definitely wasn't one of those. Instead, players had to train on the nearest public playing fields which they shared with teams from several Watford schools. With a deepening sense of apprehension, he asked to see the training kit. The shirts were frayed and full of holes, while the elastic in the shorts had perished years earlier. In order to stop their shorts from falling down when they ran around, players had to tie a knot in their waistbands.

Nobody had their own kit. Before each training session a large sack would be tipped onto the dressing room floor and everyone would grab whatever they needed. The socks were particularly vile, Graham saw. As well as being very smelly, they were stiff to the touch. Crusty even.

How often was the kit washed, he asked.

Once a week, he was told proudly.

One of the first things Graham did as the new manager was to make a list of everyone who worked at the club – from the chairman right down to the tea lady. It didn't take him long: there were only three administrative employees, including a shorthand typist and a man referred to simply as 'a retired gentleman'.

Even so, he wanted to know who got on with who, and who didn't. Who were the trouble-makers and who were the diehards who were bound to resist any kind of change? He also went round all the pubs in the area, introducing himself to the landlords and landladies and giving them his card. He didn't mind players coming in for a drink now and again, he told them, but if anyone was overdoing it, or drinking the night before a game, he wanted to know.

Graham then wrote individual letters to all the players asking them to come and see him. 'You can work out quite quickly who has a spark in their eyes and fire in their belly and who doesn't. Some of them had been bumping around in the lower divisions for years and had lost any sense of direction; others were young players who had a lot to learn.'

From the start, he had decided that he wouldn't be reckless

with Elton's money. Determined to prove that he could make big improvements without it, he also wanted to earn his chairman's trust. But already he'd begun to suspect that the experience of losing had become so ingrained in the team that Watford had forgotten how to win.

Do the players look at the game from any other perspective apart from their own? Graham wrote in his diary. Do they understand and appreciate the roles of each of their team-mates and know how the team fitted together?

The answer to both questions was staring him in the face, he realized: they didn't have a clue.

Among the first players Graham saw was the first-team goalkeeper, Steve Sherwood. Six foot four inches tall and twenty-three years old, the mild-mannered Sherwood had joined Watford from Chelsea the previous season for a fee of £4,000. 'I remember going into his office and sitting down on this very low chair – it was like something from primary school,' he recalled.

With some difficulty, Sherwood lowered himself into the chair. For one of the few times in his life, he found himself looking up at someone. 'That was odd enough, but what surprised me the most was that Graham already knew all about me – where I'd been brought up, my family, my interests, all those sorts of things.'

To begin with, they discussed what life had been like under the old regime. For instance, did he train in the afternoon?

Sherwood racked his brains. He vaguely remembered one occasion when he'd been asked to train in the afternoon, but it had stuck in his mind only because it was so unusual.

What about specialized goalkeeper training?

What about it, he asked.

Had he ever done any?

Confidently, Sherwood shook his head.

'Well, I'm going to take this club places,' Graham told him. 'Do you want to be a part of it?'

Sherwood thought about this too. 'I was aware that my career wasn't really going anywhere; I'd started off in the First Division and now I was in the Fourth. But I was still ambitious and I wanted to become a better player. The trouble was that I'd always rather lacked confidence.'

He gave what he hoped was an emphatic nod.

'How easy do you want it to be?' Graham asked.

Without thinking, Sherwood said, 'As easy as I can make it.'

The moment he had spoken, he realized his mistake. 'I kicked myself for saying the wrong thing, but I felt as if I was in a job interview and I was really quite nervous.'

Leaning across his desk, Graham stared down at him.

While he tried to hold his gaze, Sherwood felt himself quailing.

There would be no room for the lazy or the lackadaisical here, Graham said. What he was looking for was total, unflagging commitment. 'You're going to work harder than you've ever worked before. You're going to run and sweat and get fitter than you've ever been in your life. Do you understand?'

Sherwood swallowed, then nodded again.

As he left, Graham offered a parting shot. 'You've got a lot to prove,' he told him.

While Steve Sherwood was still near the start of his career, Tom Walley was plainly nearing the end. A midfielder who had once played for Arsenal and been capped by Wales, Walley was now thirty-two years old.

As soon as he sat down, he said, 'I'll be honest, gaffer. My knee is fucked.'

Graham was immediately impressed. Most players would have tried to conceal any injury. To own up to one without being asked was almost unheard of.

Like Graham, Walley was blunt, no-nonsense and a keen disciplinarian. And as they talked, Graham realized this might be just the man he was looking for. Given that the club scout's assistant was ninety-five years old and there was no youth policy to speak of, he badly needed someone who was able to combine talent-spotting with running a youth team. Watford was such a small club that it was vital they developed their own young players. That way they'd be able to save on transfer fees, and maybe even make a bit of money if they were able to sell players on to other clubs.

And there was something else that made Graham feel that Walley just might be the right man for the job. 'If I'm honest, he frightened the life out of me.'

What did he think of Watford's young players, Graham asked.

There were some decent players among them, Walley told him, but they needed proper guidance.

Was there anyone in particular that he rated?

'Luther Blissett,' answered Walley.

Two years on from the defeat at Darlington, Luther Blissett was still on the substitutes' bench. Despite scoring on his first-team debut, he had failed to hold down a regular place and was back playing for the reserves. Now aged nineteen, he'd come to England from Jamaica as a child – his father worked at the McVitie's biscuit factory in Harlesden and his mother was a cleaner.

Like everyone else, Blissett had no idea what to expect when he was summoned to see the new manager. What he didn't know at the time was that the previous regime at Watford had already decided to let him go. He clearly had talent, but was considered too raw, too immature, to be worth persevering with. Although he possessed a powerful kick, Blissett's shooting was none too accurate – hence his being dubbed 'Luther Missit' by some fans.

Graham, however, thought he could see something in him. 'He had a positive energy about him that I liked straightaway.' Elton too had spotted a glimmer of something promising in the young Blissett. 'He was quick, very quick. I hadn't seen a player like that at Watford before.'

Blissett sat down in Graham's office, eager but nervous.

Graham looked him in the eye. 'Luther Blissett . . .' he said.

He continued to look him in the eye.

Blissett stared back, as confused now as he was nervous.

'Loother Blissss-iitttt . . .' Graham repeated more loudly this time, stretching out the words.

Blissett was even more nonplussed.

Graham then stood up, throwing out his arms. 'Loooooooo-thuurrrr. Bliisssittt!' he repeated. 'With a name like that, son, you're bound to be a star.' He then told him he would have a year in which to prove himself.

Afterwards, Graham was taken aback by his own behaviour. 'I have no idea where it came from, but I think it made an impression on him.'

It did more than that. Without being quite sure what had gone on, Blissett left feeling more optimistic than he had done in months. 'He filled me with this sense of belonging, which was something I'd never really had before. I remember going away thinking, "This guy might just give me a chance."'

## Excerpt from Graham Taylor's diary

Saturday 25 June 1977.

Scouting: No one watches opposition games and there seems to have been no work done in this direction at all. Will have to look into the whole system.

Youth Policy: Almost non-existent.

Kit: No one seems to know who is in charge of it. Not impressed with how the kit is packed and would hazard a guess that no one really knows what we have got or not.

Equipment: We have a weights room . . . Apart from that, there are a few cones and absolutely nothing else at all.

Ground: A lot of mess about from the greyhounds and this is obviously going to be a problem. Ground staff is Les Simmons and two or three part-time helpers. Simmons pays a lot of attention to the pitch, even to the extent of not liking the players to go on it.

The more he thought about it, the more apt it seemed that Watford should have a groundsman who blew his top whenever a player set foot on his pitch.

One player in particular prompted peculiar reactions in people, Graham noticed. Whenever Ross Jenkins's name was mentioned, they would scrunch up their faces and blow air out of their cheeks. Although no one said anything nasty about him, they didn't really have anything good to say either.

At this point Jenkins was twenty-six years old, about to turn twenty-seven. As Graham would write later in his autobiography, *In His Own Words*, 'If he wasn't careful, he was going to find it hard to stay in the professional game. He was the archetypal ugly duckling in that he was six feet four inches tall, all arms and legs.'

In short, he was a prime candidate for the scrapheap. But however ungainly Jenkins was, however erratic his ball control, spindly his legs and hopeless his heading, there was something that made Graham feel he wasn't a completely lost cause. While he lacked much in the way of an aggressive streak, he was fast, difficult to mark and never panicked under pressure. He was also particularly good at controlling a high ball, chesting it down to his feet, then using his body to shield it from opposition players. 'If we fired a ball out of a cannon at him, he'd have a better than fifty-fifty chance of bringing it down.'

Although Elton was not that convinced by Jenkins's abilities, he had noticed there was something out of the ordinary about him. 'Physically, he was like a giraffe. But he was also a bit of a hippie. You could tell straightaway that he was a clever man who thought deeply about things.'

Unusually, Jenkins had other interests apart from football – natural history being one of them. At the time this was almost unheard of. Footballers tended not to have outside interests, still less hobbies, although the Chelsea goalkeeper Peter 'The Cat' Bonetti was known to collect dolls dressed in national costume.

Asked to come into Graham's office, Jenkins took one look at the tiny chair he was expected to sit in and decided that he had no intention of falling for such an obvious ploy. But just a few seconds later, he changed his mind. 'Normally, I like to stand up, especially when I get heated. Under the circumstances, though, I thought I'd better show willing.'

Jenkins too lowered himself down to near floor level.

Graham told him that he was going to 'dust the ship down', and that Jenkins was going to have to do whatever was asked of him. However, he would get his chance to prove himself, he told him. 'I felt Ross could be coached to use his assets and ability more effectively,' Graham recalled. 'And that, in a nutshell, is the essence of football management.'

What was abundantly clear was that Jenkins's career had reached a critical fork in the road. While he had no way of knowing where one path might lead, he had a pretty good idea where the other would end up. 'You got off your low seat and left the room in no doubt that you were going to toe Graham's line. Either that, or you'd be out on your ear.'

# 21.

On his first day of training, Graham took the players to the nearest park and asked them all a question: 'Which of you thinks that he's a Fourth Division player?'

No one put their hand up.

'Well, you're all Fourth Division players,' he told them, 'and there's no point in fooling yourselves by pretending otherwise. If you really believe you're better than that, you'll have to prove it by winning enough matches to win the Fourth Division Championship. Then and only then can you call yourselves Third Division players.'

If they were going to win promotion, not only would the Watford players need to be fitter than ever, they would also need to look the part. In future, they would be expected to clean their own kit. On the field, their shirts should be tucked into their shorts, while their socks were to be pulled up at all times. What's more, socks had to be neatly folded over at the top with the same number of stripes showing on each leg.

Off the field, the rules were just as strict: players should always be smartly dressed – jeans were banned – and were expected to be polite and considerate to others. Any transgressions would result in hefty fines.

As they were struggling to take this in, he told them they were going on a ten-mile run. Although Graham's words had made a big impression on Steve Sherwood at their first meeting, their implications can't have sunk in completely. When Graham blew his whistle everyone started running – everyone except Sherwood and the club's other goalkeeper, Andy Rankin. They just stayed where they were, looking more puzzled than ever.

'What do you two think you're doing?' Graham demanded.

'We're the goalkeepers,' they pointed out.

'So?'

'Well, do we have to do this as well?'

'Do you want to be in the team?' Graham asked.

'Yes', they said.

'Then you'd better catch everyone else up, hadn't you?'

A fortnight later, after the players had trained twice every day, doing long-distance runs in the morning and high-speed shuttle runs – 'doggies' – in the afternoon, a group of them came to see Graham and said they were feeling very tired. Really exhausted, in fact. Could they have the rest of the day off?

'No,' he told them.

Instead, they were set a new challenge: they had to keep running back and forth through a children's sandpit to build up strength in their calves. By now Sherwood was under no illusions about how tough the road ahead was going to be. While he set off willingly enough, he soon developed cramp in both legs as his feet slithered about in the dry sand. When he was no longer able to walk, let alone run, two players had to carry him back to the dressing room.

After Graham had been at Watford for a few weeks, he went to the physio's room. He found the door closed and a player sitting outside.

Someone was in there, the player told him.

Who was it?

The man said he had no idea.

Pushing open the door, Graham was astonished to see a greyhound standing on the physio's bench. 'What the hell's going on here?' he asked.

Quite unfazed, the physiotherapist explained that the greyhound was feeling poorly and needed treatment for a pulled muscle.

As it happened, Elton was at the ground that day. Immediately, Graham went to see him. 'Are we running a football club, or a bloody greyhound stadium here?' he asked. 'Because it's got to be one or the other. Either the dogs go, or I do.'

It was their first confrontation – at least it could easily have been. But far from being taken aback, Elton found himself more convinced than ever that he had made the right choice. 'I loved the fact that Graham was incredibly blunt; he clearly wasn't someone to shy away from expressing an opinion. Whether or not I agreed with him didn't matter; I adore opinionated people. Besides, I hated the dog track even more than he did. I said, "Graham, it's going, it's gone – we'll get rid of it."'

While Graham was still wary about having a rock star as his chairman, and Elton plainly had a lot to learn, he couldn't help but be impressed by his decisiveness. Sitting down to write his diary that evening, he thought back to their exchange:

'No grip of board meetings', he noted of Elton. 'But has a mind of his own and is no fool.'

Before he arrived at Watford, Graham had predicted that it would take five seasons for the club to climb from Division Four to Division Two. After just a few weeks at the club, he had begun to suspect this might be on the optimistic side. But in case anyone worried that he might walk off if he didn't get the results he was looking for, Graham made it clear he was at Watford for the long haul.

Rather than rent a house, he bought one – a 1960s-built three-bedroom detached property in a cul-de-sac called Mandeville Close. When his elder daughter, Joanne, then aged eleven, started at her new school, Graham drove her there on the first day of term. Joanne had assumed that her father would come in with her, perhaps introduce himself to some of the other parents. Instead, he dropped her off outside, then swiftly drove away. 'It really wasn't like him, but I realize he must have been very preoccupied. He used to get this look in his eye when his mind was somewhere else.'

That morning, before training started, Graham put another question to the players: 'Do you want to get to the top?'

Again they looked at one another uncertainly.

'Well, that's where I'm going,' he said. 'To the top. So who among you is coming with me?'

This time they all raised their hands.

Although Graham had kept faith with several players who'd been there before his arrival, he had got rid of others who he felt were too stuck in their ways, or over the hill, or simply lived too far away from Watford. He had also drafted in some new blood. He paid £6,000 for Sam Ellis, his old granite-headed captain at Lincoln, and £12,000 for Ian Bolton, who'd also been at Lincoln, but was now on loan to Notts County.

Both of them were reliable central defenders, and Bolton could play in the midfield if required. Before Bolton joined Lincoln, Graham had heard that he was an unusually accurate passer of the ball. Wanting to see for himself, Graham had marked out a small patch of grass and asked Bolton to land the ball as near to it as possible from fifty yards away.

He hit it first time.

Maybe this had been a fluke Graham thought, so he asked him to have another go.

Once again Bolton hit the spot.

Just conceivably, this too had been a fluke, Graham thought. Perhaps he could move back a few paces and try again?

For the third time, Bolton landed the ball on the spot.

Later the same day, Graham signed him up. As he said to him at the time, 'I've been looking for two of the meanest, ugliest bastards I could find. Sam Ellis is one, and now you're the other.'

If any Watford supporters were having doubts about his choices, Graham sought to put their minds at rest. It was true that Ellis was 'not the most elegant of players', he conceded. 'However, he will never try to hide and he is the sort of commanding defender I have been looking for.'

In essence, Graham's tactics could hardly have been more straightforward. Watford would look to attack the whole time, constantly pressing forward, with the midfield players sending long passes out to the wings, or down the middle to one of the strikers. If they could keep this up for ninety minutes, he believed, then they stood a good chance of running the opposition ragged and harrying them into making mistakes.

By this point Graham had been at Watford for two months and reckoned that he now had the makings of a decent team. 'I felt we were ready to give it a go,' he recalled.

At the next training session, Graham arrived with an A4 file tucked under his arm. Before he started, he opened the file, then put it on the ground in front of him. As he did so, Ian Bolton glanced down. Written in large black letters at the top of the first page, he saw the words, 'DAY ONE'.

# 22.

Shortly before the start of his first game in charge, a League Cup tie against Reading, Graham took his seat in the manager's dugout – an uncovered bench beside the touchline. Looking up, he saw his chairman walking towards him. His heart sank. Elton, though dressed soberly enough in a pale blue suit, was tottering along on a pair of enormous platform shoes. This, Graham felt, was not appropriate footwear for the chairman of a football club.

Meanwhile, Elton continued to walk towards the bench where he was sitting. Turning to the person sitting next to him, Graham asked, 'Where on earth does the chairman think he's going?'

The answer soon became clear. Walking to the other end of the bench, Elton sat down 'as if it was the most natural thing in the world'.

Graham was appalled. As far as he was concerned, a club chairman had no business sitting alongside the manager; he should be out of sight in the directors' box. But it was far worse when the chairman happened to be a rock star. For a start, he was bound to distract attention from the game. Let's say Elton threw his arms in the air because someone missed a chance to score, what sort of impression would that make? Plainly, a very bad one. It might even stir up crowd trouble.

Even so. Graham resolved to keep his mouth shut, for the time being at least. Better err on the side of discretion than risk making a scene, he decided.

Watford's largest crowd in years – almost 6,000 people – had come to see how they fared under their new manager. Expectations were running high. 'Watford Ready For Big Start', ran one headline in the local paper.

Their opponents, Reading, were no pushovers. Their goal-keeper, the memorably named Steve Death, would go on to set a Football League record by not conceding a goal in more than 1,000 minutes of play.

Watford won that first game 2-1, but any optimism was shortlived. A week later, they lost the second leg of the tie 1-0. Midway through the first half Ross Jenkins was carried from the pitch on a stretcher after colliding with Steve Death's outstretched fist.

As there was no club doctor, Jenkins was examined by the Watford physio who saw no grounds for concern – despite the fact that he 'couldn't control his eyes and his head kept slumping to one side'. Rather than take Jenkins to hospital, the physio decided that a cup of sugary tea would be sufficient to set him back to rights.

While it was bad enough that his star striker had been stretch-ered off with concussion, Graham was also dismayed that Elton had once again sat on the managerial bench wearing the same enormous platform shoes. At the end of the game he decided that he couldn't keep quiet any longer.

Waiting until there was no one else around, Graham broached the subject as delicately as possible. While he was aware that as the owner of the club Elton could sit anywhere he liked, he really did feel that his being on the bench sent out quite the wrong sig-nals. If they were going to be taken seriously, then Elton, as chairman, would have to set an example.

Braced for a confrontation, Graham was surprised – and relieved – when Elton immediately backed down. In future, he would sit in the directors' box, he said. At least he would start off there. However, he couldn't rule out the possibility that he might get carried away during the course of a game and find himself inching ever closer towards the touchline.

Two months in, the full implications of Graham's regime had become plain. Every morning the players would be sent off on cross-country runs in nearby Cassiobury Park. These could last for anything up to five hours. Anyone who asked, even begged, for a glass of water was told to pull themselves together.

But it wasn't just the fact that the players found these runs gruelling, Graham also seemed to have an uncanny ability to tell which of them had been slacking. Another few weeks went by before they realized he was climbing trees in the park in order to have a bird's eye view of what was going on.

This, though, was only the start. After the cross-country run came the training itself. Later in his career, Graham would write a book, optimistically titled *Football Training Can Be Fun*, in which he outlined a number of useful warm-up exercises. They read like something even the SAS would have blanched at. 'Players gather in piggy-back pairs,' runs one exercise. 'Each "jockey" has to react to instructions made by the coach – e.g. down through the "horse's" legs, run round the circle and get back onto his partner's back.' The pair that come last 'have to do press-ups as a forfeit' – this sentence runs like a refrain throughout the book.

At the time, few managers took much notice of statistics. As well as being difficult to interpret, they were considered too bookish and scientific for real football aficionados. However, Graham carefully recorded everything the players did in his black A4 files – the time they took to complete their runs, the accuracy of their passes, the number of tackles they made, their speed on the ball and so on. Subsequently, he would spend hours poring over the information he had accumulated, seeking to maximize efficiency and devise new ways to unlock the opposition's defences.

There was one lesson above all he sought to instil in the players. No matter how exhausted, dazed or dejected they were feeling, they should never abandon hope. There was no such thing as a lost cause, he told them. Always – always – there was something to fight for.

By now, there had been further changes. A full-time mainte-nance man had been taken on at Vicarage Road, with special responsibility for fixing 'dangerous guttering'. Graham had also given his first in-depth interview, to the *Watford Observer*'s foot-ball correspondent, Oli Phillips.

He made no attempt to sugarcoat his message: 'I feel there is a complete lack of discipline at the club,' Graham told him bluntly. The two men hadn't been talking for long before Phillips decided that he didn't think much of the club's new manager. As well as being unimpressed by his ideas, which struck him as verging on the crackpot, he found him arrogant and full of hot air. 'He was very confident, quite brash and I also noticed that he tended to repeat himself; he would never use twenty words if there were another one hundred lying idle.' An unimpressed Phillips went away thinking that Graham was bound to come unstuck sooner or later.

It was simply a matter of when.

For their third game of the season Watford travelled north to Stockport County – by coach rather than on the train this time. Now able to see straight once more, Ross Jenkins was back in the team. As he always did whenever he headed north for a game, he was aware of a mounting sense of foreboding. While the changing rooms at Watford were nothing to get excited about – the rows of broken wooden pegs, the lockers that didn't lock, the communal bath in which sightless creatures of the deep were reputed to lurk – the ones in northern clubs were even worse. 'Everything always seemed to be freezing. There would be no hot water for showers and, if you were lucky, just a single nail for you to hang your clothes on in the dressing room.'

But on this occasion, Jenkins didn't stay downhearted for long. Before the game started, Graham explained what he wanted him to do. 'The most important thing was never to be caught offside, because that just gives the ball to the opposition. I remember him saying that we had to get twenty attempts on goal throughout the game. If we did, then we'd probably score twice and that would usually be enough to win the game.'

It wasn't long after the kick-off that Jenkins became aware of something that he'd seldom, if ever, experienced at Watford before. 'I could tell that we were starting to get a shape to the team. For once, everything seemed to fit together.'

He was not the only one who felt that something had changed. Watching from the terraces, long-time Watford fan David Harrison found it hard to believe what he was seeing. 'Big Ross, reinstated and visibly loving every minute, bore no similarity to the dispirited figure we'd seen slouching round the same pitch just four months earlier.'

In the second half, a Watford penalty was 'crashed home' by their captain, Sam Ellis, who then 'stood motionless, facing the crowd, both arms aloft'.

That gesture alone, Harrison felt, 'eloquently demonstrated the passion lacking under the previous regime'. The game ended in a 3-1 victory for Watford with Jenkins scoring the other two goals, one of them a 'silky, glancing header'.

After the players had had their cold showers, they got on board the team coach and were being driven away from the ground when they heard a loud crash. The driver slammed on the brakes and the coach shuddered to a halt.

It turned out that an enraged Stockport County supporter had thrown a brick through one of the windows. Fortunately, the brick hadn't hit anyone and was now lying on the floor of the coach surrounded by broken glass. The players gazed at it in astonishment. Nothing like this had ever happened to them before – in the past, the only people who had ever hurled anything at them had been their own supporters.

In its own peculiar way, it seemed like a good omen.

# 23.

While Graham was busy instilling the virtues of restraint and self-discipline into the Watford players, Elton's life was heading rapidly in the opposite direction. At a televised concert he gave in Edinburgh at the end of another lengthy tour, he topped up his glass at frequent intervals from a large jug of Bloody Mary on the piano in front of him.

'I don't want people at home to think I'm an alcoholic,' he told the audience. 'I want them to *know* I'm an alcoholic.'

A few months later came a concert at the Empire Pool Wembley, in aid of the Royal Variety Club and a charity providing football facilities for underprivileged children. Elton had recently engaged a new backing band called China, formed by his long-time guitarist, Davey Johnstone, and this was to be their first public appearance.

Before the concert started, it was clear that Elton was in a touchy mood; anyone hoping for a word was warned to keep their distance. When he came on stage, he did so on his own wearing a black jacket and a matching black beret. By contrast, his skin appeared unusually white – paler than marble according to one onlooker. Without any preamble, he launched into a song called 'Better Off Dead' from his *Captain Fantastic and the Brown Dirt Cowboy* album.

It was noticeable that he seemed to sing the song's last verse with particular intensity:

> If the thorn of a rose is the thorn in your side,
> Then you're better off dead if you haven't already died.

'Better Off Dead' was followed by the equally melancholy strains of 'Candle in the Wind'. This was dedicated to 'someone in the audience who really likes Vera Lynn – Mr Graham Taylor. He hasn't been to one of these concerts before, but he likes this song, because it's slow and soft, you see – just like it used to be when he played right-back for Lincoln.'

It proved to be one of the evening's few light-hearted moments. Another twelve songs went by before Elton started playing what were later described as 'some strange chords' on the piano. After these had died away, he said that he had an announcement to make. 'It's very hard to put into words,' he told the audience. 'I haven't been touring for a long time and it's been a painful decision whether to come back on the road or not. I've really enjoyed tonight, but I've made a decision that this is going to be my last show. All right?'

This news was greeted by gasps and anguished cries of 'No!'

'There's a lot more to me than playing on the road,' Elton went on. 'And this is the last one I'm going to do.'

It wasn't just the audience who were stunned by his decision. So were his backing band who found themselves in the awkward position of being sacked halfway through their first concert. It also appalled John Reid, who was seen frantically shouting 'Stop him! Grab him!' from the wings. By then, though, it was too late; the damage had been done.

However, the person who was most shocked by the announcement may well have been Elton himself. Before going on stage he hadn't intended to say anything about giving up touring, and found the words coming out of his mouth before he had really thought through their implications.

'I was just exhausted, and sometimes when you're very tired, you say things you don't mean. There was this sense of things getting on top of me. I'd never actually wanted to be famous; popular yes, but not like the huge star I'd become. The truth was, I didn't enjoy being Elton John that much any more.'

★

By now Elton had been living at Woodside, a large 1920s-built Queen Anne-style house in Old Windsor, for several years. He had loved the property from the moment he saw it, but as the pressures of fame mounted, he spent more and more time on his own – reluctant to venture out, and unsure who to go with whenever he did. For all his popularity, he had few close friends and – as he had already learned from experience – scarcely anyone he could trust.

'By then, quite a lot of people I thought were my friends had talked to the press. I'd even taken to keeping a little black book in which I noted down the names of everyone who had betrayed me.'

And that wasn't all. 'I just felt lost. I'd dress up in these outrageous clothes and become Elton John, but once I came off stage it felt very different. I never brought the Elton persona home; he just stayed on the side of the stage. Then I'd come back here and just rattle around by myself. It didn't help that everyone I knew seemed to be famous, or in the music industry. I didn't know any ordinary people – people who would treat me as if I was normal. In my world, no one dared confront me because I was king.'

Yet there was one place where no one would fawn over him, or treat him like a creature from another planet. Just as his bedroom in Pinner Hill Road had been Elton's sanctuary when he was a child, so Watford Football Club became the only place where he felt safe and secure.

'It was a lifeline back to my childhood. When I went to Watford, I felt I could leave Elton behind for a while. I'd go to the Supporters Club and have a drink and chat to people about football, and I never felt any pressure to be someone I wasn't. No one cared about who I was, or my sexuality, and no one bowed and scraped. I enjoyed myself far more there than I did anywhere else. The ridiculous thing was that I felt more at home at Watford Football Club than I did in my own home.'

The trouble was these moments of warmth and security lasted only so long. At the end of the evening, Elton would get into his chauffeur-driven Bentley, and go back to his enormous house with only the staff and an ever-increasing number of possessions for company. He was now the owner of more than 25,000 singles, nine cars including a Ferrari and an Aston Martin DB5, one of the world's largest collections of Fabergé eggs, along with the dress worn by Judy Garland in *The Wizard of Oz*.

To fill the hours that he spent alone, Elton was not only drinking more and more, but taking increasing amounts of drugs – mainly, but by no means exclusively, cocaine. 'I used to shut myself away in my bedroom, sometimes for days on end. I was always an isolationist drinker and drug-taker, so no one else knew about it – not at first anyway.'

In part, he took cocaine simply because it was available; because he was a rock star and that – increasingly – was what rock stars did. But it was also a way of dealing with a degree of fame that he had never anticipated and which he found increasingly hard to handle. 'I was lonely, that was the truth. Lonely and confused.'

While taking drugs may not have made Elton's life any less bizarre, it allowed him to feel more in control than he did the rest of the time. He liked the jolt of confidence and euphoria that cocaine gave him, and the way it seemed to make his insecurities melt away. But at the same time, it erected another barrier between him and the outside world. Having spent much of his adult life believing he had to hide his sexuality, he now found himself keeping another big secret.

Although Elton didn't want anyone to find out just how much cocaine he was taking – his family, his colleagues or even his friends – the person whose disapproval he most dreaded incurring was that of his new manager.

By this point, Elton and Graham still didn't know one another well. But what had become clear was that they were even more like chalk and cheese than either of them had first thought – 'I was Mr Fancy Pants and he was Mr Down to Earth.' In theory,

Mr Fancy Pants should have been the one in charge; after all, he was the chairman, while Graham was his employee. But from the very beginning, Elton always deferred to Graham – the only person in the world he was happy to play a junior role to. 'I knew that I could trust him implicitly, and I felt instinctively that he had my own best interests at heart.'

Elton was also desperate for Graham's approval. He was hardly short of praise, of course. People were drenching him in plaudits all the time. However, the time when this had meant anything to him had long gone. What Elton wanted more than anything was approval from someone who might not normally have been inclined to give it. Someone far removed from the people who usually danced attendance on him. 'One of the great things about Graham was that he didn't have a sycophantic bone in his body.'

If Elton wanted Graham's approval, it was clear that he was going to have to earn it. Under the circumstances, this was likely to prove tricky. As much of a stickler for good behaviour as he was for discipline, Graham was certain to be appalled if he found out about Elton's drinking, let alone his drug-taking. But worse than that – far worse – he would be disappointed.

# 24.

Watford's triumph against Stockport was followed by another hiccup – a 3-1 loss to York City. During the game, just as Elton had predicted, excitement got the better of him. Stealing out of the directors' box, he came down to the touchline where he led Watford fans in what was later described as some 'vigorous cheerleading'. It proved to be so vigorous that it prompted a pitch invasion at full time. Much to Graham's annoyance, the police had to step in and restore order. A chastened Elton went back to his seat in the directors' box.

Afterwards, through gritted teeth, Graham gave a statement vowing that this would never happen again: 'The chairman realizes that his going down to the pitch may have had something to do with subsequent events.'

A few days later, Elton arrived at the club wearing what Ian Bolton described as 'some really lairy gear, even by his standards: the glasses, the hat, the jacket, the flares, the platform boots – all completely over the top.'

Immediately, Graham pulled him to one side. 'We're a football club here,' he told him. 'We have standards and it's important that we maintain them.' He went on to deliver a similarly charged rocket to the players: if they hoped to get anywhere, they had to show more skill and a lot more backbone.

Both rockets had the desired effect; like their chairman, the players were desperate for Graham's approval. Putting their defeat behind them, Watford chalked up five victories on the trot. A 3-1 win against Reading, with substitute Luther Blissett 'cracking home' Watford's first goal, took them up to third place in Division Four.

For Blissett, it was as if he had suddenly been released from all the shackles that had held him back before. 'I felt that I was still learning my trade, but I was now full of self-belief. I think Graham had made us all feel like that.'

Having stayed away from Vicarage Road in ever increasing numbers – whether through boredom, dejection or both – Watford supporters at last found themselves with something to cheer about. Cautiously at first, as if they feared this winning streak could never last, people started streaming back through the turnstiles.

So far no one outside Watford had paid much attention to the club's success. But all that changed on 3 October 1977, when they went to Brentford and beat the home side 3-0. Sam Ellis scored one of the goals, striker Alan Mayes another and Ross Jenkins the third. After just two months of the new season, Watford were now top of Division Four. Not only had they won nine out of their first eleven games, they had scored thirty goals in the process.

Elton's once empty pockets were steadily filling up with old Orbit wrappers.

Even Graham was taken aback by the speed of Watford's turn-around. 'Although I expect to win every game we play, I didn't necessarily expect to be taken at my word.' In case anyone was inclined to smugness, he drove them harder than ever – more cross-country runs, more training sessions, more fines for slacking or stepping out of line. When one player collapsed with cramp, Graham told him sternly, 'You don't get cramp at this club.'

In years to come, whenever he was asked about those early days at Watford, Graham would emphasize that he hadn't inherited a bunch of no-hopers who couldn't kick a ball without tripping over their own feet. What he had done, he said, was to take players who didn't have a lot of faith in their own ability and give them a degree of self-confidence that they'd never had before. 'Some of them may have been hesitant at first, but they soon realized that by training the way I asked them to, doing the simple things effectively and supporting their teammates on the pitch, they would win many more matches than they lost.' In the process, they would learn another important lesson – 'a winning dressing room is a wonderful place to be.'

And still Watford's winning streak continued. By the end of the season, they had racked up more points than they'd ever done before, and won thirty-five of the fifty-four games they had played – eleven were draws and eight defeats.

Ross Jenkins, the hopeless beanpole who had once been a prime candidate for the scrapheap, was the team's top scorer with eighteen goals. 'Graham had turned us into a proper team,' he recalled. 'Everyone knew exactly what they were supposed to be doing – so much so that, even if you were blindfolded, you could still point to where each of your colleagues were.'

Watford won the Fourth Division Championship with seven games to spare. A 1-0 away victory against Scunthorpe sealed their promotion to the Third Division. For Graham, it was a particularly poignant occasion. As he had done throughout his childhood, he climbed the steps to the wooden press box at the Old Show Ground to join his father, who was covering the game for the *Scunthorpe Evening Telegraph*. 'I sat beside him, just as I had done as a boy, and we shared the moment.'

Also there to witness Watford's coronation was Elton, who had flown in specially from America. 'Tears rolled down Elton John's face at the end of the match,' noted Oli Phillips in the *Watford Observer*. 'Tears of pure joy.'

While Elton was sobbing with delight, 'Manager Graham Taylor was embraced by his wife, his two daughters, Elton John's mother and just about everyone else who could get anywhere near him.'

A few days later, a special evening was held in Bailey's nightclub for the club's supporters. Tickets were £2 each. Supper was not included, although a special turn from comedy/cabaret act the Grumbleweeds – 'Guvnors of Live Comedy' – was. Graham also threw a party at his house in Mandeville Close to which all the players were invited, along with their wives and partners. During the evening, Sam Ellis allowed himself a cigar to celebrate Watford's promotion. After puffing away in a corner and confident that no one was watching, he stubbed out it out in a potted plant.

The following day, Graham called him in and fined him £25.

# 25.

That summer, Graham once again took his family on a caravanning holiday in France. When he returned he found an envelope lying on his desk. By now he was used to receiving letters, often from irate supporters – letters he always replied to, often in painstaking detail. However, there was something different about this one. Before opening the envelope, he noted the thickness of the paper, as well as the handwriting: the 'rich blue ink' and the 'gently sloping lettering'.

Inside were two handwritten sheets of paper. Glancing at the signature, Graham saw that the letter was signed Bertie Mee.

A few months earlier, Mee had retired as manager of Arsenal at the age of fifty-eight. Once the club's physiotherapist, he'd risen through the ranks to become manager – a role he occupied for the next eleven years. During his time in charge, Mee had transformed Arsenal's fortunes. Having failed to win a trophy since 1953, they had gone on to win both the FA Cup and the League in 1971 – only the second time a club had won the double in the twentieth century.

A small man with ferret-like features and thinning hair anchored in place with lashings of pomade, Mee always dressed in exactly the same way – a grey suit and a club tie. If anything, he was even more of a stickler for discipline than Graham. He expected his players to wear a collar and tie – not just to the ground on match days, but to training sessions as well. He also shared his attitude to facial hair – no bearded player was ever picked for Arsenal during Mee's years in charge.

At the time the shaggily hirsute George Best was reckoned to be the most gifted player in the country. While every other manager in the league would have been thrilled to sign him, Mee refused to countenance the idea, saying he didn't think Best would conform to the standards at Arsenal.

When he was the club's physiotherapist, Mee would even inspect the players' hands to check they were clean, and their trousers to make sure they were properly pressed. But while he was fiercely traditionalist in some respects, in others Mee was a keen innovator. He placed a great deal of importance on both fitness and diet – and, like Graham, he drove players to their limits.

At Arsenal, Mee inspired such fear that one player was physically sick twice a day, before each training session. He also felt that managers should never think themselves higher or mightier than their supporters. Throughout his time at Arsenal, he refused to go ex-directory and insisted that his number stay in the phone book.

When he retired from Arsenal, Mee thought about resuming his old career as a physiotherapist. But, as a friend gently explained, the world had moved on since then. 'If you go back, the staff are not like they were when you were there,' the friend had told him. 'They will wear scruffy trainers and they won't take kindly to having their hands inspected every morning.'

At the age of fifty-eight, Mee was keen to carry on working and remained convinced there was still a place in football for someone who believed in courtesy, discipline and personal hygiene. He also liked the idea of a challenge. While he wasn't looking for a job, Mee wrote in his letter, he was happy to help out at Watford if he could be of any use.

However surprised he was to receive the letter, Graham's first instinct was to chuck it in the bin. Although Mee had plainly forgotten about it, the two men's paths had crossed before. When Graham had been manager of Lincoln, he'd phoned Mee up asking if he could borrow one of the Arsenal reserve centre-halves for a few games.

Mee was one of the managers Graham most admired and he couched his request in suitably respectful terms. But far from being helpful, Mee had addressed him as 'young man', been generally high-handed and effectively told him to get lost.

After that Graham rang another of his idols, Bill Shankly, the legendary Scottish manager of Liverpool. Again, he asked if he could borrow one of his centre-halves. 'Listen, son,' Shankly told him. 'Do you like your centre-halves to be tall, quick, strong and brave?'

'Yes, Mr Shankly,' Graham said.

'Call me Bill,' said Shankly. 'That's good. But let me tell you this: Liverpool defenders have to be tall, quick, strong and brave, even the ones in the reserve team. And that is why ye cannae have any of them – but good luck.'

The incident taught Graham yet another valuable lesson. 'One man had turned me down in an obnoxious manner and the other had done so in a wonderful manner, and it taught me something about how to deal with people a little lower down the ladder. I resolved that if I ever reached the top of the game, I would not speak to a lower division manager the way Bertie had spoken to me.'

But the more Graham thought about it, the more he realized he would be mad to turn Mee's offer down flat. He talked to Elton who agreed that Mee's experience would be invaluable. Putting his qualms to one side, Graham phoned him up and asked him to come in for a chat. In the flesh, Mee proved to be even more sergeant-majorish than he had expected; everything about him seemed to bristle with pent-up energy.

Yet he wasn't remotely snooty, as Graham had feared. What's more, it soon became plain how much they had in common. How they both believed in a style of football that involved constantly pressing forward and piling as much pressure as possible on their opponents: Attack! Attack! Attack! at every opportunity. And while Mee might have an abrasive manner, he wasn't a hothead. His wife, Doris, had noticed that at moments of high tension, a little muscle would twitch in Mee's cheek. Otherwise, there was no reaction.

Graham, as he was only too well aware, was apt to fly off the handle, while his chairman was famously combustible. Perhaps the pair of them needed a calming influence? Someone older, more mature and who had seen it all before. 'I think on some level I understood that I needed someone to keep me in check and to question what I was doing from time to time.'

By the end of the meeting, Bertie Mee had become Watford's assistant manager. News of his appointment was received with disbelief among Fleet Street football pundits. Why on earth was someone with Mee's track record wasting his time with a small club like Watford? But it also sent out a clear message of intent, Graham believed: 'His arrival showed people we were not messing about and that we meant business.'

Just as Elton had when he'd first met Graham, he instinctively sensed that Bertie Mee was a kindred spirit. 'Bertie wasn't a demonstrative person, but he was a very good thinker. And although he didn't say much, what he did say made perfect sense. In some respects, we were poles apart, of course, but all three of us were quite similar personality types. All three of us cut straight to the quick and we could all spot a bad egg from miles away.'

However pleased Graham was with Mee's appointment, he was aware that he needed to show him who was boss, just in case he became uppity again. He soon hit upon a foolproof method of making it plain who was in charge.

Every morning at 8.30 sharp, there would be a staff meeting in the Kremlin. Mee would always be there in his suit and tie, raring to go. Usually, Graham, every bit as punctual, would also be present. But now he deliberately started turning up ten minutes late. By the time he arrived, a delighted Graham saw that the muscle in Mee's cheek was twitching away uncontrollably. 'I knew it drove Bertie mad, but he never said anything.'

As it turned out, Mee, far from trying to usurp Graham, was only too happy to play second fiddle. Indeed, he proved to be the least egotistical of men; he never tried to interfere, or imposed his views, or harped on about his glory days at Arsenal.

He also turned out to be much less starchy than people had anticipated. At one of the first away games that Mee attended, there was an animated discussion among the host club's directors over whether Elton, dressed in a jacket with enormous flapping lapels and his customary platform shoes, should be allowed into the boardroom. 'Gentlemen, I gather there may be a problem with our chairman's attire,' Mee said to the club's directors. 'Can you please confirm your dress code?'

Certainly, they told him; they expected any visitors to wear a jacket, necktie, trousers and shoes.

Mee pointed out that, strictly speaking, Elton was wearing all these items – albeit of a style and combination none of them had ever seen before. 'Now, they may not be to your taste,' he said, 'and frankly they may not be to mine either, but they do not bar him from entry.'

After another round of hurried discussion, Elton was granted admission.

# 26.

Graham always maintained that he had no idea Elton was gay when they first met. Although Elton had effectively come out eighteen months earlier, Graham was hardly an avid reader of *Rolling Stone* – it's highly unlikely he'd ever heard of it – nor did he bother to look at newspaper gossip columns.

As far as he was concerned, homosexuality was something he vaguely knew about, but had never actually witnessed. Thinking back to his time at Lincoln, he remembered the communal baths with all the macho conversation – and 'everything swinging away' – and reflected how difficult it must have been for anyone who was gay.

Having never – to his knowledge – met anyone who was gay before, Graham was not quite sure how to react. After giving the matter some thought, he decided to try to make a joke of it. 'I don't care what you do, Elton,' he told him. 'As long as you don't try to kiss me.'

Later on, he wondered if he could have phrased this better. But for all his awkwardness, Graham was instinctively sympathetic to anyone who was the victim of prejudice. Just as Luther Blissett had to contend with racist taunts, so Elton had become used to rival fans shouting abuse at him. 'Don't bend down when Elton John's around!' was a familiar chant; variations on the same theme would be repeated at almost every away game he went to.

From the start, Elton had decided that he wouldn't let it get to him. That he would simply grin and bear it. 'They're doing it to test you out and if you get uptight about it, that's the wrong thing to do. Besides, I found a lot of it genuinely funny.'

Graham, though, had a less forgiving attitude. 'Being singled out for your footballing or managerial shortcomings is one thing, but being abused for your sexuality is quite another,' he reflected. 'It struck me immediately that there was simply no place for this sort of thing in the game.'

He resolved that in future, while he wanted Watford supporters to be as noisy as possible, he wasn't prepared to put up with any swearing or abuse. He was also very struck by Elton's refusal to take offence. 'His ability to brush off the chants of a crowd amazed me, but it also saddened me. There's something about the anonymity of a crowd that gives people the impression they have the security to say things they would never dream of saying if they were on their own.'

Not that the two of them ever discussed Elton's homosexuality. 'We never talked about it, not once,' Elton recalls. 'Graham certainly wasn't homophobic; it just wasn't a necessary thing to bring up. That never bothered me in the slightest; I always felt that he loved me for who I was.'

In September 1978, the two of them travelled north to watch Watford play Rotherham – a game Watford lost 2-1. Usually. Elton loved going to Watford away games. Ever since childhood, forever rooting for the underdog, he'd believed that the real spirit of football could only be found in the little clubs, with their loyal cluster of fans, their quagmire pitches and their crumbling stands. 'That was where you saw people playing for the sheer love of the game, with no thought of ego or money. The clubs would be run by local businessmen. In Grimsby, they would all be in the fish trade; in Workington, they were potato farmers. In York, there was even a coal fire in the boardroom; the whole thing was very Dickensian.'

But this occasion was to prove rather different. After the game was over, Elton and Graham walked into the club bar where they found the Rotherham directors, almost as unused to victory as Watford had once been, in a state of high exultation.

'We had to take a deep breath and walk in with our heads up and our lips tight,' Graham recalled.

Elton had taken the defeat particularly badly and went off to the toilet to sit in one the cubicles until he had calmed down. While he was in there, two of the Rotherham directors came in.

As they stood at the urinals, he heard one say to the other, 'Well, we showed that poof today, didn't we?'

Although he usually let everything slide off him, on this occasion the men's casual homophobia and tone of quiet smugness infuriated Elton. When he emerged from the toilet, Graham had never seen him look so angry. At first Elton wanted to go and confront the two men responsible. However, Graham persuaded him not to. There was no point in letting them know they had hurt him, he said. If he did that, it would simply confirm all their prejudices: 'Instead of thinking of you as a poof, they'll think of you as a poof and a bad loser.'

Possibly he might have phrased this better too, Graham thought later. Even so, he was convinced that provoking a confrontation would be a mistake. Rather than make a scene, they should simply look the men in the eye, offer their congratulations and wish the club well for the rest of the season. That, he felt, would create much more of an impression.

Both of them went over to where the Rotherham directors were sitting, stuck out their hands and, in the most sincere-sounding tones they could muster, offered their congratulations and said that the best team had won. They then walked away, noting, with satisfaction, the air of considerable puzzlement they left in their wake.

Although Graham tried to be as supportive as he could, it was his wife, Rita, who worked out what Elton needed above all – a sense of peace, of normality. After their experience at Rotherham, she suggested that Graham should invite Elton round to Mandeville Close for a family supper. It was an invitation he was a bit nervous about delivering, but which turned out to be gratefully received.

There was only one rule, Rita told the two of them: they could talk about anything they wanted as long as it wasn't football. Soon these suppers became a regular occurrence. Every few weeks, Elton would join the Taylors at their dining-room table – he was particularly fond of Rita's shepherd's pie, ideally followed by her rhubarb crumble.

To begin with, they struggled to find a topic they could all talk about – football was off the menu, while Graham knew nothing about rock music. But the more they got to know each other, the more relaxed the atmosphere became. Although Graham didn't have too many interests outside football, he was interested in history, especially the Second World War, and sometimes the three of them would find themselves discussing key moments of the war such as D-Day, or the Battle of Britain.

As far as Elton was concerned, it was a glimpse of something he had never experienced before. When he was growing up, his parents had argued the whole time, with family mealtimes being particular hotbeds of fury. And now that he was an adult, his fame prevented him from leading anything resembling a normal life.

'I remember I would look around very enviously and think to myself what a stable life Graham and Rita had together. How settled they were, how happy. I used to wonder if the day would ever come when I could live like that. When I could have some stability, some normality. Or was I just going to spend the rest of my life hurtling round the world and sleeping in endless hotel rooms?'

After supper was over and the three of them had done the washing-up, they would often play cards. Both Elton and Graham were intensely competitive. On one occasion, it slowly dawned on Graham that Rita and Elton had colluded in a plan to make sure he lost. To make matters worse, the two of them started giggling like schoolchildren when they were found out. Far from being amused, Graham blew his top. Jumping to his feet, he tipped the coffee table over, sending the cards flying, and stalked off – thereby sending Rita and Elton into hysterical laughter.

For the most part, though, their evenings together were oases of calm. Years later, Graham would look back on them as some of the happiest times in his life. 'Those are the days I remember most fondly, when we were making our way and beginning to ruffle a few feathers in the game.'

Whenever he and Elton were allowed to talk about football, they would keep going for hours, carried along on the same wave of enthusiasm. 'I remember the long conversations I'd have with Elton about the club, the team, the opposition and certain players. What comes to mind above all is the energy we both had and our drive and determination to take the club forward. I loved talking to him because, although he wasn't what I call a "football person", he was very knowledgeable and he always had an interesting point of view. He always wanted to know my thoughts, but he left the football management to me and he never, ever blamed me for wasting his money if a player I'd signed turned out to be a dud.'

What bound them together more strongly than anything else was a sense that it was the two of them against the world. While they may have been facing enormous odds in their quest to achieve Elton's dream, this only made them more resolute, more bloody-minded – and more united.

In future, Graham resolved to do whatever he could to shield Elton from any personal attacks. As for Elton, he always tried to be on hand to boost Graham's morale if he was suffering any twinges of self-doubt, or feeling uncharacteristically downhearted. Whenever that happened, his response was always the same.

'Come on Graham,' he would say, putting an arm round his shoulder. 'We'll show them.'

# 27.

That summer, a recently appointed assistant Baptist minister called John Boyers had a peculiar experience; God, he became increasingly convinced, was trying to tell him something. Having come to live in Watford with his wife, Boyers was working at the St James Road Baptist Church in the west of the town.

One day, at a Bible-reading group he attended, someone asked him if his church was anywhere near Watford Football Club. Very near as it happened, Boyers told the man, before adding quickly, 'Although they don't trouble us at all.'

'Have you ever thought of becoming involved with them?' the man asked.

'Never,' said Boyers truthfully; the idea hadn't crossed his mind.

The man then introduced himself. He was, he said, the chaplain at Aldershot Football Club. An awkward silence followed. Boyers was baffled. 'I can remember thinking: how can you believe in an all-loving and all-powerful God and still be chaplain at Aldershot Football Club?' But when he went home, he forgot all about their conversation.

Six weeks went by, and then a former captain of Watford's long-time rivals, Luton Town, called Alan West came to talk to him at the church. Having retired as a professional footballer, West had subsequently become a devout Christian. The two of them began talking, and once again Boyers found himself being asked if he'd ever thought about becoming involved with Watford Football Club.

This time when he went home, he didn't forget all about it. Instead, he knelt down and began to pray. 'Lord, are you really saying something to me?' Boyers wondered. If so, a certain amount of clarification was needed; ideally a sign of some kind. On the next two nights – a Thursday and a Friday – Boyers offered up the same prayer. But nothing came through that could be interpreted as any sort of response.

On the Friday afternoon he bought a copy of the *Watford Observer* and began to read the long interview that Oli Phillips had recently conducted with Graham Taylor – the same interview that had left Phillips convinced that Taylor was much too full of himself and bound to come unstuck.

While there can't have been many people who believed that God was trying to communicate with them through the pages of the *Watford Observer*, Boyers was galvanized. 'I read, at first with interest and then with amazement, the manager's words about his hopes for the football club,' he recalls. 'Graham wanted the club to be part of the community. He wanted to take his players into schools, factories and hospitals – to make Watford Football Club not just a football club in Watford, but a football club belonging to the town and the area and the people of Watford.'

This, Boyers had no doubt, was the sign he'd been hoping for. 'I really did feel God was saying something.' But still he hung back, unsure what to do next. He consulted a fellow Baptist minister, together they did some more praying and both of them came to the same conclusion: God, they decided, was challenging them to become involved with Watford Football Club.

Boyers wrote a carefully phrased letter to Graham in which he volunteered his services as club chaplain. Always a conscientious replier to correspondence, Graham suggested that they meet up to discuss the idea. When Boyers presented himself at his office, it was not at all what he'd been expecting.

Seeing the look on Boyers's face as he gazed around at the rickety furniture, the threadbare carpet and the general air of dilapidation, Graham apologized for the state of the place – 'I'm afraid sorting out the furniture is the least of my priorities,' he told him.

What benefit could having a chaplain bring to the club, he wanted to know. Boyers explained he had no intention of conducting mass baptisms, or trying to convert anyone; it was more a matter of offering comfort to anyone who might have personal problems, or was feeling stressed about their careers.

Graham agreed to put the matter to the Watford board, and Boyers went away feeling that he had done everything he could. In the weeks that followed, he heard nothing and braced himself for disappointment. Perhaps he'd been mistaken, or somehow got his wires crossed? But actually the board proved to be far more enthusiastic about the idea than he had expected. Graham duly passed on the good news; he was welcome to join the club in an unofficial capacity.

Boyers was delighted; he had, he believed, answered God's call.

Shortly afterwards, Graham told him there was something he wanted him to do. 'You need to be involved with this club,' he told him. 'What I would like you to do is come and join in training on Mondays.' Boyers pointed out that he was not an athlete – nor had he ever been one – but Graham said this wasn't a problem. 'It's an easy morning,' he reassured him. 'We do music and movement work. It's just a bit of a loosener, getting the lads over the aches and pains of the weekend.'

The following Monday Boyers turned up at the local YMCA where Graham and the players were waiting. 'I'd like to introduce you to John Boyers,' Graham told them. 'He's one of the ministers of the local church and he's going to be involved as a sort of friend to the club. He's there to help and support and be available to you.'

As Boyers recalls, Graham's announcement was met with stunned silence broken only by a few snorts of laughter. This made him all the more determined to prove himself. But Boyers hadn't been going long before he realized that what Graham considered an easy morning was far harder than anything he'd ever done before. He lasted fifteen minutes before collapsing onto the nearest bench, with more derisory snorts ringing in his ears.

Despite this, Boyers turned up the next Monday, as determined as before. And week by week, he felt that not only was he becoming fitter than he'd ever been in his life, but that he was slowly winning the players' respect. He was even more pleased a few months later when Graham asked him to become the club's official chaplain – an invitation that, to Boyers's delight, the players enthusiastically endorsed.

Even so, there were limits to their cooperation, he discovered. On one occasion he joined the players on one of Graham's now notorious cross-country runs. Part of it involved running along the towpath of the Grand Union Canal. Trying to keep up with the others, Boyers lost his footing and toppled into the canal. Splashing about in the muddy water, he watched forlornly as the players all streamed past.

Nobody stopped to pull him out.

# 28.

'No grip of board meetings,' Graham had noted of Elton in his diary when he first came to Watford. To begin with, no one, least of all Elton himself, would have argued with this. Apart from anything else, he found board meetings numbingly dull: the long hours spent discussing defective guttering, or the dire state of the toilets. Naturally impatient, as well as easily bored, he would find himself sitting at the head of the table in the Kremlin seething away. 'Board meetings in general are useless; they don't achieve anything. Besides, I wasn't interested in the minuscule stuff, only in the bigger picture. I remember I'd be thinking to myself; Oh for God's sake, just get on with it!'

But having started out nervous, then become increasingly frustrated, Elton too found something unexpected happening as the months went by. 'Although there were boring things we had to discuss, there was something inspirational about it as well because we all shared the same vision.'

Far from being unfocused, he was determined to run the board meetings as crisply and efficiently as possible. Muir Stratford, one of the Watford directors, saw how swiftly he settled into the role. 'Elton was an extremely good chairman. Some of us might have had misgivings about having a rock star in charge, but they very quickly went away. While he encouraged everyone to speak and say what was on their minds, it was always clear just who was in charge.'

Whenever Elton was away on tour, he would still try to be back for the board meetings. And if he couldn't make it, he would often arrange for the entire board to fly to wherever he was, then hold the meeting in his hotel room. All this, of course, was a far cry from what the club's directors had been used to. Perhaps not surprisingly, they tended to treat Elton rather differently from their former chairman. 'I was the cash machine, so I'm sure that influenced how they treated me.'

At the same time, he'd made it plain from the beginning that he wasn't the possessor of a bottomless wallet. 'I never promised anything I couldn't deliver and everyone knew that whatever money I gave them, I was going to have to go out and work for.'

As for Graham, his dislike of spending any more of Elton's cash than he considered strictly necessary verged on the pathological. 'There was never any sense that I was the golden egg and Graham wanted more of my money. Quite the reverse; he wasn't remotely greedy. I could see how much he hated to ask for anything, and when he did buy a player, he made sure that he always got him for the best possible price.'

Just as Graham never took advantage of Elton, so Elton was equally careful not to step on his manager's toes. 'We were perfectly in sync from the word go. We would always talk about buying a player and I loved that sense of being a part of what was happening. While I never tried to influence him, I did know all the players across four divisions of the Football League, so I could always suggest names. It wasn't just that I was interested; I felt it was part of my job.'

However much Graham may have wanted a particular player, he would never agree to pay him much more than everybody else was earning. 'He knew that it destroys a dressing room if one player is on far more money than the others.' And if someone couldn't make up his mind whether to come to Watford, Graham knew he had a colossal ace up his sleeve. 'He used to say to me, "Give this bloke a ring, will you, and try to persuade him to come?"'

Far from thinking that such things were beneath him, Elton

loved this more than anything else. 'I adore talking to footballers, and it was so exciting. I'd never had that before.' As Graham had anticipated, hearing Elton on the other end of the line tended to have an electrifying effect on any doubters.

By this point Elton had been chairman of Watford for two years. As well as becoming a kind of home from home, Vicarage Road had given him a feeling of belonging that he hadn't found anywhere else. But it wasn't only that; he had another reason to feel excited. There was a growing sense at the club that all the elements were starting to come together. That after decades stuck in the doldrums, the wind finally was at Watford's backs.

A few weeks after arriving at Vicarage Road, Bertie Mee went to Coventry to watch the club's reserves play their Coventry counterparts in a pre-season game. At least that was his official reason for going. But it turned out Mee was much more interested in talking to Coventry's general secretary, a man called Eddie Plumley. A former goalkeeper for Birmingham City, Plumley had gone on to become one of the most respected administrators in the Football League.

Mee explained that he had recently joined Watford as assistant manager, and that the club had some big – very big – ambitions. 'We're looking for an executive manager,' he told him.

'What's that?' Plumley wanted to know.

'Well, someone like you,' Mee said.

Plumley agreed to pass on some names of possible candidates.

This, though, wasn't quite what Mee had in mind.

'Why don't you do it?' he asked.

Plumley roared with laughter until he realized that Mee wasn't laughing.

'What, are you being serious?'

Mee nodded.

As delicately as possible, Plumley pointed out that he was

general secretary of one of the most successful clubs in the Football League. Without wishing to labour the point, Watford existed in another universe – a universe of perpetual under-achievement and broken dreams.

Mee agreed that the club faced a formidable challenge, possibly an impossible one, but he persuaded Plumley to come and have a look at the ground.

The following weekend, without being quite sure what he had let himself in for, Plumley drove down to Watford. Although he'd braced himself for a shock, the reality proved to be far worse than anything he had expected. As he was being shown around, a phrase kept bouncing around inside Plumley's head: the whole place looked just like 'a corrugated graveyard'.

Peering aghast at the uncovered stands and the primeval dressing rooms, Plumley thought back to a time several years earlier when he'd come to watch a game at Vicarage Road with his wife, Fran. Much to her surprise, she had been told that she wasn't allowed to go into the boardroom with her husband. Instead, she had to go into the Ladies Room next door, where Mrs Bonser solemnly unlocked the drinks cupboard and presented her with the usual thimble-full of sherry.

As he listened to Graham outlining his plans for the club, Plumley's first thought was how quickly he could excuse himself and head back to Coventry. But the longer Graham kept talking, the more Plumley found his attitude starting to change. 'There was something about Graham that was unlike anything I'd ever come across before. He was the epitome of a perfect club manager – someone who is prepared to give everything for the club and who knows exactly what he wants.'

A couple of days afterwards Plumley was asked if he'd like to meet Elton. 'I remember we met him first in a hotel, then he asked if we would like to come and stay at his house with our two boys.' Although Plumley had never thought of Elton as a dilettante pop star who was just indulging some extravagant whim, he was still amazed by how knowledgeable he was. 'I'd spent my whole professional life in football and I'd literally never met anyone who knew as much as he did. The man was a walking encyclopaedia. He didn't just know the results in all four divisions of the Football League, he knew what was going on in all the other little leagues dotted around the country.'

Plumley saw too that there was something special about Graham and Elton's relationship. 'You could tell straightaway that they had this amazing chemistry. While they may have been completely different on the surface, they just clicked. It was clear that Graham really valued Elton's advice and that Elton had nothing but respect for Graham.'

What Graham, Elton and Bertie Mee wanted was 'the last piece in the jigsaw'. And, as far as they were concerned, they had found their missing piece. But there was something other than Plumley's abilities that swayed them. However good an administrator he was, Plumley was still a romantic, especially where football was concerned. Behind his club tie and clipped manner, Bertie Mee was also a romantic. As for Graham and Elton, neither of them would ever have done what they'd done if they hadn't been hopeless romantics too.

Being at First Division Coventry was glamorous enough, but it didn't exactly set Plumley's pulses racing. As he drove back to the Midlands after meeting Elton for the second time, another thought was bouncing around in his head. Maybe, just like Mee, what he needed to restore his passion was a challenge. Something as crazy as it was daunting.

A few weeks later, to the astonishment of his colleagues at Coventry, Eddie Plumley gave in his notice. Asked what on earth had possessed him to join a Fourth Division club when he was at a First Division one, Plumley paused, and then said simply, 'A man's got to do what a man's got to do.'

*

Eddie Plumley had only just settled in at Watford when the full enormity of what he had let himself in for became clear. Having never had an executive manager before, the club had no office to put him in. Instead, Plumley worked in what had once been the Ladies Room where Mrs Bonser had held sway over the drinks cupboard. 'I remember I just looked at it and thought: Jesus wept!'

One day a team of engineers came to see him. They had been sent by the FA, they said, to conduct various tests to see if the metal barriers on the Vicarage Road terrace conformed with safety regulations. After showing them where to go, Plumley left them to it and went back to his office.

Ten minutes later, the engineers came back.

'That was quick,' Plumley said. 'Was everything all right?'

Not exactly, the engineers told him. The first barrier they tested had lifted straight out of its concrete base, while the second had crumpled like a pipe-cleaner. If they carried on with their inspection, they were worried there would be no barriers left.

Although the ground was falling to bits around him, Plumley was determined that the club should have a new image. The club's badge featured a cheery-looking cartoon hornet dressed in Watford's colours of gold and black. This, Plumley felt, looked more like something you found in the bottom of a cereal packet than the symbol of a club that wanted to be taken seriously. In the end, the advertising agency he had hired came up with a male red deer – a hart. As well as possessing a sober sort of dignity, the hart had an impressive pair of antlers with which to gore its opponents.

There were other innovations too. A couple of weeks later, Elton's stepfather, Fred, bought a battered Portakabin in a sale and brought it on a flat-bed truck to the car park beside the stadium. It now housed Graham's office and what there was of the club's administrative staff.

The club also had a new electronic scoreboard. This was

generally assumed to be the result of Elton's generosity; in fact it had been provided for free by a company in St Albans who had built a prototype they wanted to test out. While the new scoreboard looked impressive enough, it soon became apparent there were a number of teething problems. Every time it rained, it would either flash up a series of incomprehensible messages, or erupt in a cacophony of exploding bulbs.

As well as going on a family caravan holiday to France, Graham had ventured further afield over the summer – to America. There, he had witnessed something that he found himself thinking about more and more in the months ahead. In Los Angeles, he learned that 47 per cent of the people who came to watch the LA Aztecs soccer team were women. In England, the figure for women attending football matches was less than 4 per cent.

There were very good reasons why women stayed away. While the atmosphere might not always have been actively intimidating, it was far from welcoming. There were no female toilets, while incidents of violence and threatening behaviour were increasing all the time. In an attempt to curb, or at least contain, football hooliganism, several First and Second Division sides had erected chicken-wire fences between the stands and the pitch. Rival fans were kept apart in what were effectively cages for the duration of the game.

Did it always have to be like this, Graham wondered. Was it too much to ask that one day women might feel able to come to football games? Might they even feel able to bring their children along?

Admittedly, this seemed an absurdly pie-in-the-sky idea in the current climate – the few people Graham mentioned it to tended to give him funny looks and change the subject. Even so, he wasn't deterred. Often, he had found, the most unlikely schemes proved the most successful. It was all a matter of picking the right moment to put them into practice.

*

Before the start of the new season, there was one more arrival. Having spent two years playing for Vancouver Whitecaps in the North American League, former Blackpool left-back Steve Harrison was now keen to return to England. His first attempt to meet Graham had not ended well. Harrison had set off in a borrowed car from his home in Blackpool, but it broke down halfway and he had to be towed back.

The next day he tried again, this time by train. When Harrison arrived at Watford Junction station he went out to the car park where he'd been told Graham would be waiting. But there was no sign of him, and for the next twenty minutes. Harrison paced about wondering what had happened. As he did so, he noticed that there was a man sitting behind the wheel of one of the parked cars – a man who looked remarkably like Graham Taylor.

Rather than approach him, Harrison decided to wait and find out what was going on. Another few minutes went by, and then he felt a tap on his shoulder. Turning round, he saw Graham.

'Hello,' he said. 'I'm sorry I'm late.'

'You're not late,' Harrison told him. 'You've been sitting in your car all along.'

An unabashed Graham admitted that this was the case. He'd been watching Harrison the whole time to see how he moved, how light he was on his feet or if he showed any signs of injury – and, just as importantly, to see how he coped with being kept waiting. Would he froth and rage with frustration, or was he made of steadier, less flappable stuff?

Graham plainly liked what he saw because a few days later. Harrison joined Watford for a fee of £25,000. As it happened, this was the last time that Graham took it upon himself to go to the station to meet prospective players. In future, the job would fall to Eddie Plumley.

Rather than go straight to the ground, Plumley always took a more scenic route, driving round the local beauty spots while he waxed lyrical about the delights of life at Watford to his increasingly confused passenger. But there was method to Plumley's madness. The longer he could keep anyone away from seeing the full horror of 'the corrugated graveyard', he reasoned, the more likely they were to agree to join.

# 29.

'We will fear no one,' Graham Taylor declared on the eve of the club's first game of the season – a home tie against Brentford. Lest anyone doubt that Watford meant business, the club noted that it was planning 'to add a further Portakabin to their Occupation Road complex'.

Watford won their opening game 4-0 and the two matches that followed. They then came up against Blackpool in their most challenging fixture so far. After the game was over, Oli Phillips tried, not entirely successfully, to strike as detached a tone as possible in his match report for the *Watford Observer.*

'Last night, Blackpool were gunned down coolly, cleanly and with a clinical application that often forced the unbiased viewer to blink in disbelief,' Phillips wrote. Once so dismissive of Jenkins's abilities, he now sang his praises in extravagant terms: 'The towering marksman cracked an inspired hat-trick in Watford's 5-1 victory.' And he did not stop there. 'The ugly duckling has turned into a swan,' he went on. 'The gangling pylon of ungainly awkwardness has become galvanized into honed athleticism.'

As he read Oli Phillips's report, Jenkins could hardly believe his eyes. No one had ever called him a towering marksman before, let alone a gangling pylon. 'I must say it did wonders for my morale.'

Previously, Jenkins had become used to people giving him a wide berth whenever he went shopping on Watford High Street. Sometimes they would even scuttle away with alarmed looks on their faces. But now people came up to greet him, offering congratulations, shaking his hand and asking for autographs. For the first time since turning down Huddersfield's offer three years earlier, he felt sure that he had made the right decision.

Not that Jenkins and Graham always saw eye to eye – far from it. Alone among the Watford players, Jenkins had no qualms about standing up to Graham. Whereas the others would knuckle down and obediently do what was asked of them, Jenkins was less obliging. If he disagreed with something that Graham was saying, he would stand up – after his initial interview, he'd vowed never to get caught sitting down again – fix his manager with his disconcertingly direct stare and tell him flatly that he was making a big mistake.

While no one suggested that Graham was scared of Jenkins, it was noticeable that he tended to back down whenever he was challenged, or else hurriedly change the subject. And just occasionally his composure would crack completely.

'There were a few times when Graham would tell me to stop looking at him like that,' Jenkins recalls. But far from looking away, he would simply harden his stare. 'That's when I really knew I was getting to him.'

At first, it bothered Jenkins that the two of them didn't get along too well. But the more he thought about it, the more he realized that perhaps it hardly mattered. Maybe it even worked to their advantage, with his antipathy spurring Jenkins on to greater heights. 'Whatever I thought of Graham personally, I always wanted to impress him and prove that I could do whatever he was asking of me.'

A week after beating Blackpool, Watford met Second Division Newcastle at home in the second round of the League Cup. At half-time, they were one-nil down. They were still one-nil down with twenty-five minutes to go when Graham decided the time had come to summon twenty-year-old Luther Blissett from the subs' bench.

Jenkins looked on approvingly. For several months now, he'd been hoping that Blissett would get his chance. 'I always liked

Luther very much as a person and as players we just seemed to gel. It was one of those strange things that doesn't happen very often; I always knew exactly where he was without needing to look.'

Before Blissett went on, Graham gave him one very simple instruction: 'Go on, son, show us what you can do.'

Far from being daunted, Blissett was raring to go. 'My only intention was to influence the game and make a difference to all my teammates.'

As he ran on to the pitch, he was greeted by a chorus of racist chants from the visiting supporters. Often, the chants were accompanied by volleys of bananas. Rather than get upset or infuriated, Blissett remembered the advice Graham had given him earlier. 'You can't hope to confront these people,' he had said, 'because they've got a louder voice than you. But if you stick the ball in the back of the net, that'll shut them up soon enough.'

With Blissett working smoothly in tandem with Ross Jenkins, the pair of them pierced hole after hole in Newcastle's defence. Luther Blissett scored two goals in less than twenty minutes and won the game for Watford.

The dust had barely settled on their victory in the second round of the League Cup before the draw was made for the third round. Having just weathered one stern examination, Graham was hoping that they might have a relatively easy ride. In the event, it didn't exactly work out like that. When the draw took place, there was a sharp intake of breath from several of those present – Graham included. Watford, it was announced, would play Manchester United away, at Old Trafford on 4 October 1978.

No one was in any doubt what this meant. It would be their biggest test by far since Elton and Graham had taken over.

# 30.

'We would like to extend a very warm welcome to our Third Division visitors, Watford,' declared Manchester United's manager Dave Sexton in his programme notes. 'To play United is often a memorable experience,' he added, before carrying on in the same lofty tones. 'I have no doubt that win or lose tonight, Watford will remember the occasion in years to come.'

The home side, supporters were reminded, had won the Division One championship six times, as well as the European Cup. Watford, of course, had never won anything, apart from the Fourth Division championship and the Southern League championship – and that was back in 1915. But it wasn't just their respective records that separated them; everything did.

Anyone going to Old Trafford who was feeling hungry could, for a price, visit the Directors' Lounge where they would be served 'prize-winning à la carte meals accompanied by the finest French wines'. At Vicarage Road they'd be lucky to get a leathery pie with something brown and indeterminate in the middle of it.

Those Watford supporters with long memories could still recall Manchester United's visit to Vicarage Road in January 1950. It was the biggest game the club had ever played. They met in the fourth round of the FA Cup, and expectations were high that Watford would give a creditable account of themselves. Despite the fact that their star striker, 'Welsh Wizard' Taffy Davies, had a goal disallowed in controversial circumstances, Watford held out until the last ninety seconds when United scored the only goal.

Since then, the two clubs had met on three occasions. Watford had lost every time. Given the precedents, it was hardly surprising that no one was getting too carried away. Before the game started

Graham reiterated what he had been telling the players at every training session – that speed and surprise were paramount. If they moved the ball with pace and purpose; if each player worked on his movement so that as soon as he released the ball, he took up a fresh position; if he then managed to shake off his marker so he was available to receive the ball again, if they could do all this without leaving themselves vulnerable to a counterattack, then they could beat teams that were supposedly much better than them.

And there was something else they needed to remember, Graham told them. Something that harked back to when they'd all first started playing football. 'When you were kids, you never really knew who you were playing against, did you?' he said. 'You never knew what their reputations were. You turned up, and you would just play. That is how football should be played – you just give your all.'

For only the second time in his career, Luther Blissett found himself in the starting eleven. The first time had been the week before when Watford played their Third Division rivals, Gillingham, a game they won 3-2.

Afterwards, Bertie Mee had taken Blissett aside and told him, 'With the ability you have, you have to stay in the team now.' The only thing that took the lustre off Bertie Mee's praise was the fact that Blissett had been booked for arguing with the referee during the game – something Graham warned him was completely unacceptable. 'You do not get booked for dissent at this club,' he said. 'I won't have it.'

Just to make sure the message had sunk in, he fined Blissett a week's wages.

Elton travelled to Manchester by helicopter, taking Rita Taylor and her two daughters, Joanne and Karen with him. They joined 45,000 other spectators at Old Trafford. Among the Watford faithful was long-time supporter Ian Poole. Like many others, Poole had wondered beforehand if there was really any point going all the way to Manchester, but nagging feelings of loyalty narrowly edged out his misgivings.

Poole had never been to Old Trafford before and was stunned by the size of the place. 'The huge North Stand swept imperiously away to our left, while off to our right was the seething mass of inhumanity that was the Stretford End. Having spent the last decade or so in the cathedral-like calm of Vicarage Road, I was unprepared for the sheer volume that 45,000 screaming Mancunians could achieve.' By contrast, the Watford supporters were 'a little island of yellow' amid an ocean of red.

It wasn't just Ian Poole who was overawed. Despite Graham's pre-match talk, it soon became clear that several Watford players were feeling a lot more jittery than usual. Throughout the first half, Manchester United launched attack after attack on the Watford goal, and only some spectacular acrobatics from their goalkeeper, Andy Rankin, stopped them from scoring.

On the few times Watford got hold of the ball, it seldom made it past the halfway line, leaving Ross Jenkins and Luther Blissett marooned deep in United territory. Shortly before half-time, Rankin's resistance finally gave out. The Watford defence failed to clear a corner and in the ensuing muddle, the United centre-forward, Joe Jordan, pounced, hooking the ball into the Watford net from close range.

When the whistle blew, the Watford players trudged disconsolately back to the visitors' dressing room, where Graham was waiting for them.

To begin with, he was on unexpectedly mellow form. 'Come in and sit down,' he said.

They all did as they were told.

'OK boys,' he went on. 'We've done all right so far. Little Watford against mighty Manchester United and we're only one-nil down. Let's pat ourselves on the back. It's a good effort. That's great. I'll tell you what, let's get our clothes on now and all go home. We've had a nice day.'

Mystified, the Watford players weren't sure how to react. One of them, winger Brian Pollard, made the mistake of standing up – whereupon Graham suddenly snapped.

'Sit down you!' he shouted. 'Do you seriously think that's it? That you've really done enough? Get out there and show some fucking self-respect! Do something to make people proud of you!'

By now Elton had seen enough of Graham's temper to know that he was every bit his equal when it came to hot-headedness. Although he'd only ever witnessed him lose his temper once, it was not an experience he ever wished to repeat. 'Graham was absolutely terrifying when he was angry; I remember it really scared me.'

And once he had let rip, Graham showed no inclination to stop. It was far better that the team should get absolutely hammered, he went on, rather than 'meekly slip out of Old Trafford without leaving a mark'.

When half-time was over, the Watford players went back onto the pitch, by now imbued with an uneasy blend of fear and resolve. Watching from the stands, Ian Poole immediately noticed the change in them. 'They hardly seemed like the same side who'd spent the first half vainly chasing the ball.'

Suddenly, Watford's defence looked to be both well organized and in control. Slowly but surely, the Watford midfielders Roger Joslyn and Dennis Booth wore down their United counterparts and 'the red tide started to ebb'. A scrappy clearance from the United goalkeeper Paddy Roche was headed back towards his goal. Running out of his penalty area with his feet flailing, Roche completely failed to connect with the ball. The Watford winger Bobby Downes then crossed into the goalmouth – whereupon a rising Luther Blissett headed it past Roche's fingertips into the net.

Ian Poole wasn't the only one who found it hard to credit what had just happened. 'For a second or two there was an eerie silence until we leapt to our feet, more in disbelief than celebration.'

A game that had seemed to be drifting towards an all too pre-dictable conclusion had burst into life. Watford were a team transformed; it was as if they'd been stung into action by a gigantic cattle-prod. Instead of going forwards, a shocked Manchester United now found themselves frantically back-pedalling, harried by Watford players at every turn.

Whenever Blissett touched the ball, a chorus of monkey noises rang out. But he kept remembering Graham's advice and refused to let it upset him. In the seventy-first minute, the Watford winger Brian Pollard hared up the length of the pitch and crossed the ball to Ross Jenkins, who was standing just outside the United penalty area. Running towards the touchline, Jenkins took two Manchester United defenders with him. With United's defence pulled out of shape, Watford's Dennis Booth hoisted the ball into an almost empty goalmouth.

It wouldn't stay empty for long; Blissett sprinted forward – 'from nowhere', as one football correspondent would put it – to meet Booth's cross. Blissett himself had no doubt what was going to happen next. 'I knew that if I got a firm contact with my header, I was going to score,' he recalls. 'I could see what was going to happen a split second before it actually unfolded.'

Once again, he took to the air, heading the ball past Paddy Roche, who this time made no attempt to save it. Instead, he just stood there with his arms by his sides, seemingly rooted to the spot as if he too couldn't believe what was happening.

Watford were now leading 2-1. Finally, belatedly, Manchester United organized themselves into some semblance of order and began piling on the pressure. Although the Watford defence stood firm, the cracks were starting to show. In the last minute of the game, the Watford keeper Andy Rankin saved a shot from outside the box, but only managed to parry it to the United centre-half Gordon McQueen.

Immediately, McQueen headed it back towards the top of the net. Somehow Rankin managed to twist himself round and tip

McQueen's shot over the bar. 'I placed that header perfectly,' McQueen recalled. 'I knew it was a goal. And then I saw a green thing appear with a hand on the end of it.' According to many people there, it was one of the finest saves they had ever seen. The Watford full-back Steve Harrison was equally impressed. 'I remember walking past Andy and saying, "I'll tell you what, that was a magnificent save" – to which Rankin muttered drily, "I was still going for the first one."'

By the time the final whistle went twenty minutes later, several thousand red-scarved figures had already started streaming from the ground. Fearing reprisals, the police decided to keep Watford's small band of supporters behind until everyone had dispersed. But once they got outside, they found a reception committee of hardcore United fans waiting. 'By the time they let us out only the real lunatics were still around,' Ian Poole recalled.

Heads down, they clambered on board the Watford coaches. 'Our convoy had a non-stop police escort out of town with sirens wailing, lights flashing and to hell with the traffic lights – which at least gave the neanderthals a moving target. A couple of cracked windows later and we were safely back on the motorway and able to savour a famous victory.'

The next day's papers were in no doubt about the magnitude of what had happened. The *Daily Mirror* headlined its match report, 'Night of Bliss: Fans Stunned as Luther Sends United Crashing'. It carried on in similarly dramatic style:

> Luther Blissett rammed the cruel taunts of the Old Trafford fans back down their throats last night by blasting the goals that carried Third Division Watford to the most famous victory in their history. Blissett, the target of savage abuse from moronic fans who took exception to his black skin, let the senseless jibes ride over him before producing the most devastating answer possible in this League Cup clash.

Had the abuse bothered him, Blissett was asked.

Not at all, he replied. 'People who resort to that are ignorant – and anyway I get used to this kind of treatment.'

As far as Graham was concerned, the result proved that he hadn't spent the last eighteen months in the grip of a hopeless delusion. A team of comparative journeymen really could beat a team full of stars – if they only went about it the right way. Sometimes tactics counted for more than talent, especially if everyone knew what was required of them and stuck to the script.

Watford was now firmly on the footballing map. Not only had they beaten Manchester United at Old Trafford but – the one thing that football correspondents felt able to agree on – they had thoroughly deserved their victory.

For Elton, this was the moment when he allowed himself to believe that his ambitions for Watford, however crazy they may have seemed, were not so mad after all. 'That's when I knew things were working.' As well as giving him 'possibly the greatest night of my life', the result had provided a valuable lesson in how to conduct himself as club chairman. 'After the game was over the Manchester United directors were unbelievably gracious to us. There was no rancour or bitterness; just courtesy and congratulations. I can remember how much that affected me and how I decided that I should try to behave more like them.'

From now on, whenever Elton went to an away game, there would be no more exotically dyed hair, no more flapping lapels or platform heels. 'It taught me that I had to conduct myself in as dignified a manner as possible. In future, no matter how I was feeling on the inside, I was determined that I should look the part.'

A boyhood dream come true.

2. An imp with the Imps. Graham Taylor signs for Lincoln City, 1 August 1968.

3. Elton and Rod Stewart working up a sweat at Vicarage Road, April 1974.

4. Elton is overwhelmed by multiple shots on goal at Vicarage Road, April 1974.

5. The start of a beautiful friendship. Elton appoints Graham Taylor manager of Watford FC in 1977.

. Elton plays Vicarage Road Stadium to boost club funds, raising £40,000, on 5 May 1974.

7. Elton with defender Tom Walley re-signing for Watford in 1976. He went on to become Watford's youth coach, winning the FA Youth Cup in 1982.

8. 'Looooooo-thuurrrr. Bliisssettt! – with a name like that you're bound to be a star', 1978.

Watford celebrate their promotion to Division Two by beating Hull
ity 4-0, May 1979.

ɔ. Calendar boys. Graham Taylor with Ross Jenkins celebrating promotion to the
irst Division after a 2-0 victory over Wrexham, 4 May 1982.

11. 'They all looked at me as if I was stark staring mad' – Elton at a Watford board meeting, July 1982.

12. A hard man's ha[   ] man. Watford strike[   ] Gerry Armstrong receives his Golden Boot from Elton and comedian Lenny Bennett, in recogniti[   ] for being World Cup 1982's top goalscorer while representing Northern Ireland.

13. Elton in Beijing during the club's exhibition tour of China, June 1983.

14. Dressed to impress.

15. 'A calming influence.' Elton and Graham with assistant manager Bertie Mee.

16. Yellow Brick Wall. *Left to right*: Elton, Steve Sherwood, Ross Jenkins, Luther Blissett, Martin Patching.

17. The world in motion. Elton and the team pose with a truck from new sponsors Iveco at Vicarage Road. The industrial vehicle manufacturer was the club's first shirt sponsor in a £400,000 three-year deal.

8. Riding to glory. Elton and Graham at Watford's famous 2-1 victory over Liverpool to clinch second place in Division One, 14 May 1983.

9. Legendary Liverpool manager Bob Paisley with Elton and Graham after the match in the boardroom.

20. Not always the hardest word. Graham makes a public apology to the fans, having been critical of Watford supporters in a newspaper article, April 1982.

21. The stuff of dreams. Watford celebrate finishing second in Division One, May 1983.

2. Two prodigious talents. Elton with John Barnes and Mo Johnston before the Hornets' FA Cup semi-final match against Plymouth, 11 April 1984.

3. A toast to victory.

24. Elton shares a joke with Everton fans before the FA Cup Final, 19 May 1984.

25. Hitting the peak: Graham and Elton in front of thousands of Hornets fans in Charter Place on the day after the final.

6. By their hat shall you know them. Elton with Nigel Callaghan.

7. Elton and Luther Blissett handing out Easter eggs to young fans, 6 April 1985.

28. Indomitable. Luther Blissett and John Barnes, circa 1985.

29. 'I was Mr Fancy Pants and he was Mr Down-to-Earth', April 1991.

o. Graham at the opening of the Graham Taylor Stand, November 2014.

31. Big footsteps. A mural of Graham Taylor outside Vicarage Road, February 2022.

32. Elton with husband, David Furnish, and sons, Zachary and Elijah, at the opening of the Elton John Stand, December 2014.

33, 34. Elton plays
Vicarage Road Stadium
for his 'Farewell Yellow
Brick Road' tour.

35. Watford Forever.

# 31.

Three weeks after the Manchester United game and shortly before Elton was due to fly to Paris to give a concert, he was at home in Windsor when he started feeling unwell. 'I had terrible pains in my chest, arms and legs and I couldn't breathe.' His house guest, the six-times Wimbledon Ladies Champion Billie-Jean King, called a doctor who examined him and said that he suspected Elton was having a heart attack.

An ambulance took him to the coronary unit of the London Clinic. Less than an hour later, a special BBC bulletin announced that 'Pop star Elton John has been rushed to hospital after suffering a heart attack.'

Obituaries were hurriedly dusted down while the press pack gathered outside the London Clinic waiting for more news. But after conducting various tests, the cardiologists decided that Elton hadn't actually had a heart attack; instead he was suffering from exhaustion, apparently brought on by overwork.

'Watford FC Chairman collapsed on Tuesday at his Windsor home following a hectic week even by the musician's current standards,' reported the *Watford Observer*. 'He had played charity football on Sunday afternoon, made two promotional appearances and was due to fly to Paris for a further hair transplant on Tuesday,' the piece went on. 'Doctors put his collapse down to exhaustion and hard work, but it could not prevent Elton listening to a report of Wednesday's game which Watford won 2-0. His latest condition is described as "very comfortable". "He is sleeping well," said his doctors.'

Except this wasn't quite the full story. As well as snorting several lines of cocaine before being taken ill, Elton had then proceeded to play three sets of tennis against Billie-Jean King. Given what he was doing to himself, it was remarkable that he was still functioning at all. A month earlier, he had released his twelfth studio album, *A Single Man*, which featured the staff and players at Watford singing back-up vocals on two of the tracks. To the surprise of staff in the recording studio, he insisted on singing several of his vocals lying on the floor.

Never shy in coming forward, his mother Sheila confided her worries to the showbusiness editors of the Fleet Street tabloids. His biggest problem was loneliness, she felt. 'I think he's desperate,' Sheila said. 'He's got all the possessions you could wish for, but that doesn't make him happy. He says he'd like to have a family. Unfortunately, his lifestyle doesn't allow him to meet anybody. And he won't allow himself; it's as if he holds back all the time.'

In short, Elton was someone whose wealth had failed to buy him what he wanted, still less what he needed. 'I feel as if he's got everything,' Sheila went on. 'Everything, but nothing . . .'

She also came up with an unexpected explanation for her son's sexuality. 'I don't think he'd ever have been the way he is if it hadn't been for showbusiness. Showbusiness did it, definitely.'

In spite of everything, the songs continued to pour out of him – 'Sorry Seems To Be The Hardest Word', 'Song For Guy' and 'Part Time Love' all date from this period. But however fertile he remained creatively, physically he was running on empty. The doctors told him that what he needed above all was to rest. To ease up for a while and not do anything remotely stressful.

For several weeks Elton stayed at home, put his feet up and became increasingly frustrated. 'The trouble is I'm not someone who can just sit around and do nothing; it's just not in my nature.' After a few more days of this, he did the one thing he had been expressly told not to do: he announced that he was coming out of retirement and embarking on a lengthy European tour. With the despairing cries of his doctors ringing in his ears, he headed off to Stockholm for the opening night.

Apart from some first-night nerves – he had a bad attack of the jitters during his solo spot – the concert went well. So did the ones that followed. The only problem was that out in the far-flung reaches of Europe, Elton was no longer able to keep track of Watford's progress. Television crews scarcely ever went to Vicarage Road – Watford were nowhere near important enough for that – and even if they had done, the coverage would never be broadcast abroad. Very occasionally, there might be a brief snippet of radio commentary, but that was about it.

Then one day Elton had an idea. At every home game, a man called Mike Vince used to broadcast a live match commentary for the benefit of patients at Shrodells Hospital in Watford. 'By this point I'd been doing it for several years,' Vince recalls. 'On an average night, my audience was around a hundred people' – all of them lying stretched out in their hospital beds just a few hundred yards from the ground.

Might it be possible for him to listen in to Vince's match reports, Elton wondered.

Once he had got over his shock, Vince was only too keen to help. It proved to be surprisingly easy to sort out. All Elton had to do was call up Vince's engineer before a game started. He would then trip a switch, plugging Elton in to the commentary. While his phone bills may have been ruinously expensive – the cost of listening to a single game often exceeded a thousand pounds – as far as he was concerned, it was worth every penny.

There were emotional benefits too. It meant that no matter how far away from home Elton was, or how far he may have drifted into the stratosphere, from now on, an umbilical cord of telephone cable would ensure that he remained tethered to Vicarage Road.

By a strange coincidence, shortly before Elton had a suspected heart attack, his father had a real one. By now, Stanley Dwight and his new family had moved to North Wales. They lived in a modest house with their four sons, and Stanley worked for the chemical company Unilever in nearby Ewloe. Privately, his wife, Edna, believed that the pressures of being hounded by journalists had contributed to Stanley's health problems. They would routinely knock on their door offering him money to talk about his son – offers he always turned down.

After a spell in hospital following his heart attack, Stanley went back to work at Unilever. However, he would never be the same again. At the time it was widely assumed that anyone who suffered a heart attack in their fifties was likely to have another, quite possibly fatal, one, a few years later.

When Stanley heard that Elton was in the London Clinic, he sent him a bunch of flowers and a get-well card, without mentioning that he had just come out of hospital himself. Shortly afterwards, Edna also wrote to Elton. Since she didn't have his address, she sent her letter to him 'Care of Graham Taylor' at Watford Football Club. She thought he should know that his father had been ill and that his health was declining, she wrote. As soon as Elton received his stepmother's letter, he also sent Stanley a bunch of flowers and a get-well card.

It was the first contact they had had in years.

# 32.

Watford had knocked mighty Manchester United out of the League Cup. They had silenced their critics, given their supporters plenty to cheer about and were finally being accorded some respect. As the 1978/9 season entered its final stretch, Watford were in fourth place in Division Three – within touching distance of promotion.

But as Graham lay in bed in his house in Mandeville Close, a single thought kept churning around in his head: something was wrong. The trouble was he couldn't put his finger on what it was. Nor did he feel he could talk to anybody about it. Elton was away on tour and, under the circumstances, anyone else might have thought he was off his head. But the more he thought about it, the more convinced he became.

Something was wrong.

Despite their success – or perhaps even because of it – Watford had stopped believing in themselves. Self-doubt had started nibbling away at their confidence. It was as if they'd come so far in so short a time that no one felt quite able to accept what had really happened. At any moment the rug could be pulled from under their feet and they would tumble back to where they naturally belonged – down at the bottom of Division Four. Or so they seemed to feel.

At first, Graham did what he could to push the dark clouds away. He tried to encourage the players into thinking positively, asked them into his office to give them individual pep talks and cranked up the training regime to still more punitive levels so they were ready to face whatever challenges lay ahead.

But the problem wasn't physical, he came to see; it was mental.

And what's more, nothing he said or did made any difference. It was, he said later, 'as big a test of my man-management skills as anything I'd faced since starting my career.'

He was also feeling particularly sensitive about suggestions that he had simply bought his way to the top, using Elton's money to outspend any of his rivals. 'The facts are we haven't thrown any toytown money about just because Elton John is chairman,' Taylor told a journalist. 'In the twelve months I have been here, we have recruited thirteen players at a cost of just £83,000.'

One player appeared to encapsulate the general malaise. Steve Sims had been born and brought up in Lincoln, a few hundred yards from the Lincoln City ground. When Sims was fifteen, Graham went round to his parents' house and tried to persuade him to sign for Lincoln. In the event, he went to Second Division Leicester City, mainly because his father was convinced that Lincoln were another bunch of clodhoppers who would never amount to anything.

At Leicester, Sims matured into a combative and elegant centre-half and was picked to play for the England B team. Then in December 1978, Watford paid £175,000 for him – the most any Third Division side had ever spent on a player – this was after Ian Bolton, Graham's regular centre-half, had slipped a disc while brushing his teeth.

When Sims first travelled to Watford to meet Graham, he checked into his room in the Holiday Inn and was lying on his bed when the phone rang. To his astonishment, it was Elton on the other end of the line saying that he hoped Sims would join the club. But what astonished him even more was the tone of Elton's voice. 'Although I found it hard to believe, he sounded as if he was really excited to be talking to me.'

But Sims's transfer coincided with the club's sudden loss of confidence, and from the moment he arrived at Vicarage Road, he too felt his morale starting to sag. It didn't help that he literally wasn't able to keep up with his new teammates. On his second day there, he went on a cross-country run and finished so far behind everyone else that he scarcely made it back before dark.

Nor did he fare any better on the pitch. Sims was soon being greeted with a chorus of catcalls whenever he touched the ball, and after just twelve games, was dropped from the first team: 'Graham did it for my own good because I was getting such stick from the crowd. I'd lost my way and I felt terribly guilty that I was letting everyone down.'

Whenever he had any time off, Sims would head straight back to Lincoln: 'I was a really quiet and shy homeboy and I just didn't think I fitted in.' As Graham noted later, 'He wasn't the player I hoped I was signing.'

By this point, Sims thought his confidence couldn't sink any lower. But here he turned out to be wrong. One night he got into a cab with the Watford goalkeeper Andy Rankin. The driver recognized Rankin and began talking about the club's promotion prospects.

'Graham Taylor's doing a great job,' the driver said. After going on in similar vein for some time, he came up with one important caveat. 'The only mistake he's made is buying that useless wanker Steve Sims.'

Sitting in the back seat, a crushed Sims kept his mouth shut and gazed fixedly out of the window.

Steve Sims watched from the substitutes' bench as Watford were beaten 3-0 at home by Colchester United – 'a painfully inept performance', according to Oli Phillips in the *Watford Observer*. Next they were due to play an away game against the Division Three leaders, Shrewsbury Town.

If Graham was to galvanize the players into action, he would have to do something drastic, he decided. Something that would give them enough of a jolt to make them look at their lives with fresh eyes. Before the game started, he gathered everyone together, along with one of the Watford directors, a former soldier called Jim Harrowell.

Graham asked him to roll up his trouser leg.

Harrowell did so, revealing an old war wound that had never healed properly.

The players stared at it in horror.

'Now, Mr Harrowell fought in the Second World War,' Graham told them. 'And he has to live with that and have it dressed – how many times a week, Mr Harrowell?'

'Twice,' Harrowell replied.

'*Twice!* Twice a week!' repeated Taylor. 'And you lot – you play football for a living. You don't know you're born!'

With the memory of Jim Harrowell's still suppurating wound all-too-fresh in the players' minds, Watford drew the game 1-1. However, they lost their next two games and drew the one after that. There were three more matches to go before the end of the season and they were now lying in second place. If they finished second, they would win promotion to Division Two, but their two nearest rivals both had a game in hand, and either one could overhaul them.

Watford won their penultimate game against Sheffield Wednesday 3-2. They then had to wait for nine days before their last match – against Hull at home. During those nine days, both their promotion rivals won. As a result, Watford slipped down to third place. If they didn't beat Hull, that was it – they were going to stay in Division Three.

Several months earlier, Watford had agreed to go to France to play a friendly match against a club called Sochaux in Montbeliard, a town near the Swiss border. The plan was that Sochaux would then come to Watford for a return match. With the Hull game looming, Graham was tempted to call off the fixture, but then decided that it might be better if they went after all. Perhaps it would help take everyone's minds off their promotion battle.

Before the game started, Graham did something that he'd never done before. He told the players that they should all pretend this was the first leg of a UEFA Cup tie. Rather than make any effort to win the game, they should play for a nil-all draw. This would mean that they wouldn't expend any unnecessary effort or run the risk of injuries. Sure enough, much to the confusion of the French team, the Watford players showed no interest in venturing out of their own half – let alone going anywhere near the Sochaux goal.

The game duly ended in nil-all. The only snag was that Sochaux were so infuriated with Watford's unsportsmanlike attitude that they refused to come over to England for the return leg.

All this had proved a welcome distraction, but back at Vicarage Road, Graham could feel anxiety starting to settle once more. Again, something drastic was called for. He had already tried shock tactics, so he could hardly do that again. Instead, Graham remembered the Romantic poets he had enjoyed so much as a schoolboy. In the final training session before the game, he asked the players to jog round the pitch for fifteen minutes, then lie down on their backs.

It was a bright spring day and a few fluffy clouds were scudding across the sky. The players lay there in silence, staring upwards and wondering what was going on.

'It's a good life this, isn't it?' Graham said.

No one said anything.

'The only thing we've got to worry about is winning a game of football,' he went on. 'That's all. It's not real work, is it? We're very lucky people really. We've not got a care in the world.'

As he lay there, Steve Harrison remembers thinking 'Oh God, he's really lost it now.' What's more, he suspected he was not the only one whose thoughts were drifting along similar lines.

Graham hadn't finished yet. 'And you know who's luckiest of all?' he asked.

Again, no one spoke.

'I am,' Graham told them. 'Because I'm the gaffer and if I fancy the rest of the day off, I can just take it. So, I think I'll pop home, take the wife for a bit of lunch and then spend the rest of the afternoon sitting in the garden . . .'

He paused. 'Come on,' he said. 'What are you waiting for? Let's all have the day off and I'll see you tomorrow.'

Warily, the players got to their feet, convinced they were about to be called back at any moment and sent on another cross-country run. They then rushed back to the changing room.

The following night, fortified by their afternoon off and reflecting on the lucky hand that life had dealt them, Watford thrashed Hull City 4-0. The atmosphere proved too much for some. According to the *Watford Observer*, 'St John Ambulancemen and women worked overtime as a succession of fans were carried or helped from the ground suffering from anxiety, excitement, heat or a combination of all three.'

Of Watford's four goals, Jenkins scored one – a glancing header – Luther Blissett another, with Ian Bolton and Roger Joslyn scoring the others. As well as taking Jenkins's goal tally for the season to thirty-seven – once again making him Watford's top scorer – this earned him another plaudit: he was now the highest scorer in the entire Football League, putting him ahead of household names such as Kevin Keegan, Andy Gray and Malcolm Macdonald.

Four years since they had been lying on the bottom of Division Four, three years since Elton had bought the club and two years after Graham had taken over as manager, Watford were now in Division Two.

# PART THREE

# 33.

The moment Elton's European tour was over, he told the rock promotor Harvey Goldsmith that he wanted to go back out on the road again as soon as possible. Only this time he wanted to go somewhere off the beaten track – ideally somewhere that few, if any, rock musicians had been before.

Where did he have in mind, Goldsmith asked.

Not having given the matter much thought, Elton said the first thing that popped into his head: 'What about Russia?'

By this stage in his career, Goldsmith had become used to catering to the extravagant whims of rock stars. This, though, was way beyond anything he'd encountered before. With the unlikely exceptions of Cliff Richard and Boney M, no western acts had played in Soviet Russia. Even Cliff Richard had been considered dangerously edgy by the Soviet authorities. The idea that the Russians might allow someone who had recently come out as bisexual and sang about the delights of getting stuck into a good punch-up on a Saturday night must have seemed reassuringly remote.

Goldsmith said he would see what he could do. Expecting an immediate brush-off, he approached the Foreign Office. They in turn contacted the Soviet Ministry of Culture. To Goldsmith's disbelief, they replied by issuing a formal invitation.

Two days before leaving for the Soviet Union, Elton presented Graham with the gold disc he had received for sales of the album *A Single Man* to celebrate Watford winning promotion to Division Two.

In late May 1979, he arrived at Moscow airport accompanied by a small party including his mother and stepfather, and with a Watford scarf around his neck. 'I don't know if they've heard of

Watford in Russia,' Elton told a press conference, 'but they soon will do.'

In Leningrad, he performed in front of an audience drawn from what was described as 'approved families and schools' and afterwards went back to his hotel to eat the only thing on the menu: beetroot soup and potatoes. The next morning, plainly unsure what to make of it, the music critic of the official Soviet newspaper, *Pravda*, cautiously complimented him on his 'gay originality'.

Two days later, in Moscow, Elton was given a more frosty reception. Gazing out from the stage, he saw row after row of party officials sitting there with faces that might have been baked in clay. His first few songs drew a polite ripple of applause, nothing more. Desperate to elicit a reaction, he decided to do something that he hadn't done in more than fifteen years when it had succeeded in rousing the customers of the Public Bar at the Northwood Hills Hotel from their torpor: he launched into Jim Reeves's 'He'll Have To Go'. In a place that could hardly have been more alien, it was a link back to another world. Another world and another life.

And just as had happened back then, something seemed to click. By the end of the evening large sections of the audience had left their seats to run down the aisles to the front of the stage where they joined in with those lyrics they knew and cheered the ones they weren't so sure about. At the same time, gifts rained down from the balcony – flowers, cuddly toys, even a string of pearls.

After the show was over, thousands of people – many more than had had seats – gathered in the street outside Elton's dressing room window as he waved and threw the flowers he had been given back down to them.

But not everyone was impressed. Standing beside her son, Sheila Farebrother watched this with her customary beady eye. 'You'd be better off throwing them a tomato,' she told him.

★

Graham's foreign travel followed a less adventurous path. Once again, he took his family caravanning in France at the end of the season – and once again when he got back, there was an unexpected letter waiting for him.

Glancing at the signature, Graham saw it had been written by a man who signed himself Wing-Commander Charles Reep (Retd). Reep had some information he wanted to share with him, he wrote – information that in the right hands could prove invaluable. Like Graham, Charles Reep was obsessed with footballing statistics. Armed with the right data, he believed, you could predict not only the course of a game, but also its likely result.

As punctilious about timekeeping as he was about everything else, Reep knew the exact moment when his life had changed for ever. It was at 3.50 on the afternoon of 18 March 1950 when he was watching the second half of a game between Swindon Town and Bristol Rovers.

Along with other Swindon fans, Reep had become increasingly frustrated by the pedestrian pace at which they played, and their ineffectual attempts on goal. As he always did, he had brought a notebook with him in which he jotted down his observations. Idly at first, Reep began counting the number of passes Swindon made and how often these resulted in a goal. By the end of the game, he saw that they had made a total of 147 attacking plays. While it was true that these had eventually resulted in a goal – the only one of the match – this had been more of a fluke than the result of any systematic build-up of play.

Staring at his jottings, Reep thought that he might be on to something. Rushing home, he compiled a diagram in which he drew a map of where each pass had gone and how each move had unfolded. As the diagram was far too elaborate for single sheets of paper, he used rolls of old wallpaper that he happened to have lying around, unrolling them across his living-room floor and covering them with a baffling array of hieroglyphics.

When Reep had finished, he was more convinced than ever

that he'd stumbled upon something extraordinary. Something which amounted to nothing less than a hidden code – a code which if followed correctly would give a mediocre team a distinct edge over a vastly superior one.

A standard game of football, he estimated, consisted of 280 attacking moves which resulted in an average of two goals – a conversion rate of just 0.71 per cent. But according to Reep's analysis, it would take only a very small improvement to increase a side's average from two goals to three, thereby giving them a much greater chance of winning.

From this moment on, he was a man possessed. That season alone Reep watched a total of forty games. On dark winter afternoons, when the beam from the floodlights barely crept over the touchline, he would wear a miner's helmet to illuminate his notebook as he scribbled frantically away. Then, as soon as the final whistle went, he'd head straight home with his notebook to pick apart what he had just seen – each match would take him about eighty hours to notate and analyse. Later, Reep would devise his own shorthand consisting of more than 2,000 symbols, each one denoting a different move.

Central to his theories was one guiding principle: the more passes there were, the less chance a team had of scoring a goal. That in turn led to another principle: the more quickly a team could get the ball upfield, the greater the likelihood of their scoring.

There was more to it than that, of course. The longer Reep spent analysing football games, the more he came to see that chance played a much greater role than he'd ever realized. Although skill was plainly very important, there were other forces at work too. Mysterious eddies and currents that were barely visible to the naked eye. But if you took the time to break down a move into its component parts, then you could see just how these invisible forces worked.

The following year, Reep decided that the time had come to

put his analysis into practice. He wrote to the Brentford manager offering his services as a part-time 'statistical adviser'. At the time, Brentford were struggling to avoid relegation from the Second Division. Although no one there had much idea of what a statistical adviser was, they were prepared to grasp at any straw they were offered.

It proved to be an inspired move. By using Reep's analysis, Brentford managed to double their goals-per-match ratio and won thirteen of their last fourteen games, thereby avoiding relegation.

Two years later, Wing-Commander Reep presented his findings to the Royal Statistical Society. Among them were the following:

- It takes ten shots to get one goal.
- 50 per cent of goals are scored from zero or one pass.
- 80 per cent of goals are scored within three or less passes.
- 50 per cent of goals come from breakdowns in a team's own half of the pitch.
- Regaining possession within the shooting area is a vital source of goalscoring opportunities.

Reep's findings caused a considerable stir, especially among footballing pundits. Some of them dismissed them outright. As far as they were concerned, football was a game of skill, pure and simple, and anyone suggesting otherwise was deluded, deranged or both. The idea that statistics might have any relevance in football was equally preposterous.

Others, though, were less dismissive. Just conceivably, Reep might be on to something. However resistant purists were to the idea, it was hard to argue with his results. From Brentford, Reep had gone to Wolves – they proceeded to win three league titles in four years.

In 1955, he retired from the Air Force and was invited to come to Sheffield Wednesday as a part-time adviser at a salary of £750 a year. At the end of his first season, Wednesday were promoted from Division Two to Division One. But Wednesday's progress soon stalled and Reep and his wacky theories were held to blame. He in turn blamed the club for not paying sufficient heed to his advice.

Shunned and discredited, he found himself back in the wilderness. No other managers wanted anything to do with him, while the FA could hardly bring themselves to mention his name. He was to stay in the wilderness for the next twenty years – a solitary figure in his miner's helmet scribbling away on the terraces.

By the time Reep wrote to Graham, he had compiled a thick dossier in which he outlined his conclusions that had been drawn from more than 600,000 painstakingly analysed moves. Graham gave the letter a quick read before putting the dossier in his desk drawer – where it sat for a few months.

One evening he decided to go to bed early and took the dossier with him. As he lay propped up on the pillows, leafing through the fruits of Reep's research, Graham found himself becoming more and more absorbed. In several respects, he was already putting Reep's findings into practice, he realized. He too believed in getting the ball upfield as quickly as possible – hence the importance of the Watford backs hitting long passes all the way up to their forwards.

And, like Reep, Graham had also begun to analyse games much more closely than most other managers – a few months earlier he had started videoing Watford's matches so that he and the players could watch them back afterwards. But the club could only afford one video camera – it was mounted on the corrugated iron roof of one of the stands – and quite often the picture was so fuzzy it was impossible to make out what was going on.

Graham wrote back to Reep expressing his interest. A few days later, he drove down to his home in Plymouth. Like others before him, he found Reep to be a tricky customer. Friendly enough on the surface, he could be as stubborn as he was obsessive. Yet there was no doubting his enthusiasm. Eagerly, Reep unrolled his wallpaper rolls on his living-room floor to illustrate his points.

After he'd looked at them, Graham asked Reep if he would come to Watford to meet the players. That way he would be able to explain his theories in person. But Reep wouldn't hear of it. As far as Graham was concerned, there was only one explanation for his reluctance. 'I concluded that he did not want to be challenged by players.' Nonetheless, he drove away more convinced than ever that statistics were the key to winning games: that was how you identified and exploited an opposing team's weaknesses. That was what gave you the vital edge.

If Reep wasn't prepared to meet the players, then perhaps he would be prepared to give Graham his thoughts on how they played? This idea fell on more fertile ground. While he wouldn't come himself, Reep said, he would organize for a former pupil of his called Simon Hartley to come instead of him. And so every week Hartley would watch Watford play, then compile a report for Reep to pore over. Once he'd done so, he would send his analysis to Graham.

At around this time a friend of Hartley's decided that for a bit of fun he would use Reep's research to place a few modest bets on football games. Like so many others before him, he was sceptical about Reep's findings and didn't hold out much hope that his bets would amount to anything. But in the event, he did rather better than he had expected. In the course of the following year, Hartley's friend won more than £100,000 – over half a million pounds in today's money.

*From the* Watford Observer

# MEDIEVAL MERCHANTS HOUSE FOUND IN WATFORD HIGH STREET

For generations, the bland modern façade in Watford High Street, part of Stapleton's Tyre Depot, hid an astonishing secret. Behind it lay an intact building, thought to have once belonged to a medieval merchant, that went all the way back to about 1450. At the same time, archaeologists discovered another medieval building, this one hidden behind what is now DER Rental Televisions.

How could Watford have gone so long unaware of the age of these old buildings? An expert in ancient structures saw the wagonway at the side of the DER building and realised what might be hidden inside. It must have been an exciting moment when he climbed into the dark and dirty attic, turned his torch on and saw the magnificent crown-post roof. It also begs an intriguing question, of course: what other jewels might lie hidden away in Watford, just waiting to be rediscovered?

The hope is now that both buildings can now be re-erected in an open-air museum. But strange enough, when preservationists asked Hertfordshire Country Council if they could offer a site for an open-air museum, they said they would prefer not to see such a project in Hertfordshire. They would not help.

# 34.

On the surface nothing much had changed. The Earl of Arran would have seen no reason to change his verdict that Watford was 'a living hell'. The few remaining historic buildings in the town centre that hadn't been flattened by a wrecking ball were now flanked by what brochures described as 'more modern, more scenic developments'.

Unemployment continued to rise while investment continued to fall. Estate agents, desperately trying to encourage people to move to Watford, no longer made any effort to extol the town's physical attractions, choosing instead to concentrate on its well-nigh limitless car parking facilities.

In an effort to show the population of Watford what dramatic plans they had for further roads and developments in the town – plans that would 'take Watford into the 1980s' – the borough council put on four different exhibitions. In over a month, they attracted just 200 people. Further efforts to drum up some civic enthusiasm met with much the same response. Undaunted, the council sent out 12,000 questionnaires asking people for their comments on yet more proposed changes to the town centre.

These elicited just 300 replies.

Among them was one from a Mr Roger Hillier of Gladstone Road who felt sure he knew the reason for such widespread apathy. 'The so-called improvements of the last twenty years were a disaster of such proportions that people scarcely knew where to begin when asked for their opinions,' he wrote. 'Watford is now such a laughing-stock that it's avoided by everyone except insatiable shoppers who regularly sweep through the town like a swarm of locusts.'

But while the council remained hellbent on dragging Watford into some cheerless concrete future, there was one part of town they had no interest in. Attempts, led by Elton and Graham, to move from Vicarage Road to a new purpose-built ground had met with a complete lack of enthusiasm.

The councillors made it all too plain they had no intention of approving such a plan. What's more, they clearly didn't think Watford FC had anything worthwhile to offer the town. While the council conceded that the club was no longer quite as much of an embarrassment as it had been, that didn't mean it was anything to be proud of. Far better to keep the ground where it was, they decided – tucked conveniently out of sight behind the sprawl of second-hand car showrooms and discount tyre warehouses.

As far as Elton was concerned, 'they had nothing but contempt for us. They didn't want to know me, they didn't want to know Graham, and they just wasted so much of our time. It was just like banging our heads against a brick wall.'

Nothing had changed – and yet something had changed. The Reverend Boyers had become aware of it as he went about his ministrations. It was nothing concrete, nothing you could pin down; it was just something in the air. 'There was a sense that people were happier, more at ease. That finally they had something to feel good about.'

The players felt it too. The Watford midfielder Dennis Booth, another Lincoln City veteran Taylor had brought south with him, was in the habit of walking to Vicarage Road on match days and smoking a cigarette on the way to settle his nerves. In the past, no one had paid him any attention. But now he turned around to see a long line of schoolchildren following in his wake.

By this time, there was nothing strange about the sight of Watford players, even Elton himself, strolling around the town centre, or turning up at school fêtes, or touring the wards at the town's hospitals, chatting to the patients. For Ian Bolton, as for others, it was an enormously rewarding experience. 'Imagine going to hospital and seeing the reaction of children if you gave them Christmas presents. It brought it home to you how revered you were with the fans, but it also kept our feet on the ground and improved us as people.'

In the summer, the players would hand out tombola prizes and compete in three-legged races in the pedestrianized precinct. At the same time, Graham continued to engage with Watford supporters whenever the opportunity arose. He insisted on replying to every letter he was sent. One man who angrily questioned Watford's tactics was surprised to receive not only a letter by return of post, but also a follow-up phone call inviting him for a drink. They got on so well that Graham ended up being best man at his wedding a few months later.

As well as replying to letters, Graham decided that he should make himself more available for supporters who wanted to question him more closely. An announcement in the *Watford Observer* headlined 'The Manager Wants to Meet You' appealed to supporters not to be shy, but to come and 'give the manager a piece of your mind'. Several hundred people turned up. The meeting, which had been scheduled to last for two hours, went on for a marathon four and a quarter. When it finally finished, people reeled out, as dazed as they were exhausted. Only one figure was left – not only still standing, but as full of beans as he had been at the start of the evening.

'I could have carried on all night,' said Graham afterwards.


*From Watford FC programme, August 1979*

A message from the Chairman
It looks like being the most exciting season the club has ever enjoyed. Yet I will have to miss some of it. I have to go on tour again because I just cannot ignore my career. It's three years since

I last played Los Angeles, for example. So I have opted to get all the touring over and done with in one large dose, but my return to the road does not signal a loss of interest in Watford FC.

Much has been said about the fact that I am chairman and that I have spent a lot of my own money. That is not true. Money was made available but of late it has been down to Graham. He has been given the freedom to make the plans. He certainly opened my eyes for I did not appreciate how much hard work was needed behind the scenes in order to put this club on a proper footing.

Make no mistake, we are going for broke. This is the only approach I know. We have to aim for the top, the very top. I am not prepared to just drift along on the wave of past successes and, if I was, I would quickly lose the staff we have assembled at the club.

Hopefully, we can inject a breath of fresh air into football. So many people in the game are afraid to take a chance. The apathy frightens me and to get them to accept the need and reality of change is harder than it was to get Queen Victoria to take her corset off!

I think this attitude, this lack of initiative, goes through many facets of British sport. Certainly, there is a lot that could be improved in football. Some clubs have directors with no liaison with their supporters. We may make mistakes, but we are not and will not be afraid to break new ground in our bid to get to the top.

People say that the pressure is off us now and that no one expects us to do much in Division Two in the first year. Personally, I think we will do a lot better than people expect, but ultimately promotion is our goal and after that, the very top.

I will not rest until that is achieved and I know I am surrounded by a board and staff with the same aims.

People have said that we will never become another Liverpool. Well, a few years ago, I never thought I'd be an Elton John.

In the autumn of 1979, Elton's thirteenth album, *Victim of Love*, was released. Intended as a tribute to Studio 54 in New York where he had spent many happy hours, the album was only thirty-six minutes long and contained no original compositions. In America, it made it to number 35 in the American charts. In the UK, it fared even worse, peaking at 41.

The reviews were universally bad. 'This album can't even be blithely dismissed as a bore,' wrote Colin Irwin in the *Melody Maker*. 'There are moments when it's thoroughly objectionable.'

In the *Village Voice*, Lester Bangs was just as dismissive, but wondered shrewdly if other factors might be to blame. 'There is no getting away from it,' he wrote. 'Elton's got problems.'

# 35.

Despite their fighting talk about going for broke, Watford finished their first season in Division Two in eighteenth place – fourth from the bottom. This may not have been languishing exactly, but it wasn't far off. True, they escaped relegation and enjoyed a good run in the FA Cup before losing in the quarter finals to Bertie Mee's old club, Arsenal. Even so, it wasn't what people had been hoping for. Having grown used to success, they had come to expect it, almost to take it as their due.

Some made no attempt to hide their displeasure. A Mr H. Jordan of Meadow Lane, Beaconsfield was in no doubt where the biggest problem lay, 'Sir,' he wrote to the *Watford Observer*, 'I am writing because I am very concerned with what is happening at Watford Football Club and I think someone needs to speak up. At one time Watford was run by one person – i.e. Mr Bonser – and I see it happening again . . . Also there seem to be two sets of players at the club, the ones the manager likes and the ones he doesn't, regardless of form on the field.'

Throughout the season, the newspaper headlines became gloomier and gloomier: 'Watford Are Moving Into Dangerous Waters', 'Worried Taylor Wants Answers', 'Few Crumbs To Share as Watford Are Routed' . . .

For Graham, there had been an early warning sign that all was not well. In September 1979, Watford had played Chelsea away. When their coach pulled up outside Chelsea's ground, Stamford Bridge, none of the Watford players left their seats. Instead, they just stayed where they were looking out of the windows with worried expressions on their faces.

'I looked around and realized they were waiting for me to

make the first move,' Graham recalled. 'As a group, they seemed hesitant. Perhaps they weren't sure where the dressing rooms were. It struck me that there wasn't a leader among them who had a great deal of experience at this level.'

Watford went on to lose the game 2-0 – but far worse than the actual result was the way in which Watford had played. 'We lost in a very meek manner,' he said afterwards. The more Graham thought about it, the more he came to see that he no longer enjoyed the way Watford played. A team that had prided itself on confounding people's expectations had become predictable, doing the things they thought they should be doing, rather than what they were best at.

He had been here before, of course – only a year earlier. Yet this was different: back then Watford had suffered a collective lack of confidence, whereas now they just seemed spineless. Maddened by the players' attitude, Graham took the unusual step of launching a public broadside against them in a newspaper interview, even threatening to leave if things didn't improve: 'I don't want to stay here if they haven't got the guts.'

It didn't help that Elton had once again been away on tour for much of that year. As a result, there was no one Graham could confide in, no one he felt was on the same wavelength. Perhaps because he had been away so much, Elton appeared to be the only person who wasn't worried. Far from becoming disenchanted with Graham, he had just offered him a new five-year contract.

'I had complete faith in him. I knew from my experience in the music business that if you have a record that goes in at number one, and then your next one goes in at number eight, you immediately think, "Will I ever get to number one again?" But sometimes you just have to be patient and trust in your ability.'

Despite Graham's threat to walk away from Watford, he hadn't hesitated to sign his new contract. But Elton's confidence in him did nothing to banish his anxiety; in some respects it only made it worse, leaving him feeling guilty that he was letting his chairman down. If Graham needed any reminders of how precarious the life of a manager was – and what short memories football clubs had – it came in the shape of news from Lincoln City. Everything he had achieved there was in the process of being dismantled or destroyed, he learned – the new manager had even told the groundsman to burn the paper and pencils from his old office.

There was only one way to stop the rot at Watford, he decided: he would have to go shopping. Together, Graham and Bertie Mee would often go and check out players they had heard about. In order not to alert anyone to their presence, they always stood on the terraces and Bertie Mee would disguise himself by pulling a baggy cap down over his face. This was not quite as successful as he had hoped. On one of their early trips, Mee was standing there seemingly concealed beneath the folds of his cap when someone walked past and said, casually, 'Hello Bertie.'

When Elton came back from touring, he would occasionally join Graham on these clandestine missions. Like Bertie Mee, he would also disguise himself – albeit with rather more success. 'No one ever recognised me; we would just stand on the terraces along with everyone else. I remember once we were locked into the ground at Rochdale. They had such small crowds that they didn't want anyone to leave, so they simply locked the gates.'

As far as Elton was concerned, these visits offered him a chance to slip briefly back into anonymity. That alone was a welcome novelty, but once again what he loved most was the sense of involvement. 'It was one thing to be chairman and sit in the boardroom, but for me the really fulfilling thing was being part of the football side. Although Graham made the final decision about a player and I would never have dreamed of trying to influence him, we would always talk about the players we'd seen. And the extraordinary thing was that we never once disagreed.'

By now Watford's needs were so pressing that Graham decided

that he had to step up the frequency of his trips to other clubs. Every few weeks, without telling anyone what he was doing, he would drive down to London, park his car, then catch a train north. Before setting off, he would already have bought a ticket to a game that interested him – always paying his way as if he was an ordinary supporter and never alerting the club in advance.

Arriving at his destination, Graham would walk to the ground, usually buying himself some fish and chips on the way. Just as Elton relished the anonymity of their scouting missions together, so there were few aspects of Graham's job that he enjoyed quite as much as the opportunity to stop being Graham Taylor for a while. Above all, he loved the subterfuge, the thrill of moving unnoticed through huge crowds of people.

At Watford, Graham was renowned as a tremendous chatterbox; words poured out of him in an unbroken stream. But here he kept his mouth firmly shut. Instead, he would listen to what people standing around him were saying. 'I'd keep my ear on the conversations to see if I could pick up what people were saying about the player I was there to see.'

As Graham had discovered when he was at Lincoln, he could learn a lot by sly eavesdropping. 'Supporters can be often very revealing about their team, especially when they have no idea they're being overheard by a manager.'

If, for instance, he was thinking of buying a team's winger, he would be able to work out very quickly what supporters felt about him. What sort of man was he? Was he willing to drop back into defence and help out his teammates? Or was he a bit of a show pony who was only out for himself?

During the game he would move around, watching the play from different areas of the terraces. Here too there was a lot to be learned. 'It always surprised me what a different impression I'd get from a game of football standing behind the goal compared to sitting on the halfway line.'

Invariably, Graham headed north on these expeditions for one simple reason. Always careful not to spend any more of Elton's money than necessary, he knew that players up north tended to be cheaper than those down south. Once the match was over, he would walk back to the station and catch the overnight sleeper back to London, allowing himself 'a little glass of something' on the way to help him sleep.

The next morning, Graham would turn up at Vicarage Road without anyone having any idea where he had been. If any player had caught his eye, he would discuss it with both Bertie Mee and Elton. ' "I think I've got one, if we can afford him," I would say.'

Having secured Elton's agreement, Graham would then conduct detailed background research, both on the player and his family. 'I knew I was not just signing the player, I was signing his wife and children too. A good player can easily be unsettled if his wife is unhappy, or if the children have difficulty at school. I wanted to get to know a player's family and show them what sort of club we were and what sort of man I was.'

On one of his early trips north, Graham had been very taken with Sunderland's left-winger, Wilf Rostron – before joining Sunderland, Rostron had played for Bertie Mee's Arsenal. In October 1979, Watford paid £150,000 for him. Moving south with his wife and young baby, Rostron had assumed they would buy a house. But he was in for a nasty shock. Looking around local estate agents, Rostron believed at first they must have added an extra zero to their prices by mistake. Slowly, it dawned on him that property was far more expensive down south.

To make matters worse, building societies routinely turned down applications from footballers on the grounds that they were an unacceptably high risk, with no job security and next to no long-term prospects; the sort of people they really didn't want cluttering up their books. Unable to find anywhere to live, Rostron, his wife and their baby son joined a large group of similarly marooned players who had gone to stay at the local Holiday Inn, often for months at a time.

In fact, two of the five players Graham bought that autumn were from London clubs. Both were Irish.

Pat Rice was a former captain of Arsenal who had made more than 500 appearances for the club at right back during Bertie Mee's time as manager. At thirty-one, Rice was coming to the end of his career, but Graham thought he was such a natural leader that he was worth taking a chance on. The first time he introduced him to the other players, he told them, 'This is Pat Rice. He's going to be our captain, but because of his age he may have the odd day off to recover.' As it turned out, Rice never needed a day off – although he was made to work harder than he'd ever worked in his life. 'If you were injured, you still had to come in at 9 a.m. If you were two minutes late, then you had to buy lunch for everyone.'

But there was still something Graham lacked. Back when he had bought Dennis Booth and Ian Bolton from Notts County, he had told them he was looking for 'a couple of uglies' – unreconstructed brutes who were prepared to soak up any amount of punishment and still keep pressing forward. Now he wanted a kind of hard man's hard man – someone big, brave and belligerent. Again, it wasn't long before Graham became convinced that he had found exactly what he was looking for.

Gerry Armstrong was a 27-year-old Tottenham Hotspur centre forward who had played more than twenty times for Northern Ireland. Armstrong hadn't actually started playing football until he was seventeen. Prior to that he had played Gaelic football for Bangor, where he had enjoyed somewhat mixed fortunes. Despite Gaelic football being one of the most violent games ever devised, sendings-off are rare. Armstrong had managed to be red-carded on his debut – something that was thought never to have happened before. He came on as a substitute with twenty minutes to go, but lasted only ten of them.

Having scored a goal as soon as he came onto the pitch, Armstrong was told by the opposing team's centre-half that 'the next time you go by me, I'm going to do you.' He may only have been seventeen, but Armstrong had played enough Gaelic football to know that you had to get your retaliation in first – 'and so I whacked him.' Off he went.

But an unchastened Armstrong soon carried on in much the same vein. A few weeks later, he went up to catch a ball and was flattened by two opponents. As he fell to the ground, one of them landed on Armstrong's hand. In considerable pain and with the red mist descending once more, he smacked the man in the jaw. Again, there was nothing odd about this; fights broke out all the time in Gaelic football. At the time, though, Armstrong was wearing a plaster cast on his hand to protect a broken knuckle. As a result he ended up breaking the man's jaw in three places.

This time he was banned for six months.

The more Graham heard about Gerry Armstrong, the more he liked the sound of him. He was beefy, he was fast, and anyone who showed any inclination to tangle with him plainly needed their head examining. The only problem was that Spurs were asking £250,000 for him, far more than Watford had ever paid for a player before.

When the two men met – in a car park at Tottenham – to discuss a possible move, the first thing Armstrong said to him was, 'I want to play up front.'

'Good,' said Graham. 'Because that's where I want to play you.'

Before they shook hands on the deal, there was something Graham wanted to ask him. £250,000 was a lot of money and people were going to expect big things of him. How would Armstrong feel about having that weight of expectation on his shoulders? Possibly it might affect his morale, as it had done with Ross Jenkins? Perhaps even tap into his buried insecurities?

As far as Armstrong could remember, no one had asked him about his insecurities before and it wasn't a subject he had any desire to pursue. I couldn't give a damn, he told him.

'Right,' said Graham, 'you're the man for me.'

Between August 1980 and January 1981, he spent almost £600,000 of Elton's money on five new players. That should have been enough to set his mind at rest, except it wasn't. Still the questions kept fluttering around in his head. Had he – and his core players – reached their natural level?

It would hardly have been surprising if they had. After all, three of them had been at Watford ever since the club had been stuck in Division Four. A fourth, goalkeeper Steve Sherwood, was stuck on the subs' bench, seemingly for eternity. Even when armed with Wing-Commander Reep's rolls of wallpaper, surely there had to be a limit to what a bunch of journeymen could achieve? To how many rockets Graham could put up them? To how long they could carry on playing out of their skins? Was this the end of the road, he wondered. Had Watford gone as far as they reasonably could?

Had they, on some fundamental level, been found out?

# 36.

One night in the summer of 1980, Graham caught a taxi in Watford town centre. The driver, chatty even by taxi-driver standards, told him about a seventeen-year-old boy he'd just seen playing for a team called Sudbury Court in North London.

Conversations like this were an occupational hazard of a manager's life. People were always telling Graham about prodigiously talented teenagers who, on closer inspection, turned out to have rather more donkey in their DNA than thoroughbred. In this case it didn't help that Graham remembered he had been driven by the same man in the past. On that occasion he had also banged on about two other dazzling prospects that he'd seen. Both of them turned out to be hopeless.

Even so, he was loath to ignore any recommendations. However slim the possibility, there was always a chance he might be missing something. Too busy to have a look himself, Graham sent Bertie Mee to watch Sudbury Court's next game. Mee had a set protocol on such occasions, just as he did for every other aspect of his life. He would stay until he had satisfied himself that he'd seen enough – usually about fifteen minutes – then quietly slip away.

On his visit to Sudbury Court, Mee stayed for even less time than usual. But on this occasion his reasons for leaving were rather different. Instead of feeling that he'd come on yet another wild goose chase, he was anxious that if anyone recognized him, they too might have seen what he had just seen. Rushing home, Mee called the secretary of Sudbury Court and asked if he could have the phone number of the boy's parents.

But when he rang it up, he learned that he had been put

through to the Jamaican embassy. The boy's father, a Colonel Kenneth Barnes, turned out to be the Jamaican military attaché to the UK. In London on a four-year posting, Colonel Barnes was due to return to Jamaica in six months time, taking his family with him. This made time even more of the essence. Could he possibly pop over to the Jamaican embassy and see him, Mee asked. There was something important he wanted to discuss.

A naturally gregarious man, Kenneth Barnes invited Mee for a drink. Before becoming the Jamaican military attaché, Barnes had been the manager of the Jamaican national side. He would go on to play a key role in founding Jamaica's bobsleigh team which, to widespread incredulity, succeeded in qualifying for the 1988 Winter Games at Calgary – this despite Jamaica never once having had a significant fall of snow.

As the two men talked over their gin and tonics, they realized they had met before. Several years earlier, Mee had taken Arsenal to Kingston for what was supposed to be a friendly match against the Jamaican team – in fact, the game had proved anything but friendly and ended in a riot. Barnes was one of the Jamaican officials who had helped usher Mee and the Arsenal side to safety.

While Mee's military career hadn't been that spectacular – he'd worked as a physiotherapist in the Royal Army Medical Corps before ending up as a sergeant – both of them had a love of service life.

Meanwhile, Colonel Barnes's son, John, was in the next-door room doing his best to listen to their conversation through the embassy's stout oak doors. 'I couldn't make out what they were saying, but it was obvious they were talking about me, and I got the impression it was something important.'

What Mee was proposing was that the colonel should leave his son behind when he and the rest of his family went back to Jamaica. Mee would act in loco parentis and make sure that John was properly looked after and didn't get into any trouble.

Initially averse to the whole idea, Colonel Barnes found his resistance beginning to melt. The good impression that Mee had made in Jamaica grew steadily more favourable: the bristling bearing, the immaculately knotted club tie, the way he insisted on calling Colonel Barnes 'Sir' . . . all this went down especially well. If he and his wife were going to leave their son in the care of anyone, it was hard to imagine a more suitable candidate.

By the end of the evening, they had come to an agreement. John Barnes would join Watford for the upcoming season. At seventeen, he was too old to be an apprentice and would have to be signed as a full professional. Given that Watford were taking away Sudbury Court's star player, it seemed only fair they should give them something by way of return. As Sudbury were amateurs, Watford couldn't give them any cash. Instead, they offered the team a new set of football shirts, shorts and socks – an offer that was gratefully accepted.

The first time John Barnes joined the senior squad for a training session, Graham sent them all on another cross-country run. Assuming that Barnes would never be able to keep up with the other players, Graham drew him a map so that if he got lost or left behind, he'd be able to find his way home.

But once again, things didn't go quite as planned. Far from being left behind, Barnes set off at a blistering pace, swiftly moving to the front of the field. Having done so, he just kept on going, his lead stretching all the time. By the time they had been going for an hour, Barnes was so far ahead of everyone else that he decided to stop and wait for them all to catch him up.

# 37.

On Saturday 26 August 1980, long-time Watford supporter David Harrison and several of his friends drove down to the South Coast for the first leg of a League Cup tie against Southampton. None of them were feeling optimistic.

Southampton had three former England internationals in their team – Charlie George, Kevin Keegan and Mick Channon. A fourth, Alan Ball, who had played in England's World Cup-winning team of 1966, was on the substitutes' bench. While all four may have been getting a little long in the tooth – two of them would never see thirty again – Southampton had still managed to finish in the top half of Division One the previous season.

They'd started the new season in some style too, clocking up four wins and a draw from their first five games. Watford had also made a bright start to the season. But after winning their first three games, the wheels once again came off the wagon and they lost the next three. As puzzled as he was depressed by this loss of form, Graham felt that changes were needed – one in particular.

He decided to put Ross Jenkins on the substitutes' bench. As soon as he heard the news, Jenkins went to see Graham and told him bluntly that he was making a big mistake. Some prolonged eye-balling followed before Jenkins stormed off.

For David Harrison and his friends, their visit got off to a pleasant-enough start. 'We had a moderate pint in a forgettable pub on Southampton Common and strolled down to the ground on a balmy August evening.'

That, though, as he recalled later, 'was very definitely as good as it got.' From the starting whistle, Watford were picked apart by the home team. By half-time they were two-nil down. In the second half, Southampton banged home another two goals. What made it worse, as far as Graham was concerned, was that Watford showed the same pathological reluctance to venture into their opponents' half as they had done when they were back at the bottom of Division Four.

Any satisfaction that Ross Jenkins may have felt watching from the substitutes' bench was drowned out in the general sense of dejection. Looking over at the visiting managers' dugout, David Harrison could see that Graham Taylor was 'embarrassed by his team and incandescent with rage'. Afterwards, when asked what he thought of Watford's performance, Graham did not stint himself. 'I considered our display inept and awful,' he said. 'We let down ourselves and our supporters.'

Driving back home that night, David Harrison and his friends tried not to dwell on what they had just witnessed. And they tried even harder not to think about what lay in store for Watford when they met Southampton for the second leg of the tie one week later.

In the programme notes he wrote for each match, Graham usually tried to sound as cheery as possible. But the piece he wrote for the second leg of Watford's League Cup tie against Southampton revealed him in an uncharacteristically downbeat mood. They faced what he called an 'impossible task'. The most he, or anyone else, could reasonably hope for was that they might get through to the final whistle with a few shreds of dignity left intact. 'Whatever tonight's result, I expect all Watford players to walk off the pitch and be able to look people in the eye.'

Taking his usual place leaning against a concrete pillar at the Vicarage End of the ground, David Harrison shared Graham's sense of foreboding – 'I wasn't exactly in a state of fevered anticipation, put it that way.'

Despite this, it would never have occurred to Harrison not to come. Indeed, Watford had sold a very respectable 16,000 tickets for the game – usually their gate hovered around the 11,000 mark. However, most had been bought by people who wanted to see the famous faces in the Southampton team.

On the morning of the match, Graham gathered the players together and told them they should forget about the previous result. Instead, they should treat the match just as if it was a league game. If they managed to score two goals, Southampton would be annoyed, though not too worried. But if they could score three, Watford 'would be starting to get to them'. For the time being, he went on, they should aim to be two-nil up at half-time.

However impassioned Graham's delivery, no one was under any illusions that this was just fanciful, pie-in-the-sky stuff. He had made one change to the team, bringing back Ross Jenkins from the substitutes' bench. If being omitted from the team had produced an instant, combustible reaction, news of his reinstate-ment prompted nothing more than a quizzical lift of Jenkins's eyebrow. But as he watched the Southampton players warming up, he saw something that gave him a glimmer of hope. 'You could see they weren't mentally prepared. They clearly felt that all they had to do was get off the bus, play a bit and they would be through to the next round.'

Indeed, so confident were Southampton of victory that they had left some of their famous faces behind, including Kevin Keegan. There were also suspicions that for all their glitz and glamour, the team possessed an Achilles heel in the form of their Croatian goalkeeper, Ivan Katalinić. On his arrival at the club two years earlier, Katalinić had been nicknamed 'The Kat' by admiring fans. But that hadn't lasted long. After a series of less than impressive performances, he had been given a new nickname – 'Katastrophic'.

David Harrison watched in surprise as Watford swarmed for-ward from the kick-off, apparently uncowed by the previous result. After just eleven minutes, Steve Sims, deep in the opposition half, threw a long ball to Ross Jenkins, who then flicked it to the Watford midfielder, Malcolm Poskett. From the edge of the penalty box, Poskett blasted a shot past a flailing Ivan Katalinić.

At this point Southampton might reasonably have expected events to take a more predictable turn. Now that Watford had clawed back a few shreds of self-respect, normal service could be resumed. Yet still the home team came forward, leaving several of the Southampton players plainly bemused. What was the matter with them? Why were they bothering? What were they trying to prove?

Watford kept at Southampton, launching attack after attack, until ten minutes before the end of the first half, Wilf Rostron passed back to the Watford defensive midfielder Ray Train. From twelve yards out, Train loosed off a shot that Katalinić could only waft an ineffectual hand at.

Southampton were now leading 4-2 on aggregate.

Just as Graham had wanted, Watford went in at half-time with a two-nil lead. In the dressing room, he told his players that they should also put this straight out of their minds. In the second half, they should just give it everything they had, playing without fear and always looking to attack. Almost as an afterthought, he added, 'You never know where it might take you.'

This made a particularly strong impression on the Watford midfielder Kenny Jackett, who four months earlier had made his first-team debut, at the age of eighteen. Having been brought up next to Vicarage Road – he could see the ground from his bedroom window – Jackett had been steeped in Watford folklore since infancy. As a young player, under Tom Walley's tutelage, he had always taken a keen interest in how a manager's attitude affected a team's performance.

'One of Graham's great strengths was the way he could talk to a group of people,' Jackett recalls. 'He could hold them completely in the palm of his hand, and he had this natural ability to pick up on the general mood and get the pitch just right.'

As he listened to Graham's half-time speech, Jackett felt his spirits starting to lift. 'It was very clever man-management because he took away our fear of failure completely. He put all the emphasis on effort, application and performance, not on the result. If we played positively and did all the right things, then he would be satisfied.'

As the second half got under way, Jackett was one of several Watford players who noticed that something odd appeared to have happened to Southampton. Their fluency had disappeared, and so had their blithe assurance that the result was a foregone conclusion. It even seemed to Ross Jenkins that Southampton's star striker, Charlie George, was so out of sorts that he kept casting longing glances towards the touchline in the hope that he might be substituted.

Midway through the half, Jenkins sent a low cross into the Southampton penalty area. Luther Blissett lunged forward, but couldn't quite reach the ball. Instead, it came straight to another Watford midfielder, Martin Patching. As Oli Phillips would write in his match report, Patching 'lashed the chance past a despairing Katalinić'.

Southampton were now leading 4-3 on aggregate.

Then, eight minutes later, came disaster. Steve Sims, trying to deflect a shot from a Southampton forward, succeeded only in sending the ball into his own net. Watching the ball fly past his own keeper, Sims felt sure that he had just snuffed out what slender hope they had. 'There's nothing to compare with the feeling of scoring an own goal,' he recalls. 'I just wanted to hang my head and apologise to everyone.'

The score was 5-3 on aggregate.

But Sims didn't have long to brood on his mistake. Just a minute later, the game took another dramatic turn. Ross Jenkins was fouled inside the Southampton box. Immediately, the referee pointed to the spot, and Ian Bolton fired the ensuing penalty past the now 'hapless' Katalinić.

That made it 5-4.

By this point, David Harrison was finding it increasingly hard to credit what was happening. He wasn't the only one. Looking around, he saw that everyone had the same dazed expressions on their faces. With just four minutes left, Watford launched yet another attack on the Southampton goal. Standing on the edge of the Southampton area, and so near the goal-line that he could barely make out any gap between the posts, Ross Jenkins saw the cross bouncing towards him. 'My aim was simply to keep it low and not sky it. That was all I was thinking about.'

The moment Jenkins made contact with the ball, he knew exactly where it was going. Neatly bisecting the posts and evading the the now 'utterly flummoxed' Katalinić, it ended up in the far corner of the net.

It also took the game into extra-time.

Assuming that a number of Watford supporters would want to make an early escape after their inevitable defeat, the club had opened a pair of sliding wooden gates at the Vicarage Road end of the ground. But instead of anyone leaving, hundreds of people began pouring in as word got about that something extraordinary was going on.

Shortly after the start of extra-time, the Watford striker Ray Train clashed heads with a Southampton player. Graham took him off and brought on seventeen-year-old Nigel Callaghan for only his third first-team appearance.

Having also come up through Tom Walley's youth team, Callaghan was unquestionably talented, but reckoned still to be some way short of being the finished article. He had been on the pitch for only a few seconds when Watford won a corner. Just as he had been told to do in training, Callaghan took up a position on the edge of the penalty area. The corner was intercepted by one of the Southampton defenders who was unable to clear it. Instead, the ball fell at Callaghan's feet.

'I hit it first time, instinctively,' he recalled.

As everything seemed to slow down around him, Callaghan watched as the ball sailed into the net. 'It was the sort of thing I'd fantasized about so much as a child.' Running back towards the halfway line, he happened to glance over his shoulder. A double-decker bus was stationary in the road beyond the Vicarage Road end of the ground. 'I could see all these people on the top deck. They must have seen the goal because they were jumping up and down in celebration.'

The score was now Watford 6, Southampton 1.

Watford were leading 6-5 on aggregate with just three minutes of extra-time left to play. And still they kept pushing forward. In the last minute of the game, Malcolm Poskett danced past the sliding Ivan Katalinic to score Watford's seventh.

When the referee blew the final whistle seconds later, the Vicarage Road crowd let out a roar the like of which, it was generally agreed, had never been heard before. Among the onlookers was the recently retired president of FIFA, Sir Stanley Rous.

Asked for his reaction, Rous said, 'I cannot remember seeing anything in my lifetime to compare with it.'

As Steve Sims came off the pitch, Graham said simply, 'One hundred per cent'. And in that moment all the doubts and uncertainties that had beset Sims earlier disappeared. 'It sounds a ridiculous thing to say, but I felt like a completely different person.'

Later that evening, the BBC announcer reading out the final score paused, clearly thinking he must have made a mistake. Then, rather more slowly than before, he read out the result again.

Having made three goals and scored another, Ross Jenkins, like Nigel Callaghan, found himself thinking back to his childhood – and to the Roy of the Rovers comic strips that he too had once read. Things like that aren't really supposed to happen in real life, but very occasionally they do.'

Meanwhile, the Southampton manager, Lawrie McMenemy,

was described as 'looking like a man who has just suffered a particularly harrowing bereavement'. After the match, Graham saw him standing in the corridor outside the dressing rooms. He noted with satisfaction that McMenemy was 'white as a sheet'.

Six thousand miles away in a hotel in California, Elton had cut short rehearsals for the opening night of another world tour to listen to his phone link-up with Watford Hospital radio. Once again, Mike Vince, the hospital's match commentator, found himself in the strange position of broadcasting to an audience that comprised a scattering of patients in varying stages of consciousness and an international superstar on the far side of the world.

For Elton himself, the experience, if anything, was even stranger. 'The weird thing about listening to a match down a phone line is that I didn't have anyone to share it with; it was just me with a phone clamped to my ear. I remember it was a superb, sunny afternoon and I was lying by the pool. Every time Watford scored, I would shout "Goal!"'

Soon he found he had the pool to himself.

No television cameras were there to record what had happened – the game wasn't considered worth covering. Nor, apart from Watford's hospital broadcast, was there any radio coverage. Instead, it existed only in the memories of those who had been there. Struggling to take in what he'd seen, David Harrison was aware that once the initial rush of euphoria had subsided, there was a peculiarly private air to people's celebrations. 'You could see these small groups of bewildered fans, reluctant to leave the scene, as if everyone was still lost in their own little worlds.'

Standing in the same spot twenty minutes later, Harrison was struck by 'the most terrible thought. I found myself wondering, Is there any point ever coming to another game? Because I knew that whatever happened in the future, I would never see anything like it again.'

Others suffered no such melancholy twinges. 'Had Hollywood produced it, people would have scoffed, or shunned the screenplay as being composed by dreamers,' wrote Oli Phillips. Not to be outdone, one of the *Watford Observer*'s readers, a Mr C. F. Edwards of Croxley Green, put it in even more hyperbolic terms: 'It was,' he wrote in a letter to the paper, 'the result of the century.'

# 38.

It wasn't only Elton who was feeling the pace. So was Bernie Taupin. While there was never any acrimony between them, they both decided they needed a break from one another. In the meantime, Elton started working with another lyricist, Gary Osborne. That Christmas, Osborne was at home with his family and about to sit down to Christmas lunch when the phone rang. It was Elton calling from Woodside in tears. He was there on his own, he told him. His latest boyfriend had failed to appear – later, it turned out that he'd run off with a stewardess he had met on the flight from Los Angeles – and Elton had sent his staff away for the holidays.

Piling into a car, Osborne and his family set off for Windsor. When they arrived, they found Elton in the kitchen, still in tears. On the table was an enormous cooked turkey with a single slice carved off it. Alongside, was an equally big Christmas cake – again with one slice missing.

The next day, Boxing Day, Elton paid a visit to Vicarage Road. While he had vowed never to go to another away game wearing anything inappropriate, the same rules didn't apply when he was on home turf. On this occasion, he was wearing a new coat that he'd just paid £1,500 for. Long, multicoloured and with a matching belt that tied around his waist, it gave a raffish twirl whenever he spun around. Although not everybody was as taken with it as he was, no one could dispute that it made a big impression.

Apart from Gary Osborne's visit, Elton had spent most of the past ten days shut away in his bedroom at Windsor. Under the circumstances, he didn't think he was looking too bad, but he was feeling a little ropey and, by way of a pick-me-up, poured himself a large Scotch from the boardroom drinks cabinet.

As he was doing so, Graham walked in.

During the previous two years there had been numerous signs that Elton's life had gone past the point of self-control. On one occasion Rita remembers Elton's mother phoning up and saying how worried she was about him – how he spent all his time cloistered away in his bedroom, seldom emerging even at mealtimes.

Although Elton himself was confident that no one at the club had spotted anything amiss, this took no account of Graham's powers of observation. Far from passing unnoticed, everything Elton did had been noted and filed away. On several occasions Graham and Rita had discussed what, if anything, he should do. It was an awkward situation. Ultimately, Elton was Graham's boss. Quite possibly he might resent any interference in his private life. If any attempt to broach the subject went badly, it might even signal the end of their friendship. On the other hand, Elton was the club chairman. As such, he was the – very – public face of Watford. Any embarrassment he caused was sure to reflect on everybody else.

In the end, Graham decided to wait until events took another lurch towards the abyss. When he walked into the boardroom and saw Elton about to lift a large Scotch to his lips, he realized the moment was coming ever closer. Partly it was the fact that Elton was drinking whisky that sounded the alarm – it wasn't yet lunchtime – and partly it was his appearance: he had neglected to shave for several days. But more than anything it was his coat. Never one to pay attention to the ebb and flow of fashion, Graham assumed that Elton had simply forgotten to take off his dressing gown before leaving his house that morning.

Once again, he decided to keep quiet – however much this taxed his own powers of self-control.

The next morning, there was a board meeting. Having spent

the night brooding, Graham made sure he arrived early so that he would be the only person there when Elton walked in.

When Elton did arrive, Graham was horrified. Although Elton had in fact put on a suit and tie, Graham didn't know it: they were hidden under the same coat he had been wearing the day before. The moment Elton sat down, Graham walked over to the drinks cabinet, picked up a bottle of brandy, walked back to where he was sitting and slammed it down on the table in front of him.

'That's what you have for breakfast, isn't it?' he said.

As Elton was struggling to take in what had just happened, Graham let rip: 'What the fuck do you think you're doing?' he asked. 'You're letting yourself down and you're letting the club down. If you ever turn up looking like this again, that's fucking it as far as I'm concerned.'

A good deal followed, all of it in the same vein; all delivered in the same infuriated tone. Meanwhile Elton was still reeling. He'd seen Graham tearing a strip off players in the dressing room, and that had been bad enough. Now he found himself on the receiving end. In his entire adult life, ever since he'd left Reg Dwight behind and become Elton John, no one had ever spoken to him like this. No one would have dared.

As he sat there in the Watford boardroom with his head bowed, not saying anything, Elton found himself overwhelmed by something he'd spent years trying to run away from: a sense of shame. 'It shook me to the core,' he recalls. 'It was one of those moments when all the delusions that I'd surrounded myself with, all the lies I'd told myself, fell away. I was just left there, stunned and mortified.'

In other circumstances, he might have brushed it aside. 'I certainly wouldn't have taken it from anyone else; I would just have told them to fuck off. But because Graham came from outside my world, somehow that meant I couldn't ignore it. I may have been the king of my castle, but that was completely unimportant to him. Graham just cared about me as a person. About the fact that if I carried on the way I was going, then I was going to kill myself. That was what really shone through; behind his anger, I could see that he really loved me.'

Although the whole incident lasted barely a couple of minutes, its effects would last a good deal longer. Going back to Windsor, Elton was in no doubt about what had to happen next. That day, he stopped drinking and taking cocaine. 'It launched me on the road to recovery. Although there were plenty of false dawns along the way, lots of setbacks and broken promises, it gave me the kick-start I needed. In effect, Graham saved my life; I've never had the slightest doubt about that.'

However seismic the effects of Graham's outburst, what occurred between them was never mentioned again. Far from ruining their friendship, it ended up doing the opposite. Elton was left feeling even closer to Graham. More than ever, he wanted to prove that he deserved his respect: 'I would have done anything for that, literally anything'

At the same time, he wanted to prove to Graham that he really was trying to straighten himself out. That he wasn't going to let the side down again. 'I had to become the person that Graham thought I was capable of being.'

And for Graham it confirmed something that had been floating around in the back of his mind for a while. Something he didn't like to acknowledge at first because it felt a bit embarrassing, but which now seemed unavoidable. Years later he would recall how, almost without being aware of it, his relationship with Elton had gone beyond friendship to another place entirely. 'I came to regard him as the younger brother I never had.'

Not, of course, that he would ever have dreamed of telling him.

# 39.

By now Steve Sherwood had spent so long on the substitutes' bench that it had come to feel like a second home. When Watford's first-choice goalkeeper broke his collar-bone bringing in a scuttle-full of coal, Sherwood had briefly taken his place. But then Graham bought another goalie, a man called Eric Steele, and once again Sherwood found himself back on the bench.

For all his agility, the 6′ 3″ Sherwood was reckoned to be too much of a gentle giant to succeed at the highest level. Too mild-mannered, too self-effacing and possibly just too nice. While he tried not to let this latest setback get him down, the fact that he'd been with the team since Watford were at the bottom of Division Four preyed on his mind. Was that where he really belonged, Sherwood wondered. Down on the bottom? At heart, was he just one of nature's also-rans?

But unbeknownst to him, the planets were finally aligning in his favour: Graham had begun to suspect that Eric Steele was less commanding inside his six-yard box than he should be. Once again, Sherwood was summoned from the bench. Shortly before Christmas, on 9 December 1980, Watford had played First Division Coventry City at home. It was the second leg of the fifth round of the League Cup – the first leg had ended in a 2-2 draw.

As the players trooped out onto the pitch, a pall of gloom hung over Vicarage Road, as it did over the rest of the country – earlier that day Elton's friend John Lennon had been murdered outside his apartment building in Manhattan.

Almost immediately came disaster. After just three minutes, Coventry scored. This, though, was only the start. Having noticed that Eric Steele hardly ever came out for crosses, Sherwood decided to do the opposite, rushing forward at every opportunity. The trouble was, the more he ran forward, the more exposed he was – and the more often Coventry scored.

The final score was 5-0. Although Sherwood didn't think he had been to blame for all five goals, he knew that he'd definitely been responsible for two of them. Walking back to the dressing room, he was in no doubt about the gravity of what had just happened. 'I just thought, God, this is a disaster. Being a goalkeeper, you can feel very exposed sometimes, lonely even, and I can remember wanting to dig a hole and crawl into it.'

As he saw his manager coming towards him, Sherwood braced himself for a furious tongue-lashing. Instead, Graham was perfectly friendly, sympathetic even.

'Didn't really go according to plan, did it?' he said.

Sherwood agreed that it hadn't. Not at all, frankly.

What on earth had made him come out for every cross, Graham asked.

Sherwood began to explain that he wanted to try something a bit unorthodox, but Graham just shook his head.

'Play your normal game,' he told him. 'That's why I've put you back in the team.'

And that, to Sherwood's amazement, was it. He was even more amazed when he looked at the team-sheet for the next game and saw that he had retained his place. It was a turning point, the moment when his confidence began to rise off the floor. 'Graham could easily have taken the result at face value and said, "That's your lot." But when he kept me in the side, it made me feel that he actually cared about me, and I wanted to prove that his faith hadn't been misplaced.'

A week later, Ross Jenkins was playing against Swansea when he slid in to tackle one of the opposition players. As the two of them locked legs, Jenkins heard a sound like a branch snapping in two. When he tried to stand up, a bolt of pain shot up his left side and he fell over. When Ross broke his ankle at Swansea, he limped off rather than be carried off.

With his leg encased in a plaster cast, Jenkins soon learned that life had changed. If in the past Graham had tended to step warily around him, now he ignored him altogether. Like his teammate Steve Sims, Jenkins found that having any sort of long-term injury effectively rendered him invisible in his manager's eyes. The year before, Sims had also hurt his leg. Hobbling around Vicarage Road, he tried to make himself useful, always greeting Graham warmly whenever their paths crossed.

To his dismay, his manager barely acknowledged him.

It was only later that Graham apologized and told him that he had got into the habit of blanking out injured players. They were no use to him until they had recovered, he explained. Graham, though, did not apologize to Ross Jenkins – either then or afterwards. And as soon as his ankle had healed, Jenkins learned that he had been put on the transfer list with a price tag of £100,000.

Only six weeks earlier, Watford had played Nottingham Forest in the fourth round of the League Cup. Forest were the reigning European Cup winners. They were also lying fifth in Division One. So confident was their manager, Brian Clough, of victory that he didn't bother to attend the game. Instead, he went on holiday to Majorca leaving word that he was looking forward to soaking up some autumn sun and had no wish to be disturbed.

But Graham had devised a plan which he believed, if properly executed, could render Forest toothless. Everything hinged on neutralizing their winger John Robertson. Even though Robertson was thicker round the waist than most footballers, and lumbered about with a curiously bored expression on his face, something unexpected happened as soon as he got hold of the ball: he seemed to shoot straight from first to fourth gear. And once he'd hit ramming speed, Robertson could slice through a defence with alarming ease.

But if you could shut him out of the game, Graham believed,

then Forest would lose their shape, and with it – he hoped – their composure. He decided to employ what were, by any standards, unconventional tactics. Rather than pick another winger to mark Robertson, Graham chose his second reserve centre-forward, John Ward.

By this point Ward had become such a regular fixture on the substitutes' bench that he was known as 'To travel' by the other players – whenever the team list would go upon the noticeboard, his name would appear on the bottom: 'To travel, Ward'.

As Graham knew, Ward had a remarkable capacity for fastening onto an opposition player like a limpet, never giving him any room to manoeuvre. Even so, Kenny Jackett wasn't the only Watford player to be taken aback by the news of his selection. 'For such an attacking manager, it was a very defensive move by Graham. But as well as having a lot of experience, John was also incredibly disciplined. If he was asked to do a particular job, he would do it with complete focus.'

From the moment the whistle blew, Ward was at Robertson's heels, sticking to him so closely that one observer was reminded of a single four-legged creature scuttling wildly about with its head on fire. With their main player closed out of the game, cracks duly appeared in the Nottingham Forest ranks. Shortly before half-time, Watford scored twice – the first goal a penalty scored by Luther Blissett, the second a left-footed strike by the usually right-footed Ross Jenkins. Then, during a second half in which Forest became increasingly out of sorts, Watford added two more goals. Both were scored by Jenkins.

The final score was Watford 4, Nottingham Forest 1.

It had been almost two years since Jenkins had last scored a hat-trick. That night, unable to sleep, he decided to do some wallpapering. 'We'd recently moved into this house in Cassiobury. I've always been a bit of a handyman. I hadn't got round to papering this passageway, so I decided I might as well start now. I knew it was a weird thing to do, but I was still flying. And somehow it did calm me down and give me a bit of perspective.'

Jenkins was only a week away from his twenty-ninth birthday, and as he wallpapered away into the small hours, he wondered if he had anywhere left to go. If this might just turn out to be the pinnacle of his career.

The following day, late in the morning, Brian Clough phoned up his office from his sun lounger in Majorca. 'How are things?' he asked brightly. A long and uncharacteristic silence followed as Clough absorbed the news of Forest's defeat.

But now, hardly more than a month later, Jenkins found he had become surplus to requirements. Immediately, he went to see Graham, fixed him with his death stare and yet again told him he was making a big mistake. Graham was unrepentant. Later he recalled, 'Ross was not playing too well. And when we put him on the market, no one came for him, suggesting other clubs felt he wasn't playing too well either.'

Anyone with any knowledge of football knew what this meant. If Jenkins hadn't come to the end of the line, he was plainly limping into the final furlong. With nobody showing any interest in buying him, he decided to jump before he was pushed. Jenkins went to the only club who had shown any flicker of interest – the Washington Diplomats based in Washington USA.

At the time, soccer was making its first hesitant strides into America. Hoping to dispel fears that British vices might find their way across the Atlantic, the Washington Diplomats had plumped for a name designed to emphasize their peaceable, conciliatory nature. Jenkins had never heard of them, but there was nothing unusual about that – scarcely anyone had, even in Washington. 'There was an assumption that if you went off to the States, you were going to a kind of elephant's graveyard. The US league was full of British players who were winding gently down to retirement.'

With deep misgivings, Jenkins flew off to America, hoping that it might prove to be a temporary arrangement. Officially, he was on loan and hoped to be back at Watford within a few months. The problem was that no one else seemed to feel the same way. But once he arrived, Jenkins found the reality wasn't as bad as he'd feared. 'I was earning good money and I actually found that it did me a lot of good being away from Watford. Being in America gave me a chance to look at things afresh.'

It was a long way from Vicarage Road in every respect. The pitches weren't made of grass, they were Astroturf; the players travelled everywhere by plane rather than coach or train, and while the stadiums they played in were enormous – they were usually American football stadiums – a lot of the time hardly anyone came to watch them. As far as Jenkins was concerned, it was also like being in a kind of ghostly afterlife where legendary figures of yesteryear could be glimpsed, still going through their paces.

At one stage, he even found himself playing with the great Dutch striker Johann Cruyff. Only two years older than Jenkins, Cruyff bore little resemblance to his former lightning-footed self. 'He couldn't run then – the injuries had caught up with him – but even in that state you could see what he had been.'

As Jenkins jetted from one sparsely attended game to another, he did his best to keep up with what was happening three thousand miles away. Not much, from what he could tell. Watford remained stuck in the middle of Division Two – just about holding their own, but showing little sign of moving upwards. Although they were capable of occasional stunning successes, overall the team looked to be shuddering to a halt. 'It was obvious to me that the oil in the works had thickened up and the engine was grinding.'

Watford finished the season in ninth place. For Jenkins, it was clear evidence that the team hadn't moved on in his absence. And that Watford still needed him, even if they didn't seem to be aware of it themselves. All he could do was stay fit, keep scoring goals and hope against hope that his chance might come again.

# 40.

Each year before the football season started, Elton would hold a party at his home in Windsor. The entire staff of Watford FC was invited, from Graham to the cleaners, along with everyone's families. Guests would be taken by coach from Vicarage Road to Windsor where they would be met by Elton and his mother. After a buffet lunch, there would be games on the lawn for both adults and children – egg-and-spoon races, piggy-back races, three-legged races.

Anyone who wanted to was free to wander around the grounds, or look at Elton's extensive collection of cars. For Luther Blissett – and others – it was a glimpse of a world they had never seen before. Yet what struck Blissett most strongly was not the opulence on show, or the lavishness of the hospitality; it was the fact that there was never any sense of hierarchy, or standing on ceremony. Elton knew everyone's names and was clearly delighted to see them. But there was more to it than that. He wasn't just delighted, it seemed; he was grateful too – as if he needed them every bit as much as they needed him. 'I've never forgotten those parties. There was always this magical atmosphere, this sense of camaraderie, of all of us mucking in together.'

Throughout the afternoon, the games would continue until the shadows lengthened on the grass and it was time for everyone to climb on board the coaches and go back home.

Then, a few weeks later, came a more low-key celebration: Graham's birthday. Three years earlier, he had woken up at his home in Mandeville Close, looked out of the window and seen there was an elderly Austin 100 parked on his front lawn that had been painted in Watford colours. On closer inspection, Graham saw that the bonnet had been signed by all the club staff.

It turned out to be a present from Elton.

For his thirty-seventh birthday, Elton gave him another present. Although Graham had tried listening to Elton's records and found some of them quite hummable, they didn't really appeal to him. Musically, his tastes had stalled in the mid 1950s when his great heroine, Vera Lynn – the 'Forces Sweetheart' – became the first British artist to have a US number one with 'Auf Wiedersehen Sweetheart'.

Seeing how devoted Graham was to Vera Lynn, Elton decided to play a little trick. He gave him a copy of one of Vera Lynn's albums which had been signed by her. Not only that, it bore a personalized message. Graham was even more thrilled than Elton had expected, gazing awestruck at the signed album cover as if it was a holy relic. Meanwhile, Elton was so helpless with laughter that tears were running down his cheeks. Later on, it turned out that the album hadn't been signed by Vera Lynn at all. As Elton confessed, he had simply faked her signature.

Graham had been angry enough when Elton and Rita had conspired to defeat him at cards, but this was much worse. It wasn't funny in any way, he told Elton stiffly. Not only had he toyed, most inconsiderately, with his feelings, but he'd also committed a form of sacrilege by forging Vera Lynn's signature.

Besides, this was no time for horsing about – there was far too much at stake. Watford had spent two seasons in Division Two. That was quite long enough. In many respects, everything Graham had done at Vicarage Road had been leading up to this point. Maybe the oil had thickened up, maybe there was still a cog missing and maybe Watford lacked the ability to put together a string of consistent results, but it was too late to worry about that. They would just have to work with what they had.

If they failed, there could be no more excuses. For all his promise and his enthusiasm, Graham would be remembered as just another stargazer whose daft theories had ultimately proved to be his undoing. The message could hardly have been clearer: if it wasn't now, it might well be never.

# 41.

At the end of July 1981, a small story appeared in the *Watford Observer* headlined, 'Big Ross Back To Boost Hornets', The report went on to say that Jenkins – 'the legendary Watford striker' – had recently returned from six months spent in the USA playing for the Washington Diplomats. 'Four months short of his 30th birthday, 6' 3" marksman Jenkins declared that he is match-fit, ready to play his part and "raring to go".'

Before the new season started, there was one more thing Graham wanted to do. Throughout the country, football hooliganism remained as out of control as ever. At the end of the previous season the sum of £276.43 had been raised in the pubs around Watford to pay for repairs to the roof of the Supporters Club tea bar which had been used by home fans as a refuge from rioting West Ham supporters.

A month earlier, Prime Minister Margaret Thatcher had hosted a reception for the England footballers who were off to compete in the European Championships in Italy – the first major tournament England had qualified for in ten years. The party went with more of a swing than anyone, especially the players, had expected. According to some reports, Mrs Thatcher even stood on a chair and in ringing tones told them, 'We shall love you if you win, and we shall still love you if you lose!'

But at the team's opening match of the tournament – against Belgium in Turin – events soon took a familiar turn. An early England goal was followed three minutes later by a Belgian equaliser. Immediately, bottles began to rain down onto the pitch, thrown by disgruntled English fans. The Italian police, armed with batons and tear gas, waded into the crowd. A cloud of yellow tear gas temporarily blinded several of the England players.

Few of the watching football journalists were surprised. A few months earlier, Hugh McIlvanney of the *Observer* had written: 'The Brits, having been swept into a corner economically and politically, are currently afflicted with a national sense of inadequacy that includes among its cruder manifestations, a tendency to kick foreigners in the testicles.'

It wasn't just foreigners British football fans wanted to kick in the testicles – it was each other too. When the American writer Bill Bryson, a devoted Anglophile, went to his first football match at White Hart Lane with some friends, he was appalled by what he saw: one man urinating on another, people wearing National Front badges, frequent racist chants and an underlying air of menace that felt as if it could erupt into violence at any moment. What appalled him most, though, were people's reactions – 'for my friends, it was an ordinary day out'.

No one was sure who – or what – was to blame. Some said it was the permissive society that had rotted people's morals, others that the economic climate had reduced them to the level of wild beasts. At the same time a group of Marxist sociologists argued, quite straightfacedly, that hooliganism was a response by working-class fans to the increasing commercialization of the game. This conveniently disregarded the fact that fans seemed far more interested in beating the living daylights out of one another than directing their anger at their club's owners.

Although Watford had had comparatively little crowd trouble, they hadn't escaped completely. After one game, opposition supporters went on the rampage and a milk bottle was chucked through the window of a house belonging to a 72-year-old woman, Mrs Martha Atkins, who had recently suffered a heart attack.

'My front room was filled with glass,' Mrs Atkins said. 'It has made me feel very ill.'

Trying to ensure there were no further incidents, Elton made an appeal of his own. 'We have a record at this ground for experiencing little or no crowd violence and we aim to keep it that way . . . To all supporters, I would say, please come again, and behave yourself.'

To keep rival fans apart, more and more chicken-wire fences were being put up at football grounds. There were those who thought that Watford should erect their own fortifications. Graham, however, wouldn't hear of it. He even refused to consider raising the low brick wall – barely a foot high – that separated the stands from the pitch. Anything that created more of a barrier than necessary between the supporters and the players was a bad idea, he felt.

This was to have unexpected consequences. During one match Wilf Rostron was running towards the opposition goalmouth when, to his surprise, he saw a tiny figure coming towards him with his arms outstretched and a delighted grin on his face. Rostron was even more surprised when he came closer and realized it was his three-year old son. On another occasion, Graham turned round and saw that a young boy was caught in the middle of a scuffle in the crowd behind him. Immediately, he waded in, sorted out the altercation and invited the boy and his father to come and sit with him on the manager's bench.

These outbreaks of violence made the need for a radical initiative even more important, Graham believed. He decided that a section of one of the stands at Vicarage Road – consisting of 500 seats – should be given over to families who wished to bring their children to a game. He had been mulling over the idea ever since he had returned from the States two years earlier, and, although the portents could hardly have been less promising, was determined to press ahead. He also took the then unprecedented step of appointing a woman, Caroline Gillies, to their senior management team.

In keeping with everything else at Vicarage Road, there was to be a strict code of conduct regarding the family enclosure. Players were forbidden from swearing anywhere near it and threatened with yet more fines if they disobeyed. Adults were permitted to enter the new enclosure, but only when accompanied by a child. On arrival at a game, each child would be given a present – usually a bar of chocolate – and asked to give their date of birth.

On subsequent birthdays, they would receive a card from 'All their friends at Watford Football Club'. Any child in possession of a junior season ticket would also have a seat named after them. While adults could also have seats named after them, their seats would bear only their surnames and initials, whereas the children's seats would carry their full names.

Predictably, there was no shortage of people who thought the idea was not only misconceived, but plain mad. As well as being a waste of 500 seats, it was wildly irresponsible to encourage young children to come to such an unsuitable venue. They were bound to witness outbreaks of appalling behaviour, and could well find themselves in physical danger. Amid much disapproving clucking, the naysayers consoled themselves with the assumption that it was bound to end in disaster.

But once again things didn't quite turn out that way. The first weekend the family enclosure opened, every seat was taken. At Watford's next home game, there was a queue of small children around the block waiting to get in. Far from being a damp squib, the idea caught on so fast that within a few weeks Graham received discreet inquiries from several other clubs looking to follow suit.

# 42.

Ever since returning from the States, Ross Jenkins had changed, Graham noticed. He wasn't more easygoing, not exactly – that would have been going too far. But he was not quite so touchy either, so quick to take offence. What's more, there was no longer any suggestion that he might have lost a bit of bite. Instead, he seemed more determined than ever.

Jenkins himself had noticed that there was a change in Graham's attitude towards him, although he couldn't quite put his finger on what it was. 'Somehow he gave me more recognition than he had done before.'

By this stage, Jenkins hadn't played a first-team game for Watford for nearly eight months. Rather than toss him straight back into the fray, Graham decided to wait and see what happened in the meantime. After losing two-nil to Grimsby Town at the beginning of September, Watford were now lying in twelfth place. Five days later, they had moved up to eighth.

Jenkins was not the only player who had changed. So had Steve Sherwood – out of all recognition. When Watford beat Oldham Athletic at the beginning of September 1981, a game in which almost single-handedly Sherwood kept out attack after attack, Graham took him aside afterwards, put his arm round him and said that not only had he controlled his goalmouth, he had succeeded in turning it into his own personal stockade: 'No one was ever going to get past you tonight.'

After agonizing for longer than usual, Graham decided to name Ross Jenkins in the team to face Chelsea at Stamford Bridge on 7

September 1981. 'If he doesn't do it now,' he said, 'then he never will.'

He also picked seventeen-year-old John Barnes for his full first-team debut. Two months earlier, Graham had watched Barnes play for Watford's youth team against Leyton Orient. Like Bertie Mee before him, he hadn't hung around for long. Once he'd seen Barnes send a left-footed volley past the Orient goalkeeper, Graham had turned to the person he was with, said, 'That's all I need to see,' and walked off.

Elton too was equally smitten the first time he saw Barnes play. 'He was just brilliant. You knew straightaway he was going to be a superstar.'

As a result of all the training Barnes had been put through, he was two stone heavier than he had been a year earlier. Previously, he'd come on once as a substitute, but Graham decided the time had now come to find out if he could last the full ninety minutes. Seeing his name alongside that of Barnes on the team sheet, Ross Jenkins allowed himself a moment of satisfaction. 'I can remember looking at the list and thinking, Hello, have I been waiting for you, pal.'

The author of the Chelsea programme, while welcoming Watford to Stamford Bridge, couldn't resist noting that their season had begun 'a little erratically', before ending on a more traditional sporting note: 'May the best team win!'

As John Barnes ran out onto the pitch, his reception could hardly have been less sporting. Just as Luther Blissett had been when he had made his debut three years earlier, Barnes was greeted with a barrage of racist abuse from the Chelsea fans.

It wasn't just in football stadiums that racism was on the rise. Five months earlier, the UK had seen its worst-ever race riots when Brixton in South London had erupted in violence. Poor, marginalized and repeatedly picked on by the police, the area's predominantly black population had risen up in fury after a nineteen-year-old black man was wrestled to the ground by a policeman who had assumed he was a mugger – in fact, he turned out to have been the victim of a stabbing.

Over the summer, the rioting had spread – to Toxteth in Liverpool and Moss Side in Manchester. Just about the only thing the police and the rioters could agree on was that Britain was a more racially divided society than it had ever been before.

Now, as he stood on the halfway line, Barnes listened to the monkey chants ringing out from Chelsea's Shed End and watched the volleys of bananas raining down. But however shocked he was, he never for a moment let it unsettle him. Instead, he regarded it with a mixture of disdain and incredulity.

'I can remember looking round and thinking, these people can't possibly be aiming this abuse at me. I mean, I'm an upper-class Jamaican boy who has been brought up in an embassy. Why on earth should I feel inferior to these ill-educated idiots who can barely spell their own name? It made no sense at all.'

For one of the spectators, long-time Watford supporter Graham Walker, the afternoon had already taken on a sense of *déjà vu*. 'You didn't go to Stamford Bridge expecting anything other than a good hiding on the pitch and, unless you were quick or well disguised, a bloody good hiding from the thugs on the terraces.'

Yet far from being cowed or outgunned, Watford took control of the game right from the kick-off. They ended up winning 3-1. A reinvigorated Ross Jenkins assisted in all three goals, while John Barnes ran rings around the Chelsea defence.

Watching this unfold, Graham Walker felt as if he had found himself in the middle of a waking dream. 'In the wide-open spaces of Stamford Bridge, Barnes dances around every tackle and is so good they can't even catch him to whack him. Crosses coming in from all over the place. Never seen anything like it. Where did they find him? How old is he?'

The one person who wasn't amazed was Barnes himself. 'I knew that I needed Graham's help in order to maximize my potential, but I never for a moment felt, Am I good enough? Do I belong in this company? Not once; the idea simply never occurred to me.'

As the game went on, the racist taunts died away and those Chelsea fans who stayed to watch did so in increasingly gloomy silence. When it was over, Graham was asked about Barnes's performance. As ever, he was careful not to heap too much pressure on a young player's shoulders. On the other hand, he didn't want to downplay his contribution. In the end he said carefully, 'I think we may have unearthed a gem.'

Four games into the season, Watford had moved up to fifth place.

# 43.

But not everyone was convinced. Every victory that Watford notched up brought forth another rumble of criticism. According to Jack Charlton, a member of England's World Cup-winning side of 1966, Watford were simply 'a hump-up and knock-back team'. Alan Ball, his fellow World Cup-winning teammate, was equally dismissive. Watford, he said, 'did not play proper football'.

Others were even more vitriolic. Terry Venables, a former England player himself who'd recently become manager of Queens Park Rangers, declared that Watford were just a 'hit and hope' side who had reduced football to little more than a game of pinball. Settling into his stride, Venables went on to claim that they had set back football by more than fifty years. There were those who felt that his case was rather undermined by the fact that Watford had just beaten QPR 4-1 in the League Cup.

Watford weren't without their supporters, of course. The former England captain Billy Wright came to Vicarage Road and told them there was nothing wrong with the way they played. 'He said if we were being criticized it was because we had people worried.'

But steadily the chorus of disapproval began to swell. In Fleet Street, no one had a bigger bee in his bonnet about Watford than the *Daily Mail*'s chief football correspondent, Jeff Powell. Whenever the opportunity arose – and it did so on an almost weekly basis – Powell would lash out at Watford's tactics. Not only were they crude and amateurish, he wrote, but their style of play was depressingly simplistic.

Running Jeff Powell a close second in the Watford-bashing stakes was *The Times*'s football correspondent, Brian Glanville. Like Venables, Glanville felt that Taylor had 'tainted the essence of English football'. Worse still, Watford's tactics were 'abhorrent'. While they may have succeeded against the lumpen journeymen of the Third and Fourth divisions, their crude brand of 'kick and rush' football had no place in the more rarefied air of the Second Division.

In public, Graham pretended that he was untouched by all this sniping. There was no right or wrong way to play football, he would tell interviewers. As long as you stuck to the rules, you could play in any way you wanted. Besides, if it was really that simple to play the Watford way, as people claimed, why wasn't everyone doing it?

Privately, though, it was a different story. After one game Brian Glanville saw Taylor and, provocatively, extended his hand. Graham refused to shake it. 'I can't! I can't!' he exclaimed in an agonized voice, before going on to accuse Glanville of peddling misinformation.

'You're a liar!' he told him. 'You write lies!'

Casting around for an explanation, Glanville concluded that it was 'a classical Freudian instance of displacement, unconsciously transposing emotion from one subject to another'. However, there may have been a less fanciful explanation. More thin-skinned than he liked to let on, Graham always found any criticism hard to take. The more he tried to brush off the brickbats, the more they niggled away and set his insecurities jangling. It can't have helped that he kept his feelings carefully stoppered up. Never one to take his work home, he gave his family little indication of what was going on inside his head.

With few friends and fewer hobbies, the only way he could relax was by going for a run, or by listening to his old Vera Lynn records. As he did so, Graham could at least console himself with the thought that Watford, crude, abhorrent and amateurish though they may have been, were storming up Division Two and getting closer and closer to the promotion zone.

★

Cheered on by an unlikely new audience of small children and nursing mothers, Watford won nine of their next ten games. By December, they were in fourth place. Caught up in the swell of excitement, Benskins Brewery offered customers in any of its Watford pubs a free pint of beer every time the team won or drew. In less than a week, they gave out more than a thousand free pints.

But while the family enclosure had proved to be a great success, something unexpected was going on elsewhere in Vicarage Road. Although Watford were now only a whisker away from promotion, attendances had dropped – plummeted even. A game against Leyton Orient, which Watford won 3-0, drew only 10,000 supporters, less than the club would have attracted when they were down in Division Three.

In an attempt to drum up support, Graham led the players on a lap of honour before the game started. This had some effect, but not much. Next, he took to pleading directly with the townspeople to come back. 'I live and breathe Watford Football Club and I've done everything I can to take this club forward,' Graham wrote in the *Watford Observer*. 'The town itself may have been destroyed and made into a shopping centre and my heart bleeds for this, but the football club needs the community to rally round.'

After twenty games out of forty-two, Watford had gone up to third place. In January 1982, they walloped Derby County 6-1. 'Arrogant Watford Show No Mercy,' ran the headline to Oli Phillips's match report. His description of what happened was couched in almost Old Testament terms: 'The slaughter began after only three minutes when Gerry Armstrong headed Watford in front after Ross Jenkins nodded down a long centre from John Barnes.'

That same month they also played host to Manchester United in the third round of the FA Cup. There had been a considerable number of improvements to the Watford ground in the past few years, but there was one proposed change that Graham had always refused to consider. Surely it was time that the managers' dugout had a roof on it, people had implored him. It hardly made the club look as if it belonged in the top flight if both the manager and the visiting manager sat on an uncovered bench. Again, Graham wouldn't hear of it; if the players were going to get wet, then so would he.

For several days before the Manchester United game it had rained almost non-stop. As a result, the pitch was a quagmire. Before the game started, Graham took his usual place on the bench. He saw the United manager, 'Big Ron' Atkinson – a natty dresser despite resembling a cement mixer on legs – poke the toe of one of his expensive Italian suede shoes into the mud. Clearly, he was trying to decide whether to brave the elements or watch the game from the stand. After another experimental prod, Atkinson, with all the enthusiasm of a condemned man mounting the scaffold, walked slowly towards the bench and sat down.

Watford won the game 1-0.

Afterwards, the United midfielder Ray Wilkins managed to imply that Watford's tactics had been to blame. 'The high ball is not really our style,' Wilkins said sniffily, before conceding that United hadn't done a lot better with the low one. 'We didn't really get a kick when it was on the ground either.'

While the lack of enthusiasm from supporters continued to puzzle and depress him, Graham had problems closer to home. One of his key players, Nigel Callaghan, was causing him increasing concern. No one doubted that Callaghan was prodigiously talented on the pitch, it was what happened to him off it that was the problem.

Always a bit chaotic and prone to ill-discipline, Callaghan, almost alone among the Watford players, regularly defied Graham's edicts. He would turn up late to training, react badly to criticism and eat prodigious quantities of burgers when he was supposed to be watching his weight.

He was particularly fond of disco music, and it was said that you could hear Callaghan's car coming from half a mile away. On one occasion, the music system he installed in his car was so powerful that it drained the battery. On another, flames erupted from the bonnet as he was pulling away from Vicarage Road and three fire engines had to come to extinguish the blaze.

Despite his waywardness, Graham was fond of Callaghan. 'Having never had a son myself, I sort of took to Nigel,' he said. 'I recognized him as a great talent. I did love him and I could see there was a danger he would lose his way.'

Hoping to instil some discipline into him, Graham decided to invite him to stay at Mandeville Close. As Callaghan rightly deduced, it wasn't an invitation he could turn down. 'To this day, I've no idea why Graham made me come and live with him. I think he was trying to teach me the value of life, or something like that.'

Callaghan wasn't the only one bemused by Graham's invitation. 'I got a bit of micky-taking from the lads about it: they used to call me "Teacher's Pet". That only made it worse, of course.'

Forbidden to use his car while he was there, Callaghan was forced to walk to Vicarage Road for training sessions. On the way, Graham would often drive past in his Jaguar. Instead of offering him a lift, he would sound the horn, give him a cheery wave and drive on. In the evening, Callaghan would have a meal with Graham, Rita and their two daughters. The rest of the time, he sat in his bedroom with his headphones clamped over his ears listening to music.

However much Callaghan may have hated being there, there were signs that Graham's approach might be paying off. At the end of his first week staying with the Taylors, Watford played West Ham in the fourth round of the FA Cup. They won 2-0. Callaghan made the first goal and scored the second – a casual flick when he had his back to the goal.

Afterwards, Graham asked him if he would stay for another

week, but Callaghan had had enough. 'I just said to him, "No, I want to go home."' On the following Tuesday, Graham posted the team sheet for Saturday's game against Derby. Gazing at the piece of paper in mounting bewilderment, it gradually dawned on Callaghan that he had been dropped.

By now, Watford were in second place in Division Two. If only they could remain there, promotion was assured. Yet still the crowds stayed away. At the end of March Watford beat Bolton Wanderers 3-0, a result which took them briefly to the top of the table. But once again, only 13,000 people bothered to attend. Having tried unsuccessfully to encourage people to get behind the team, Graham decided to see if he could shame them in to coming instead.

Why were supporters being so lily-livered when Watford players were giving everything they had, he demanded in the *Watford Observer*. What had happened to their pride, their self-respect?

The tone of the letters that poured into the paper the next day – high indignation verging on apoplectic fury – suggested he had gone too far. It wasn't apathy that was keeping people away, the letter writers insisted. It was unemployment that was to blame. A lot of the club's long-time supporters had been laid off and could no longer afford to buy tickets.

At the next match against Crystal Palace, Graham walked out onto the pitch carrying a large placard. On it were two words: 'I'm sorry'.

Then, with the winning post in sight, Watford had another attack of the wobbles. After losing to Cardiff at the beginning of April, they managed only two draws in succession. Thinking that the team could use a break, as well as a distraction, Graham told the players to pack suitcases and bring them to the next training session.

Speculation was rife about where they might go – some of them thought they might be jetting off to Cyprus for a few days, while others reckoned Malta was a more likely bet. Everyone then sat in confusion as the team coach drove past Heathrow airport and headed instead for the South Coast. Far from lazing around some Mediterranean swimming pool, the players ended up spending three nights at a modest guest-house in Ventnor on the Isle of Wight run by long-time Watford supporters Paul and Karen Challis.

Although this was hardly what they'd had in mind, it seemed to do the trick: Watford comfortably won their next three games. If they could beat – or draw against – Wrexham at home, that was it; they were definitely going up.

At last Graham's pleas had been answered and a crowd of more than 20,000 came through the turnstiles. All of them, or almost all, erupted in cheers every time a Watford player touched the ball.

With Nigel Callaghan restored to the team, Watford got stuck into Wrexham with what, even by their standards, was unusual vigour. They scored once before the break and once afterwards – the second goal prompting a pitch invasion from prematurely celebrating supporters. The final score was 2-0, with both the goals being scored by a familiar figure – 'Vicarage Road warhorse Ross Jenkins'.

Watford were now in Division One for the first time in their history. Amid widespread scenes of jubilation, 'even the motorists stuck in streets clogged by celebrating fans had to smile'. Elsewhere, 'Hornet supporters swarmed over town on Tuesday night, their red and yellow scarves painting a sunrise in the darkness.'

On tour in Helsinki, Elton cut his concert short by fifteen minutes to sit in his dressing room glued to a phone listening to Watford Hospital Radio. Immediately the game was over, he phoned Graham, so giddy with excitement that all he could do was keep repeating, 'We did it, Graham! We did it!'

Not surprisingly, his memories of what happened next were a

little hazy. 'I knew I had several large drinks and I couldn't stop shouting, but that was about it. It was so joyous. I was also completely stunned. I'd never thought that we'd be able to go through the divisions so quickly; it was really like this fairy tale coming true.'

Amidst his own celebrations, Graham totted up how much he had spent taking Watford from the Fourth Division to the First. Five years earlier, when they had first met at Elton's home in Windsor, Graham had told him he reckoned he would have to spend a million pounds. In the event, Graham had spent rather less of Elton's money than that – around £750,000.

For Steve Sherwood, as for everybody else in the Watford team, joy was unconfined. 'When the final whistle went, I literally got carried away – the fans chaired me off along with at least two of the lads.' In the chaos, a souvenir hunter stripped him of his goalkeeping gloves. The sense of accomplishment, of pride, of sheer disbelief at what they had achieved was 'the best feeling you can possibly have on a football pitch'.

The next morning, the chant 'We are up!' resounded around offices all over Watford. Meanwhile, Sherwood was still in a state of bliss. Nothing could diminish his delight – not even the fact that when he arrived for training minus his gloves, Graham had taken him aside. He took a very dim view of such carelessness, he told him. To ensure it didn't happen again, Sherwood would have to buy a new pair out of his own wages.

# 44.

In their school fête that year, Durrants School in Croxley Green offered an unusual first prize. Dirty grey in colour, roughly three feet long, cylindrical in shape with a right-angled bend at one end and covered in scribbled signatures, it immediately attracted a good deal of interest.

From the moment he saw it, Gary Penfold, then a fifteen-year-old pupil at the school, was determined that it should be his. 'I went mad buying tickets,' Penfold recalls. 'I have no idea how much the tickets were, or how much I spent, but I remember I bought an awful lot.'

The prize had been donated by his history teacher, Mrs Jenkins, who in turn had obtained it from her husband, Ross. After Jenkins had recovered from his broken ankle and his plaster cast had been removed, he decided that just conceivably it might appeal to a young Watford supporter.

As it turned out, Penfold was only one of a large gaggle of schoolboys who were determined to get their hands on Jenkins's plaster cast. On the day of the school fair – a Saturday – he had to leave before the result of the raffle was announced, and so it wasn't until the next Monday that he learned he had won. But while Penfold was thrilled, his victory prompted more mixed reactions at home. 'My mum and dad were pleased after a fashion that I had won. But what was I going to do with it, they wondered.'

The plaster cast lived in his bedroom for several years until the Penfolds moved from Croxley to Chorleywood in 1987, when it was put in a box in the loft. More than forty years on, it has travelled with Gary Penfold to every house that he has lived in: 'It's been in three lofts since then, and that's where it remains today' – along with the programmes from every Watford game he has ever been to.

# PART FOUR

*From the* Watford Observer

# VANDALISM IN WATFORD DOWN BY 25%

Vandalism in Watford and Rickmansworth fell by almost 25% this June compared to the same month last year. The most dramatic drop in vandalism has occurred in Watford itself. There were 69 cases last year, compared with only 39 this June. Of these 39 attacks, it was noted that 11 of them were on buildings owned by Hertfordshire County Council.

# WATFORD 'SUCH A HAPPY PLACE'

Popular television magician Paul Daniels paid tribute to Watford townsfolk after a shopping expedition to buy some new hi-fi equipment. 'People are so friendly here,' said Daniels, presenter of the BBC's *Paul Daniels Magic Show.* 'When I go shopping elsewhere, people just look straight through me, but in Watford they all come to say hello and wish me well. It's such a happy place.'

# BIG ROSS MAKES A STRIKE

Ross Jenkins, the man who has been a leading scorer in Watford Football Club's push for Division One, homed in on another target this week. Following the club's promotion glory in which the lanky striker played such an important role, he was invited to open the new cash dispenser installed at the Watford Junction brand of Lloyds Bank.

'It gives me great pleasure to declare this cash dispenser open,' Jenkins declared to the small crowd who had gathered to watch the ceremony.

He then withdrew £25 from the machine which Lloyds Bank donated to a charity of his choice.

# 45.

Three months after winning promotion to Division One, Graham was standing on the touchline as the players walked off after an away game against Southampton. Watford had won the game 4-1, with Nigel Callaghan scoring two of the goals and Gerry Armstrong and Ross Jenkins one apiece. Afterwards, the Southampton manager, Lawrie McMenemy, was once again reported to be 'white as a sheet'.

Among the Southampton players was the small, incorrigibly chirpy figure of Alan Ball – the same Alan Ball who had been such a vociferous critic of Watford's style of play. Not only did they not play entertaining football, Ball had declared, but it wasn't even 'proper' football at all.

What had rankled most of all was that Ball had said this to Graham's face when they had been on the same flight back from a pre-season tour of Australia. Possibly as a result of his having had more drinks than was entirely wise, Ball had been in an expansive mood.

'Just wait until you get into the First Division,' he had told Graham. 'We'll show you how to play proper football.'

He had then roared with laughter and helped himself to another beer. Despite feeling the vein in his neck starting to throb, Graham had managed to restrain himself.

This was Watford's second match in the First Division. They'd also won the first – against Everton, 2-0 – as well as the three warm-up games that had preceded it. Shortly after winning promotion from Division Two, Graham decided to take the players away on another break. This time round no one got carried away with excitement. Sure enough, it proved to be an even more unpleasant surprise than their trip to the Isle of Wight. They flew to Norway where a bus took everyone to what looked like an old army barracks, set in the middle of a featureless plain miles away from the nearest town. The accommodation, as Graham later acknowledged, was more basic than he'd expected, but then they weren't there to enjoy themselves. They were there for one purpose only: to get themselves in the best possible shape.

'We were a good football team, but I accepted that we might not be the best. However, I also knew that if we couldn't be the best, we could certainly be the fittest.'

He had said this before, of course, back when Watford were down at the bottom of the Fourth Division, but a lot had changed since then. Now the bar was set infinitely higher. 'I thought we had to be fantastically fit – fitter than we had ever been before.'

Before dawn each morning everyone would run up to the training ground a mile away, do some drills, and then run back again. Only then would they be allowed a frugal breakfast. There were another three sessions every day, each one more strenuous than the last. At the time, there was a heatwave in Norway and during their training session, the players pleaded to be allowed some water.

Graham refused.

This was not a club for softies, he told them. 'I was absolutely merciless,' he recalled. It wasn't just the players' bodies that needed to be in top shape, their minds had to be too. In future, he said, they should start every game imagining they were already a goal down. That way, they'd always be fighting an uphill battle, always trying to come back from adversity. And just in case anyone was showing any signs of getting ideas above their station, he still made them all clean their own boots.

Almost everybody, whether in Watford or outside, had assumed that Graham would splash out on some new signings over the summer, that he would be dipping into Elton's bank account to beef up his squad. In fact, there had been only one new signing: a player from non-league Burton Albion who had cost a few thousand pounds. Instead. Graham decided to stick with the same players – the ones who had been tried, tested and not found wanting in the heat of battle.

'We were going to stick to our guns and play attacking football from the first minute to the last. I felt we could win more than we lost by being true to the team we were.'

Now, as he watched Alan Ball walking towards him, Graham found himself feeling torn. Should he say anything, he wondered. To do so might be considered undignified, possibly even a bit cheap. On the other hand, he wasn't sure if he could hold back.

In the end, the temptation proved too great. As Ball went past, Graham leant towards him and said in his ear, 'Not bad for a side that can't fucking play, are we?'

# 46.

All this time Elton had had next to no contact with his father. One day, after he had played a concert in Manchester, one of his half-brothers came backstage and told him that Stanley had had another bout of heart trouble. He needed a quadruple bypass.

The next day Elton called him up and offered to pay for the operation. Stanley wouldn't hear of it; he was perfectly happy to wait in the queue and have the operation on the NHS, he said.

Once again, the communication channels snapped shut.

A few months later, Elton made another attempt. He was coming to Liverpool for a game, he told his father on the phone. It wasn't far from where Stanley was living, so why didn't the two of them have lunch first, then watch the game?

To his surprise, his father agreed.

Elton booked a table in the restaurant of the Adelphi Hotel. The stage was set for what he hoped would be a grand reconciliation. As the day of their lunch grew closer, he found himself becoming more and more nervous. In part, he realized, it was because his expectations were running away with him. 'What I wanted my father to say more than anything else was, "Well done; I'm so proud of you."'

Perhaps it wasn't too late for something to change, Elton thought. Perhaps the two of them might finally set their differences aside and acknowledge what they had in common. It wasn't such a mad idea. Elton, after all, had inherited the two great passions in Stanley's life: music and football. Quite possibly, he would never even have gone to a football match if it hadn't been for his father.

He'd been six years old when Stanley had taken him to his

first game, and the memory of emerging from Watford tube station, of being part of a great tide of people heading towards Vicarage Road, of his father holding his hand to make sure that he was safe, had never left him. Football had been the glue that had bound the two of them, however awkwardly, together. It was at football games – and only at football games – that Elton felt his father approved of him, that he was the son Stanley had wanted.

A lot had happened since then, of course. Meek, self-conscious Reggie had done something no one could have foreseen by turning into superstar Elton. As for Stanley, he was no longer a forbidding authority figure, but an elderly man with heart trouble living in north Wales.

When the day of their lunch came, Stanley, crossing on the Mersey ferry, saw his son's private helicopter coming in to land at Speke Airport.

Elton arrived early at the Adelphi, and sat in the dining room waiting anxiously. Although he had asked for a table in the corner, several of the other guests spotted him and pointed him out for the benefit of those who hadn't yet done so.

Right on time, his father arrived, and was shown to the table by the maître d'. As they shook hands, Elton was aware of Stanley's eyes flickering over him. Sizing him up. In that moment the years fell away, and Elton went straight back to being a small boy. 'I could see him giving me the once-over, looking at how I was dressed. Maybe I was being paranoid, but I immediately felt the same air of disapproval I had always felt.'

Despite all Elton's hopes that things might be different, in that moment he realized it was never going to work. The two of them were just too far apart, too 'like oil and water' for any reconciliation. 'There was just nothing, no point of contact at all.'

For the next hour and half, they struggled to think of anything to say to one another. Between the yawning silences, they discussed the fortunes of various relatives – who had been up to what. But the conversation never burst into life; it just faltered and spluttered and then petered out. Throughout the meal, Stanley didn't say anything about Elton's career. About what he had achieved, or how proud he was of him. Instead there was just awkward chit-chat. Once again Elton offered to pay for Stanley's heart operation, and once again his father refused. Then back they went to pushing their food around their plates.

Why couldn't his father say anything, Elton wondered. Perhaps Stanley wasn't proud of him at all? Perhaps he still felt that his son should have knuckled down and got a proper job, worked in an office, settled in suburbia and led a safely inconspicuous life? Was that it? Except that Elton knew from his half-brothers that this wasn't the case. Quite often, they'd said, Stanley would talk about him with both pride and affection. So why couldn't he say anything to his face? Was his father so emotionally repressed that he could no more talk about his feelings than he could turn cartwheels round the dining room?

Whatever the reason, it left Elton feeling more confused, more adrift than ever. However much he was garlanded with praise, it was painfully clear that he was never going to get it from the one person from whom it would have meant most of all.

At the end of the meal he paid the bill, and the two of them went off to Anfield in the back of Elton's Bentley. More than twenty years had passed since they had last been to a football match together. Now, father and son sat side by side in the directors' box and watched as Watford were soundly beaten 3-1 by Liverpool.

Again, they hardly spoke.

When the game was over, Elton's chauffeur dropped Stanley off at the train station to catch a train back to north Wales. In the back of the car, they said goodbye as formally as they had greeted one another a few hours earlier. Then Elton watched through the smoked glass windows of his car as his father disappeared through the station entrance.

They never saw one another again.

# 47.

Watford lost their next game, then beat Swansea at home. Four days later, they were due to play West Bromwich Albion – again at home. At this point they were lying in third place in Division One.

This had done nothing to snuff out criticism of the way Watford played. If anything, the better they did, the louder the chorus of discontent grew. The football correspondent of the *Daily Mirror* disdainfully dubbed them 'Wholesalers' – apparently this was because they had 'no need of a middleman'.

According to the Spurs manager Keith Burkinshaw, 'You don't need any sophistication at all to play like Watford.' There was no place for flair in their approach, Burkinshaw complained, only an unsophisticated mule-ish determination. At their next meeting, Watford beat Spurs 1-0 at White Hart Lane. Afterwards, a 'tight-lipped' Burkinshaw strode off without talking to any of the assembled journalists.

But far from hailing Watford's victory, the press pitched in with even more ferocity. One writer referred to them as a 'pack of mad dogs beating their heads relentlessly against a brick wall, trying desperately to find a crack'. If this wasn't bad enough, the fact that Graham had bought into Wing-Commander Reep's batty theories had turned him into a robotic 'slave to statistics'.

Graham reacted to this latest volley of brickbats by affecting mild exasperation: 'It annoyed me when people said that Watford's style was setting the game back twenty years because I felt we were playing attacking, exciting football.' Elton, characteristically, was less circumspect: 'What gave these tossers the right to tell us how we should play? I just thought, fuck the lot of them.'

With his critics' words still ringing in his ears, Graham struck an unexpectedly philosophical note when he sat down to write his programme notes for the West Brom game: 'What price freedom?' he began.

To a very large degree, within the law – which is paramount – we can enjoy the freedom of living in a free country. You can criticise your team, the directors and myself and freely express your view on how the game should be played. To walk into our stadium, you have a feeling of openness and fresh air. Compared with many clubs, we are fortunate to have the space inside the ground that we have and I am relieved that circumstances have not yet forced us to turn it into a human cage. I sincerely hope that everyone values what we have at Watford and that you, the supporters, have helped to achieve this by your good and orderly behaviour.

Under the circumstances, it seems unlikely that anyone at Vicarage Road was giving much thought to the joys of freedom and fresh air. The game itself was a briskly efficient, one-sided affair which ended in a 3-0 victory for Watford, with Luther Blissett scoring two of the goals and Les Taylor the third. But in a way that was hardly the point; there was another, far more important drama playing out elsewhere.

Once the final whistle sounded, scarcely anyone left the ground. They remained where they were, waiting for an announcement over the PA system. Shortly after five o'clock a disembodied voice asked for everyone's attention.

The crowd fell silent.

Manchester United and Manchester City had both won their games, the voice announced. Everybody knew what this meant. Both Manchester teams and Watford now had the same number of points, while Liverpool had one more. Watford, however, had a better goal difference than either Manchester United or Manchester City. If Watford's traditional blood rivals, Luton Town, could somehow beat Liverpool, or even hold them to a draw, then Watford would go top.

The irony that it should be Luton – despised Luton – standing between Watford and the top spot wasn't lost on anyone. There was a further pause before the Anfield result was announced. When it came, a collective gasp of disbelief ran around the ground, followed by an enormous roar. Despite having fielded three goalkeepers during the game – the first two had been injured – Luton had managed to draw 3-3 with Liverpool. As a result, Watford were now top of Division One.

Elton had delayed a trip to the Caribbean so that he could watch the game. Afterwards, he and Graham embraced in the dressing room. This time, neither of them could think of anything to say. They just stayed silently clasped together, until the players decided to take matters into their own hands and threw Graham into the communal bath.

That evening, Graham and Rita Taylor were Bertie and Doris Mee's guests at the Last Night of the Proms – Graham had turned thirty-eight a few days earlier and this was his birthday treat. Crammed shoulder to shoulder with the other Promenaders in the Albert Hall, for once Graham found himself part of the throng. No longer a solitary, fretful figure on the touchline, he had become, however briefly, another face in the crowd. Able to let himself go without any thought to the consequences.

As Graham cheered away and roared out the words of 'Jerusalem' and 'Land of Hope and Glory', he thought back to the time five years before when he had first joined Watford. Since then they had risen eighty-three places in the Football League – from the depths of the Fourth Division to the top of the First.

Nothing like it had ever happened before. Never before had

anyone taken a football team so far in such a short time. However improbable this was, there was something else that made it even more unlikely. Graham had taken Watford all the way from the bottom to the top with four of the same players that he'd inherited when he first arrived – Luther Blissett, Ian Bolton, Ross Jenkins and Steve Sherwood. All four had seemed destined for the scrapheap, written off either as has-beens or clomping no-hopers. But Graham had turned them into something that they never had thought they could become – top-flight footballers.

In the five years since Graham had arrived, Watford Football Club had also been transformed out of all recognition. Back then, the club's only Scout had just celebrated his ninety-fifth birthday, the players' training kit was a pile of rancid rags, rats cavorted beneath the main stand, the crowd barriers bent like willows in a stiff breeze and women were tolerated in the boardroom on match days only as long as they kept their opinions to themselves.

Now, with violence flaring and human cages springing up at football grounds all over the country, Vicarage Road, with its community spirit, its family enclosure and its quaint faith in human decency, was like a glimpse of another, more innocent world.

And Watford itself had changed. Not physically – that was too much to expect – but in other, less obvious ways. A town whose heart had been torn out by crazed town-planning, whose workforce had been decimated by lay-offs and which year by year was being engulfed by suburban sprawl, had rediscovered something that seemed to have been lost for ever: its identity, its spirit and, above all, its pride. Far from looking shifty or embarrassed when asked where they came from, people now boasted of coming from Watford. If such a thing had ever happened before, no one alive could remember it.

All this was down to Graham.

At the end of the evening, after they had sung themselves hoarse, Graham and Rita drove back to their house in Mandeville Close. As they were getting ready for bed, Rita asked him how he was feeling.

Caught unawares and still brimming with elation, Graham said the first thing that came into his head.

'It's been,' he told her, 'the happiest day of my life.'

# 48.

While Watford was enjoying the biggest purple patch in its history, football itself was going through a colossal upheaval. Transfer fees were rocketing, and so were players' wages. Three years earlier, Trevor Francis had become the country's first £1 million player when he joined Brian Clough's Nottingham Forest. In the same year, England goalkeeper Peter Shilton became the highest-paid footballer in Britain on a weekly wage of £1,200.

There had been other changes too. In the past, players had negotiated their own salaries. Now, increasingly, they had agents to do it for them. Watching this with as much dismay as disapproval, Graham believed it was taking the game further and further away from the working people who had always been its most passionate supporters. But soon he too would be caught in the changing tides.

On the final day of the season, Watford once again played Liverpool, this time at home. They won the game 2-1, thereby guaranteeing themselves a place in the following season's UEFA Cup. Five years after Elton had told Graham that he wanted to take the club into Europe, his impossible dream had come true.

When the game was over, Graham, Elton and Eddie Plumley invited Liverpool's players, staff and directors into the boardroom, along with all of Watford's staff. Graham sent two of the apprentices up the road to get fifty portions of fish and chips, and everyone sat round the boardroom table eating their chips and drinking champagne– 'It was such a fantastic evening because someone else then saw the real Watford and how we used to do things.'

For Ross Jenkins, though, that day was a much less happy experience. Ten minutes before the Liverpool game started, Graham called him into his office.

'Right,' he said. 'I'm letting you go.'

As he had done so many times before, Jenkins didn't say anything; he just stared at him. While he had always known that football was a hard-headed game, he was stunned by the breezy, almost offhand manner in which Graham had dismissed him. It was true that Jenkins had had a number of injury problems that season. Six months earlier, he'd felt something go in his stomach during a game against Spurs – it proved to be a hernia. Despite his not being match-fit, Graham had carried on using Jenkins as a kind of Trojan horse, bringing him on as a substitute to put the wind up the opposition. Now he was being told in the brusquest possible terms that he had come to the end of the road. 'The whole thing was short, blunt, impersonal and, I have to say, ungrateful. At least, that's how it seemed to me.'

As he stared at Graham, Jenkins began to suspect that he was feeling a lot more awkward than he was prepared to let on. 'I got the feeling that he had deliberately chosen a moment when time was tight so that I wouldn't be able to argue with him, or tell him that he was making another mistake.'

Still smarting but not wanting Graham to see how upset he was, Jenkins turned on his heel and walked out. Aged thirty-one, with a wife and two young children, and like so many of his now former colleagues, he had given next to no thought to what he might do next.

Watford finished the 1982/83 season in second place, eleven points behind Liverpool and one point ahead of Manchester United. Their success had finally silenced the naysayers, or at least prompted them to keep their criticisms to themselves. It had also attracted interest from abroad.

At the end of the season they travelled to China, the first British club to play there. The novelist Martin Amis, who had been commissioned to write a piece for the *Observer*, accompanied the team. Amis had paid a visit to Vicarage Road beforehand, and had been surprised to see that 'the stands and terraces are dotted with women and children' – and not, as he had expected, 'with National Fronters and bald hooligans . . . Compared to most other grounds in the First Division, Vicarage Road is a vicarage tea-party,' he wrote.

It was while they were in China that Graham heard that AC Milan were keen to buy Luther Blissett, and had offered £500,000 for him. The previous autumn, Blissett had become the first Watford player to play for England. Two months later, he was the first Black player to score a goal for England when he notched up a hat-trick against Luxembourg.

What did Elton think of AC Milan's offer, Graham wondered.

Although both of them realized it would be unfair to stand in Blissett's way, they were determined to hold out for a £1 million transfer fee. AC Milan agreed to double their offer, but still Graham hummed and hawed. He went round to Tom Walley's house and asked him what he thought.

Walley was not a sentimental man.

'Take it,' he said.

A few days later, Graham, Eddie Plumley and Luther Blissett had a breakfast meeting with representatives from AC Milan at a hotel in London. For hour after hour negotiations dragged on, with Blissett stuck in the middle watching as his future was decided. Eventually, the deal was done, hands were shaken and the men from AC Milan vanished into the afternoon.

Whereas Graham had sought to disguise his feelings about getting rid of Ross Jenkins behind a mask of brusqueness, this was quite different. 'I felt a sort of emptiness I had never felt when selling a footballer before.'

As they got up to leave, both he and Plumley were in tears.

'I suddenly became aware that we were losing so much more than a footballer,' Graham recalled. 'It felt like we were selling our son.'

The lingering sadness that Graham felt about selling Luther Blissett was exacerbated by a mounting injury crisis. One by one players fell by the wayside. At the beginning of September 1983, when Watford embarked on their great European adventure, they resembled a long crocodile of the halt, the lame and the generally crocked. In the first leg of their opening UEFA Cup tie, they were drawn away against the German side Kaiserslautern. With so many of his senior players out of action, Graham had to turn to much younger, unproven ones: seven of the team he picked were aged twenty-one or under. Several of them had never been to Europe before, let alone played there.

On the night before the game, a raucous band of Kaiserslautern supporters sang and chanted outside their hotel into the small hours. Lying in his single bed with his feet dangling over the end of the mattress, Steve Sherwood tried – in vain – to get to sleep. 'Just when you thought they'd got bored and gone home, they started up again.'

Watford didn't fare much better on the pitch, eventually going down 3-1. Nerves plainly got the best of some of the players. Twenty-year-old Charlie Palmer, recently drafted in at right-back, admitted that the final whistle couldn't come quickly enough as far as he was concerned. 'To tell the truth, I was petrified.'

For the second leg, two weeks later, Graham urged supporters to 'Remember Southampton'. To get everyone in the right mood, thousands of little plastic horns were given out for them to blow during the match. But the programme notes he wrote for the game – headlined 'We'll Give It A Go' – suggested that he was hardly letting his expectations run away with him.

Watford went one up after just four minutes, thanks to a goal by nineteen-year-old Ian Richardson making his first-team debut.

Three minutes later, the home supporters erupted in delight when Charlie Palmer's cross hit a Kaiserslautern player and the ball bounced off him into the German net. Halfway through the second half, Richardson scored his second goal.

Worried that the team might lose focus in all the excitement, Graham sent the injured John Ward over to the other side of the pitch. Lying down behind the advertising hoardings, out of sight of the linesman, Ward spent the rest of the game bellowing encouragement at the players while the Watford faithful parped away wildly on their plastic horns. As much to their own surprise as anyone else's, Watford ended up winning 3-0.

Graham described it as the greatest result of his career.

In the next round they came up against the Bulgarian side Levski Spartak. Watford drew the first leg 1-1 at home. They then travelled to Sofia where, on a bitterly cold night, 60,000 Levski Spartak supporters greeted them with a barrage of fireworks and a chorus of what the Watford players rightly identified as a rich array of Bulgarian obscenities.

At full time the score was 1-1. By this point, the Bulgarian supporters had long passed the point of verbal intimidation and moved on to more physical demonstrations of their displeasure. Fires broke out around the stadium and, as Nigel Callaghan waited to take a corner in extra-time, bottles rained down, shattering on the frozen ground and showering him with broken glass.

Callaghan appealed to the referee to do something, only to be told not to bother by Steve Sims. 'Get on with it you tart,' Sims called out. 'It means they are scared of us.'

When Callaghan eventually took the corner, he found Sims at the near post. He flicked the ball across the goalmouth where a leaping Wilf Rostron headed it into the bottom corner of the net. A few minutes later, Watford scored another goal. They ended up winning the tie 4-2 on aggregate.

A watching Oli Phillips, never one for understatement, broke into the verbal equivalent of an ecstatic war dance in his match report. 'The shrieking, whistling Balkan hordes were silenced as Watford overcame a speedy, talented and often dominant Levski to forge another emotion-charged memory which will live with them for the rest of their lives,' he wrote in the *Watford Observer*.

Watford were now in the third round. Yet still the injuries kept piling up. Trying to make light of it, Graham put an announcement in the classified section of *The Times*:

Wanted: professional Footballers. Many vacancies now available at First Division club for men (or women) aged between eighteen and eighty and prepared to work on Saturday. Some playing experience desirable but preference will be given to those with two arms and legs in good working order. Apply in writing to G Taylor, Vicarage Road Stadium, Watford.

Among several new signings Graham made that year were two Scotsmen – George Reilly and Maurice – 'Mo' – Johnston. Reilly had left his last club, Cambridge United, under something of a cloud after they refused to match his wages – £300 a week – with the money his friends were earning as bricklayers on building sites. As a result, Reilly went on strike and refused to play – he is believed to be the first player ever to do so. But Graham liked the look of him: his speed, his aggression and even his appearance – before each game Reilly would take out his false teeth and run onto the pitch with a large gap where his incisors should have been.

Mo Johnston had come from Partick Thistle and, Graham reckoned, was one of the most instinctive goalscorers he had ever seen, with an almost uncanny knack of being in the right place at the right time.

The only problem was that Johnston's appetite for scoring goals was easily matched by his appetite for hanging out in nightclubs. Just to make sure that he didn't pass unnoticed, Johnston liked to wear a gleaming white leather suit when he took to the dance floor.

Not long before, Graham would have probably dished out the same unforgiving treatment to him as he had to Nigel Callaghan. But if football was changing, perhaps he was too. Far from being unforgiving, Graham was oddly lenient, even indulgent, reasoning there was no point in fining Johnston for any misbehaviour as he wouldn't take any notice.

On one occasion, shortly after Johnston's arrival at Vicarage Road, Graham took the players to a gym off the Tottenham Court Road in London for a series of fitness tests. The night before Johnston, as usual, had been whooping it up until three in the morning. This was the dawning of the age of sports science and Graham, keen as ever to embrace innovation, wanted to find out what was involved. He looked on as the players ran on treadmills to have their lung capacity measured and were given blood tests to determine their oxygen levels.

Afterwards, one of the doctors came to see him.

'Mr Taylor,' he said, 'One of your players, Mr Johnston, has performed very well in the tests.' The doctor then paused before going on in disbelieving tones, 'However, I have to tell you that he is officially drunk.'

Watford's first foray into Europe came to an end in December 1983 when they were soundly beaten by Sparta Prague in the third round. After their triumphs of the previous, season they were also struggling in the league, seldom moving off the bottom of the First Division. But amid the gloom, there was one glimmer of light. Ever since the beginning of 1984, Graham had had an odd conviction that Watford were going to win the FA Cup.

Worried about jinxing their chances, the only person he told was Elton, advising him to make sure he wasn't playing a concert on 19 May – Cup Final day. But to begin with the portents didn't look at all promising. Watford's FA Cup campaign got off to a testing start when they came up against their old rivals Luton Town.

The game ended in a 2-2 draw.

By the time of the replay, Elton was recording a new album in Montserrat. Once again, he phoned up Watford Hospital Radio and was patched through to Mike Vince's commentary. For the next two hours, he sat with the receiver glued to his ear as the game swung back and forth. It was, he said later, the most expensive phone call he had ever made.

After ninety minutes, the score was 3-3. During the break before extra-time, the exhausted Luton players collapsed onto the turf. Seeing this, Graham once again refused to let his players sit down, believing – rightly as it turned out – that this would give them a psychological advantage.

Watford won 4-3, thanks to Mo Johnston who scored his tenth goal in eleven games.

They then beat Charlton Athletic, Brighton and Hove Albion and Birmingham City to reach the semi-finals where they faced Plymouth Argyll. After just five minutes, John Barnes raced up the left wing, dancing past Plymouth players, and neatly side-stepping a long streamer of toilet paper that had been thrown onto the pitch. He then crossed the ball into the penalty area where George Reilly headed it into the net. It proved to be the only goal of the match.

Reilly's flying header would live long in the memories of those who saw it. Nearly twenty years later, he was working as a bricklayer on a building site in Corby when another worker suddenly launched himself at him and bit off part of his right ear. By way of explanation, the man hissed the single word, 'Plymouth!'

Watford were now in the FA Cup Final for the first time in their history. In the other semi-final, Everton beat Southampton – again the score was 1-0. But just as Watford were about to hang out the bunting, an incident occurred that put a large dent in

Graham's conviction that they were destined to win. It also brought him closer to physically assaulting a referee than he'd ever come before.

Three weeks before the Cup Final, Watford played Luton for the fourth time that season. Given that Watford had overcome them in the third round, Graham asked supporters to show some tact and restraint – a call that largely went unheeded.

'We're going to Wembley. We're going to Wembley,' the Watford fans chanted repeatedly. 'And you're not.'

Before the game started, Graham had made what he considered to be a light-hearted comment to the referee: 'We've got a Cup Final coming up, so you'll have no trouble with us.' Immediately the words were out of his mouth he regretted saying them. At the very least, he was tempting fate, he felt. Worse still, he might have sown an idea in the referee's head.

So it proved. Towards the end of the first half, the Watford captain Wilf Rostron and the Luton defender Paul Elliott went for the ball and both fell to the ground in a tangle of legs. Rostron was convinced Elliott had made a reckless challenge – 'I don't know what he'd had for breakfast, but some of his tackles were ridiculous.'

Words were exchanged, along with a little light pushing and shoving, but no punches were thrown. To general astonishment, both men were sent off. Walking towards the tunnel, Rostron was in no doubt what this meant. Having been red-carded, he would automatically miss the next game – the Cup Final.

Neither, of course, was Graham. When the game was over, he stood in the referee's path outside the dressing rooms and let rip. 'I really eyeballed him in the corridor,' he recalled. '"Do you know what you've done?" I shouted. "You've cost our captain the chance to play at Wembley!"'

That night, he and Rita drove to Stratford-on-Avon to see a Shakespeare play. Graham was still so upset that the evening passed in a blur. Lying in bed back in Mandeville Close, he found he couldn't remember a single thing about the production, even which play they had seen.

There was worse to come. With a week to go before the Cup Final and just after their last league game of the season – a 2-1 victory over Arsenal – Graham did something he had never done before: he announced his team for Wembley. The moment he did so, he regretted it.

He had ignored a characteristically astute piece of advice from one of the managers he most admired – the legendary Bill Shankly of Liverpool. 'Never pick your team for the next match on the way home from a win, a draw or a defeat,' Shankly had counselled. It was far better to wait until the dust had settled and your mind was clearer.

So why had he done it, Graham wondered afterwards. 'I thought it might settle them down and help them relax if they knew they weren't fretting over their place in the side all week,' he recalled. 'I felt they needed that sense of security, but perhaps I was wrong.'

Apart from anything else – as Graham knew perfectly well – footballers didn't thrive on a sense of security. Rather, it was uncertainty that kept them on their toes. As the week wore on, he cursed his own impetuosity and wished he hadn't backed himself into a corner.

Not that there was anything he could do about it, he realized. To change anything at this point would only look like weakness, or muddle-headedness. He would just have to live with the consequences of his own actions. With his captain suspended, no training ground, his team selection set in stone and his faith in his own judgement badly holed, Graham now faced the biggest game of his life.

# 49.

To celebrate Watford reaching the FA Cup Final, Benskins, the local brewery that had once manufactured a beer reputed to change a person's entire personality, produced a special commemorative ale. This too would prove to be a never-to-be-forgotten experience. According to one customer, its after-taste was akin to being elbowed in the throat by a Scotsman.

In the days leading up to the final, the town was festooned with red, yellow and black ribbons. Shop windows were full of home-made hornets along with replica FA Cups made out of tin foil. Despite the warm spring weather, children went to school wrapped in Watford scarves. Meanwhile, Graham was being bombarded with letters from supporters begging him for tickets to the final. By nature an assiduous replier to any correspondence, he found this particularly agonizing. 'Please don't write to me,' he implored in the *Watford Observer*. 'I have to write back and that takes time I could use on other things.'

With such a high-profile musical chairman, people had assumed that Watford would record a special Cup Final single – by this point there was a tradition that cup finalists would capitalize on the occasion by singing an instantly forgettable song in raucously out-of-tune voices. But Elton made it clear he had no intention of following suit. 'It's not my scene and I'm not going to get involved with anything like that.'

Unbeknown to Graham, his goalkeeper Steve Sherwood had injured his thumb three weeks earlier. For fear of missing the final, Sherwood decided to keep quiet about it. His already fragile self-confidence was dealt a further blow when the Nottingham Forest manager, Brian Clough, said dismissively of him, 'He's as honest as the day is long, but we've put more goals past him than I've had hot dinners.'

Interest in the Cup Final was so intense that the country effectively came to a halt on the day of the match. Both the BBC and ITV would cover the game. The TV audience for the Cup Final regularly exceeded 20 million – more than a third of the UK population. And it wasn't just domestic audiences who were transfixed: every year there would be a mad scramble among broadcasters from all over the world to buy the rights.

Naturally protective of his players, Graham was determined that they should stay as far away from the media hoopla as possible. Three days before the final, the team moved into the Ladbroke Hotel, a few minutes' drive away from Wembley Stadium. In part, this was to keep them away from the media who were desperate for any whispers of gossip, no matter how faint. Cloistering them away in a hotel in one of the more desolate stretches of north London had the added advantage of ensuring that Mo Johnston didn't sneak out to a local nightclub – there weren't any. Hoping to keep the players' feet on the ground, one afternoon Graham took them all to visit a nearby hospital where they toured the wards and handed out presents to the patients.

On the morning of the final, Eddie Plumley had just finished his breakfast when the phone rang. Picking up the receiver, he heard Graham's voice. Immediately, Plumley suspected that something awful had happened.

'What's wrong?' he asked.

Nothing was wrong, Graham assured him. 'I just wanted to say thank you for everything you've done. It's been absolutely fantastic and let's hope we can finish it off this afternoon.' He also had a present which he would give to him later, he added.

Plumley, not usually the tearful type, found that his cheeks were damp as he put down the phone. 'It was such a considerate thing to do when he must have had so many other things on his mind.' Later, Graham presented Plumley and all the Watford staff with specially embroidered Cup Final team shirts – that year, in another sign of creeping commercialism, the names of both clubs' sponsors had been permitted to appear on players' shirts for the first time.

Elsewhere, something close to derangement had taken hold. As part of their coverage of the game, the BBC sent the then popular comedian Michael Barrymore to Watford. Blacked-up and wearing a curly wig, Barrymore was filmed answering questions from an interviewer in a cod Jamaican accent and quoting lyrics from Bob Marley songs. No one was sure what to make of this – either at the time, or indeed afterwards when it dawned on them that he was meant to be impersonating John Barnes.

'That wasn't particularly to my taste,' Graham noted stiffly.

But in one sense Watford escaped lightly: the Everton players had to endure the sight of another then popular comedian, Freddie Starr, goose-stepping around their hotel in a Nazi uniform.

With an escort of mounted policemen, the Watford coach drove into Wembley Stadium to be greeted by thousands of cheering fans. Looking out of the window, Steve Sherwood realized that he was feeling more nervous than he had done in years. It didn't help that he was unable to do his usual pre-match preparation – shooting practice with Nigel Callaghan – as the Royal Marine band were standing in his goalmouth. Walking down the Wembley tunnel and out into the light, all Sherwood could see were thousands of blue and white Everton scarves. 'Then I turned around and saw all those yellow, black and red flags behind us; it was an incredible sight.'

During the traditional Cup Final hymn, 'Abide With Me', the camera cut away from the players to the Royal Box where Elton was standing with tears streaming down his cheeks. Up until this point, he had thought that he'd been bearing up pretty well, but suddenly emotion overwhelmed him. 'I always cry at 'Abide With Me' because it's such a beautiful hymn, but it all at once just struck me how much we had achieved in simply getting there.'

For the first half an hour, Sherwood watched while a hundred yards away his teammates launched one attack after another on the Everton goal. Slowly, his nerves settled. Before the game, Graham had emphasized just how important it was for Watford to score first. That way, they could knock what might prove to be a fatal hole in Everton's composure. For their part, Everton knew that if they were able to soak up whatever Watford threw at them, they could hit them on the counter-attack.

From what Sherwood could see, everything appeared to be going according to plan. The only problem was that the noise of the crowd was so loud that neither he, nor any of the players, could hear the instructions that Graham was bellowing at them from his dugout.

And then, in a moment, everything changed.

With seven minutes to go before half-time, Everton launched their first concerted move of the game. One of the Everton forwards had a wild hack at goal from outside the penalty area, but scuffed it. The ball bobbled into the box where another Everton forward, Graeme Sharp, was able to transfer it from his left foot to his right, then loose off a shot. After hitting the inside of the right-hand goalpost, the ball ricocheted into the net.

All Sherwood could do was stand and watch aghast as it went in.

At half-time Graham told a subdued dressing room that they should put their disappointment behind them and do what they'd done so often in the past – come from behind. But this time the fire in their bellies wouldn't burn for long. The second half had only been going for six minutes when Everton crossed the ball into Sherwood's penalty area. As he rose to catch it, Everton's star striker, Andy Gray, also took to the air and managed to head the ball out of Sherwood's grasp. By the time Sherwood fell to the ground, Gray had already turned and raced away in celebration.

Immediately, the Watford players protested that it had been

a foul, that Gray had headed Sherwood's arm and not the ball – later, television replays confirmed this to be the case. By then, though, it was too late – the referee had awarded the goal and Everton were 2-0 up. In the forty years that have gone by, the memory of what happened has never left Sherwood. 'Even now, I still find myself thinking about it sometimes in the middle of the night. Wondering if I should have done something different.'

For Watford, it would prove to be a blow from which they never recovered. When the final whistle went with the score still at 2-0, Graeme Sharp was one of the first to offer his commiserations to the Watford players. What made the strongest impression on him was that all the Watford supporters stayed behind to applaud the Everton players as they embarked on their lap of honour. Usually, the fans of the losing side beat as hasty a retreat as possible after the final whistle.

When George Reilly was getting ready to collect his losers' medal from the Duchess of Kent, he remembered a promise he had made to his mother that he wouldn't meet a member of the royal family without wearing his false teeth – and dashed off to the dressing room to fetch them.

Despite the result, that evening there was a party at John Reid's house near Rickmansworth. Everyone who worked at Watford FC was invited, along with their families. Elton John and Kiki Dee sang 'Don't Go Breaking My Heart' and the party went on until the small hours. As far as Elton was concerned, his sense of sadness was tinged with regret. 'I think we choked, the players were overawed by the occasion and by being at Wembley. Because I'd played there myself, I wished that I'd talked to them beforehand and told them not to be intimidated. But I thought we were such giant-killers that we'd fly. Instead, they flopped.'

Although Graham did his best to put a brave face on what had happened, he found it even more of a struggle than he had expected. 'There was champagne and laughter and while I didn't exactly sit quietly in the corner, I couldn't mask my disappointment.'

But it wasn't just disappointment; there was another feeling that Graham couldn't get rid of. Over the next few days, the same feeling kept circling around in his head – a nagging suspicion that this was it. That Watford really had gone as far as they could. That something had vanished in the Wembley air which could never be recaptured. That six years and eleven months since he and Elton had sat in the Kremlin and celebrated his becoming manager by helping themselves to a drink from Mrs Bonser's cupboard, Watford's great adventure had come to an end.

# 50.

A few weeks after the FA Cup Final, Graham saw a group of Watford players standing outside the dressing room at Vicarage Road. Coming closer, he could hear that they were talking about money.

Taking a £10 note out of his wallet, he tore it into pieces and threw them on the floor. 'Here you are,' he said. 'Is this all that matters to you?'

The players slunk off, abashed. That Christmas, Graham was presented with a picture frame. Inside were the pieces of the £10 note which they had painstakingly stuck back together. He hung it in his downstairs lavatory as a reminder that he too should never get carried away by money.

If football was changing, Watford was too. Three of the four 'rocketmen' – the players who had gone all the way from the bottom of Division Four to the top of Division One – had now left, with only Steve Sherwood remaining.

In May 1987, Graham decided that the time had also come for him to move on. He was appointed manager of Aston Villa, who had just been relegated from Division One. Although he had braced himself for an emotional wrench, the reality of leaving Watford proved far more painful than he had anticipated. For several months after moving with his family to Birmingham, Graham found himself driving down to Watford on the slightest pretext – not entirely sure what he was doing, or why he was doing it.

'I must have gone half a dozen times or so. Sometimes I would go into the stadium if a gate was open, but other times I would just sit in my car outside the ground. I wanted to have a look around the place and say goodbye, I suppose. I told Rita what I'd been doing, and I think she thought I was going mad.'

At the end of 1987, Elton sold Watford FC to Jack Petchey, a property magnate. He no longer had the time to devote to the club, he said. Except this wasn't quite the full story. With Graham gone, Elton found that things just weren't the same any more. 'I still loved the club, but there had been a serendipity, a magic, about the two of us together, and I couldn't conjure up that same magic without him.'

In the eleven years since Elton had bought Watford, he had, he estimates, given between £8 and £9 million to the club – an expenditure which may have prompted much weeping and wailing among his management team, but which he had never regretted for a moment. 'I never got a penny back from my investment, but that didn't matter at all. It had enabled me to have the greatest adventure of my life.'

During Graham's first season in charge at Aston Villa, they won promotion back to Division One. Two seasons later, they were the Division One runners-up. By then he had become one of the best-known managers in the country, having inspired not just one but two spectacular resurrections.

One day, the phone rang in his office. When he picked it up, Graham heard Eddie Plumley's voice on the other end of the line. "'Graham Kelly at the FA has just been on to me asking if I had your home number," Eddie said. "He didn't say this, but I think he wants to talk to you about the England job."'

At the end of July 1990, three weeks after Graham had been unveiled as the new England manager, Elton checked into the Advocate Lutheran General hospital in Park Ridge, Illinois to begin treatment for his alcohol and cocaine addictions.

The road to reach this point had been long and bumpy, with any number of relapses and broken resolutions. But however desperate a state Elton was in, he was in no doubt where the first impetus to seek help had come from. It had been on that Boxing Day morning eight years earlier, when Graham had banged a bottle of brandy down in front of him and told him that he was ruining his life. That he was letting himself down, along with everyone he was close to.

Ever since then, Elton had often thought back to how it had felt being on the receiving end of Graham's tirade. How it had filled him with shame and a determination to change. 'Something took root inside me that day which had quietly been growing all this time. I've no doubt that Graham saved my life. Without him, I would have been lost.'

At one therapy meeting Elton attended in the hospital, the other patients were asked to make a list of his good points and bad points. He was then asked what he thought of their comments. After he had been talking for a while, someone gently pointed out that Elton had never mentioned any of the good points they had listed; he had concentrated only on the bad ones.

Back in his room, Elton wrote 'I Am Worthy, I Am a Good Person' on the front of the file that he had been given when he checked in. Six weeks later, he left the Lutheran. He has never had a drink or taken drugs since.

The news of Graham's appointment as England manager appalled his critics. Brian Glanville from *The Times* was beside himself with indignation. No good would come of it, he predicted. However well Graham had done at club level, his tactical limitations were sure to be exposed by good international sides.

As it turned out, Glanville was right – and yet everything started out so well. England lost just once in Graham's first twenty-three matches in charge. The BBC football commentator John Motson remembers going to watch England practise and hearing Graham tell their star striker, Gary Lineker, that he had to run faster. 'He definitely wasn't cowed by the job.'

Bullish with the players, Graham was equally bullish with the supporters. When he heard some England supporters taunting John Barnes with racist chants, he leapt up to confront them. 'Hey!' he shouted. "You're talking about another human being, so just watch your language, all right?'

But after such a promising start, England only just managed to qualify for the 1992 European Championship. By the time the competition got under way, Graham was already being criticized for chopping and changing his team too often. He also had a tendency to pack his sides with dogged workhorses rather than creative wizards – or so it was claimed.

England drew their first two matches 0-0, but needed to beat Sweden to advance to the next round. Not only did they lose 2-1, but Graham committed what was deemed to be an act of unforgivable heresy by substituting Lineker in his last international match. In doing so, he deprived him of the chance to equal – or even beat – Bobby Charlton's record of forty-nine England goals.

The next morning the wolf pack descended.

The *Sun* led the way with a headline that read 'Swedes 2, Turnips 1' and a photo of Graham's head superimposed on a turnip. Other newspapers – broadsheet as well as tabloid – piled in with equal ferocity. Throughout the remaining two years of Graham's time as England manager, the feeding frenzy never let up. At Heathrow airport, he and Rita were spat at by disgruntled fans.

In July 1993, at a by-election in Christchurch, a man stood as the 'Sack Graham Taylor' candidate. He gained eighty votes – sixty-two more than someone calling himself 'Alfred the Chicken'.

There was worse to come. In the interests of openness, Graham had allowed a camera crew to follow him and the England team around for four months as they prepared for the 1994 World Cup. He even agreed to wear a microphone during games so that every remark he made in the dugout was preserved for posterity.

Before their World Cup qualifier against Holland – a game England had to win in order to qualify – the Dutch FA refused to allow the director, Ken McGill, and his crew into the ground. McGill appealed to Graham who agreed to smuggle them in on the team bus. It was a decision he may have lived to regret.

Once the game was under way, Graham was heard exclaiming in exasperation, 'We're all over the fucking shop. They've done everything we told them not to.' When the Dutch player Ronald Koeman escaped without a booking after scything down England's David Platt, and then went on to score Holland's equalizer, Graham marched up to the linesman. 'I was just saying to your colleague that the referee's got me the sack,' he told him. 'Thank him ever so much for that, will you?'

At the end of the game – a 2-2 draw – Graham looked up at the sky and said despairingly, 'God, what have I done wrong? I am not a bad man.'

A month later, just as he had predicted, he was sacked.

In an interview shortly after Graham lost the England job, it was plain how much he had been affected by all the criticism. 'People have no recognition of how it hurts you,' he said. 'They think you don't care. And those people who know it hurts you, they put the knife into you so it hurts you even more . . . People say I'm bitter. I am not bitter. I'm just bloody disappointed in myself.'

Before the documentary, entitled *An Impossible Job*, went out, Ken McGill took it round to Graham's house to show him. 'As we watched it in his front room, I looked at his face to judge the reactions,' McGill recalled. 'It was an awkward situation, seeing him relive the pain.'

Following transmission, in January 1994, mockery rained down from all sides, with Graham's remark 'Do I Not Like That?' instantly passing into the dictionary of national catchphrases. Not that he harboured any grudges over the way he had been presented – he even attended McGill's wedding a few months later.

Both Rita and their two daughters are convinced that Graham was deeply scarred by the way he was treated. Having always believed that human beings were essentially decent and well intentioned, it was as if his whole worldview had been turned on its head. And there was something else, of course – for the first time in his life, he had to contend with the fact that people regarded him as a failure.

A doctor diagnosed depression and suggested he took a holiday. Instead, Graham resolved to answer his critics in the only way he knew how – by going back to managing a club. The trouble was that no one wanted him. Every day he would wait for the phone to ring, and every day nothing happened.

Six months earlier, he had been the most powerful man in English football; now he had become an outcast. And then one day, the phone finally rang. Wolverhampton Wanderers wanted to know if he might be interested in becoming their new manager. At the time, Wolves were bobbing around the middle of Division One. Graham took the job – 'I won't pretend I had many alternatives' – and steered them up to eighth place by the end of the season.

But while he remained as ebullient as ever in public, he realized he was perilously close to being burnt out. Friends begged him not to watch the 1994 World Cup. He was bound to find it upsetting, they said. Besides what was the point? Why not take Rita away, ideally to some far-flung country where no one was that interested in football?

That would be the sensible thing to do, Graham agreed. But rather than take their advice, he did the opposite – staying at home and forcing himself to sit through every game. 'I didn't invite anyone round for company. I watched most of the games alone. Some days it was not easy, but I needed to do it. It was almost as if I was punishing myself, and although this sounds like a crazy thing to say, I felt it was part of the process of getting over it.'

After each match, he would go out into the garden and kick a football around. There was something about having the ball at his feet and feeling the evening air against his skin that not only soothed him, but also sharpened his thoughts. And by the time the World Cup was over, he felt ready to move on.

Wolves finished the next season in fourth place. However, they made a poor start to the season after, winning just four of their first sixteen games. The fans turned against him, as did the Wolves directors, and in November 1995, Graham resigned.

But down at Vicarage Road, something was stirring. At the end of the year, after watching Watford be relegated, Elton said that he was willing to get involved again. While he had no intention of buying the club for a second time, he was prepared to head up a consortium that would mount a takeover bid.

Three months later, Graham came back to Vicarage Road. The ground he returned to bore little resemblance to the one he'd first visited twenty years earlier. In 1986 the Shrodells Stand, alongside which spectators had once gone blackberrying at half-time, had been torn down and replaced with a new £3 million stand – financed in part by a £1 million loan from Elton. It was named the Sir Stanley Rous Stand, after the former FIFA president and one-time sports teacher at Watford Grammar School for Boys.

Then, in 1993, the Vicarage Road stand was built: half of it housed away supporters and the other half was the Watford family enclosure. Putting away fans next to small children was seen in some quarters as an act of madness, and yet there was never any trouble – if anything, the presence of so many young faces was thought to have a calming effect on away fans' behaviour. A year later, the old Rookery Stand was also replaced.

To begin with, Graham was the caretaker manager, then the director of football, before being reappointed full-time manager in 1997. The next season, Watford were promoted to Division One, now rechristened the Premier League. But despite the club's success and the sense of coming home, Graham increasingly began to feel that he'd made a mistake. That you really couldn't – or shouldn't – go back.

Watford lasted only one season in the Premier League before being relegated again.

In March 2001, by now in his late fifties and suspecting that he didn't have the same hunger as before, Graham announced he would be retiring at the end of the season. That, finally, was it. Or so it seemed. But like so many other football managers, he found retirement hard to cope with.

After another few months of kicking a ball round his garden, Graham agreed to take another step back into the past by returning to Aston Villa. That didn't work out either – the club only just avoided being relegated at the end of his first season. But what finally convinced Graham his time was up wasn't so much the club's lack of success as an incident that happened at the end of one of his last games in charge. An Aston Villa supporter marched down the steps to the managers' dugout, came right up to Graham and with a face contorted with anger, said, 'You're yesterday's man, Taylor.'

After resigning from Villa, Graham became a very popular – and much respected – football commentator. Occasionally, as he did the rounds of the commentary boxes, he would bump into Gary Lineker who had also become a media pundit. However upset Lineker may have been about being substituted when he was within touching distance of Bobby Charlton's record, over time he had come to feel rather differently about it. 'We were always perfectly friendly, and looking back, I think Graham did me a favour. The chances are I wouldn't have scored because we weren't a very creative team, and by taking me off he actually made a martyr of me.'

Ever since Graham had first left Watford, he and Elton had talked regularly on the phone. 'We would just phone one another up from time to time for a chat,' Elton remembers. 'We'd talk about football, about what we'd been up to. While we may not have seen one another as often as we once had, we never lost that sense of closeness, of being able to pick up just where we had left off.'

In November 2014, Graham returned to Vicarage Road for a ceremony to mark the renaming of the Sir Stanley Rous Stand. In future, it was to be known as the Graham Taylor Stand. As supporters sang, 'One Graham Taylor, there's only one Graham Taylor', he walked onto the pitch flanked by a guard of honour made up of old Watford players, including Ian Bolton, Steve Sherwood and Luther Blissett, to be presented with an inscribed silver salver.

At one end of the ground, supporters unfurled an enormous yellow banner with a picture of Graham and key Watford players on it inscribed 'We're Still Standing'. Flattered though he was to have had a stand named after him, it was the affection in which he was held by Watford supporters that meant more than anything.

'I have never changed my opinion that football is a game for the people. During my career, I tried not to lose sight of the fact that we were striving to be successful for the supporters as well as for ourselves. Yes, we could carry on playing the game without them, but there wouldn't be anything like the sense of enjoyment and satisfaction when things go well. So to be recognized and appreciated by those supporters means a great deal to me.'

Every once in a while, Graham would go and sit in the stand that bore his name. But while people were always delighted to see him, he became aware that as time had moved on, so something else had happened: memories had faded.

'Whenever I visit Vicarage Road to watch a match, people are so kind,' he wrote in his autobiography, 'although I notice it is usually older people who come up to me asking for a photograph or autograph. It pulls me up short to realise that someone would have to be in their mid-thirties to remember the tail-end of my first spell as Watford manager. Sometimes the supporters have their children with them and occasionally they will say, "This is Graham Taylor, our greatest-ever manager", which is very nice to hear, although I smile to myself when I look down at a blank little face and realise it means nothing to an eight-year-old.'

In December 2014, Elton opened the new Elton John Stand at Vicarage Road – it had been built on the site of the old East Stand. Wearing a Watford scarf and accompanied by his husband, David Furnish, and their two sons, he told the crowd that 'I love football and I always will and Watford is embedded in my heart.'

The Elton John Stand and the Graham Taylor Stand now face one another across the pitch where more than sixty years earlier Reggie Dwight first saw Watford play.

It had been here that Reggie had first lost his habitual shyness and been swept up in the emotion, the passion, of a crowd. Where he had first roared and hollered and let himself go. And it had been here that he had first gazed awestruck at the Watford players as they raced about in their baggy shorts. As he did so, he had felt that these impossibly glamorous figures lived not only in a different world from him, but in a completely different universe. A universe he was quite sure he could never hope to inhabit, no matter how unexpected a course his life might run.

In the early morning of 12 January 2017, Graham died of a heart attack at the age of seventy-two. Elton was at home in Windsor when he heard the news. 'It was one of the biggest shocks of my life. I'd talked to him a couple of days before and everything was fine. Then Rita phoned to say that she had gone downstairs to make a cup of tea and when she came back, Graham was dead.'

Later that morning, Elton issued a statement. 'Graham was like a brother to me. We shared an unbreakable bond since we first met. We went on an incredible journey together and it will stay with me for ever . . . I love you Graham and I will miss you very much.'

For an hour before the start of Graham's funeral, old Buddy Holly songs boomed out of the tower of St Mary's church. On its way there, his cortège passed by Vicarage Road for one last time. Outside the church, more than a thousand mourners had gathered to pay their respects as Graham's coffin, draped in a Union Jack and topped with a wreath in Watford colours, was carried inside.

Not everyone could be there. Elton, who was performing in Las Vegas, sent an enormous wreath and a statement which was read out by the BBC football commentator John Motson. 'While I was very flattered to be asked, I remember feeling very nervous,' Motson recalls. 'I only received Elton's speech about an hour before, but I did my best and managed to get through it.' In his speech, Elton wrote that Graham had been the most honest and open man he had ever met.

Oli Phillips, who had confidently predicted that Graham would quickly come a cropper when he joined Watford, sat next to Ross Jenkins, who he had once referred to as the worst signing in Watford's history. The two of them had gone on to become firm friends.

Around the town speakers relayed the service to hundreds of people who stood in silence in the thin winter sunshine, listening. Afterwards, when the hearse containing Graham's coffin drove away, they burst into applause that kept rippling round the churchyard long after the hearse had disappeared. One of the mourners, asked for her opinion of Graham, chose not to dwell on his career in football, but on his less obvious accomplishments. 'Watford was just another suburb until Graham came along,' she said. 'He put the town on the map, and it became a much nicer, friendlier and safer place as a result.'

Occasionally, towards the end of his life, Graham would find himself back in his car, just as he had done when he first left Watford thirty years earlier. Half-surprised by what he was doing and how he had got there. Not outside Vicarage Road this time, but driving around the rural lanes and villages that surrounded the town. Aimlessly pottering about the Hertfordshire countryside, with no destination in mind, simply going wherever the fancy took him. As if something inside him, something he could hardly control, was leading him back to the place where his heart belonged.

# Curtain Call

Ever since Ian Bolton had slipped a disc while brushing his teeth, he had been troubled by a recurrent back problem. In 1981, he began to suspect that his playing days might be over. But in a pioneering operation, dynamite was injected into his spine and a reinvigorated Bolton was able to carry on at Watford for another two years.

It was only after he left Vicarage Road for Brentford in 1983 – for a transfer fee of £5,000 – that everything fell apart. The move didn't work out, his marriage hit the rocks and six months later he was working as a car salesman. Overnight, Bolton went from earning £350 a week to £90. Made redundant, he spent a few months working on a building site, and then signed on the dole.

By this point he was thirty-two years old with next to no money. 'I was a typical thick footballer; I didn't have a clue how to do anything because I was so used to being mollycoddled.' Salvation came from an unlikely source. One day, while leafing through the local paper, Bolton saw a job vacancy advertised at a company in Watford that manufactured industrial doors. Despite having barely any qualifications and no idea what an industrial door was, he applied. When he arrived for an interview, it turned out that the boss was a huge Watford fan. Not only that, Bolton had always been his favourite player.

He got the job and, with it, a second chance. 'Without it, I have no idea what I would have done.' These days, Ian Bolton lives in Abbotts Langley with his second wife, Tina. On a shelf above his desk are two of his most treasured possessions – a framed photograph of the gold disc Elton John won for his 1978 album *A Single Man*, on which he and other Watford players sang back-up vocals, and a much thumbed Christmas card from Graham and Rita Taylor.

Beneath their signatures, Graham had written, 'Still pound for pound, my best-ever signing.'

Gerry Armstrong was Northern Ireland's top scorer in the 1982 World Cup. A year later he left Watford, and after a spell in Spain signed as player-coach for Brighton and Hove Albion. A lot of people find that age knocks off their rougher edges, and they turn into much milder versions of their old selves. This, however, did not happen to Gerry Armstrong.

Halfway through one game, he decided that he'd put up with enough abuse from opposition fans. Jumping into the stands, Armstrong laid two of them out. To no one's surprise, this signalled his rapid exit from the club. He then went to non-league Crawley Town, but once again Armstrong's patience was soon tested. 'A couple of hundred people were calling me names, so I went to the touchline and asked if any of them wanted to take me on. And not one came forward – they all bottled it.' Shortly afterwards, he also bid farewell to Crawley Town.

After his retirement in 1998, Armstrong now works as a football commentator.

Sam Ellis played his last game for Watford in November 1978 when they were beaten 4-0 at Hull City. Oli Phillips who was at the game with his friend the *Watford Observer*'s cartoonist Terry Challis, recalled Challis saying that Ellis reminded him of a wounded bull, standing on the centre circle with his hands on his hips and plumes of steam coming from his nostrils. Ellis went on to become manager of Blackpool for seven years, taking them from the Fourth to the Third Division, then went on to be the manager of Lincoln City – where he had first met Graham.

During his time as a manager, Ellis often found himself reflecting on the conversation he and Graham had had twenty years earlier – when he'd been all set to walk out of Lincoln and Graham had persuaded him to change his mind. It was, Ellis still believes, the single most important conversation he has ever had. 'Graham not only rescued my career; he rescued my life.'

In August 1992, the Reverend John Boyers left Watford and became Manchester United's first-ever chaplain. Two years earlier, he had founded Sports Chaplaincy UK, a charity providing pastoral and spiritual care to anyone involved in professional sport. While he was at Old Trafford, Boyers wrote a book, *Beyond the Final Whistle: A Life of Football and Faith*, in which he updated the teachings of Christ and recast them in footballing terms. 'Just like a football transfer, the spiritual transfer is the start of a new adventure, not the climax of it,' Boyers counselled. 'It is a commitment that leads on to other things. A new manager must coach us, prepare us and integrate us into his squad, but we can be assured that ultimately we will receive a victory medal when the final whistle blows.'

Just a year after being sold to AC Milan for £1 million, Luther Blissett was back at Watford. In May 1985, during a game with Manchester United, he collided with the United goalkeeper and had to be stretchered off. It turned out that Blissett had fractured his skull. After he had come out of hospital, the Watford groundsman, Les Simmons, presented him with a square of turf that he had cut from the Vicarage Road pitch. When he examined it more closely, Blissett saw that the grass was stained with his blood.

Blissett went on to play fourteen times for England. Shortly after his international debut, he received an anonymous letter telling him he would be shot the next time he appeared in an England shirt. He took no notice, declaring it to be the work of 'a crank and a coward'.

In 1988, he was transferred again – this time to Bournemouth. But, like a homing pigeon, he soon returned to Vicarage Road. In his final season there, in 1991/92, Blissett was once again the club's top scorer. In all, he made more than 500 appearances for the club and scored 186 goals. In 2022, he was made an honorary life president of the club. Today, almost thirty years after his retirement, Luther Blissett remains Watford's most capped player.

During the course of Wing-Commander Charles Reep's long life, he went from being an outsider to a sage, and then back to outsider again. For half a century, he notated and analysed a total of 2,200 matches, in his spidery, barely legible hand. But while Reep's ideas were taken up by other managers after Graham, within a few years he had largely been forgotten.

Dismissed as a crank who was obsessed by the long-ball game, Reep's theories – so it was held – not only didn't stand up to close analysis, but put paid to any idea of attractive, flowing football. Reep insisted that he had no interest in telling anyone how to play. 'I must emphasize that my methods are not a declaration of how football should be played,' he explained. 'But it is the most efficient way,' he added.

In the 1990s, back in obscurity once more, Reep found an unexpected champion in the shape of Norway's then manager Egil Olsen. After travelling to his Devon home to consult him, Olsen arranged for Reep to be guest of honour when Norway played Graham Taylor's England in 1993.

He looked on as Norway won the game 2-0.

When Reep died in 2002, aged ninety-seven, there were a few brief obituaries, but otherwise his death passed unnoticed – the FA ignored it altogether. Reep himself wouldn't have been surprised. 'They dismiss me as a rather eccentric chap,' he said once of the FA. He had no doubt why. 'Obviously, it's because I've put a question mark against so many aspects of the game.'

Tom Walley was Watford's youth coach from 1977 to 1996, during which time he launched the careers of Kenny Jackett, John

Barnes, Nigel Callaghan, Ashley Young, David James and Steve Terry. Just as Graham had suspected when they first met, Walley proved to be a man after his own heart: tough – unrelentingly so at times – but always encouraging and devoted to his players' welfare.

When he first started as youth coach, the Hertfordshire FA refused to allow Watford to have an Under-15 team on the grounds that any players would be too young to make up their own minds about what they wanted to do. 'Graham and I went to see them and said, "If the parents want them to play, what's the problem?"' Watford duly got approval for their Under-15 team.

As Walley travelled the country in a beaten-up Transit van looking for promising young players, he was always keen to stress how uncertain the life of an apprentice footballer was. 'You can see a lad of fifteen who looks the part, but he could have lost it by the time he's eighteen. You just have to be honest with them, don't promise anything and never fill anyone's heads with dreams.'

Inducted into the Watford Hall of Fame in 2018, Tom Walley was described as the best youth coach England has ever produced.

Just as Elton had anticipated when he first saw him play, John Barnes went on to become a footballing superstar. In 1987, he left Watford and joined Liverpool for a fee of £900,000. Barnes would go on to score 106 goals for the club in 403 matches. Capped seventy-nine times for England, in 1983 he scored what is still considered to be one of the greatest ever goals when he danced his way through a befuddled Brazilian defence before threading a shot past their keeper. Despite this, Barnes was regularly booed and catcalled during the match by a group of National Front supporters.

If he had started his career under any manager except Graham, Barnes believes, he would probably have gone off the rails. 'I was a maverick and mavericks need discipline. At the same time as teaching me discipline, Graham taught me humility and I hope that's stayed with me ever since.'

During his time at Liverpool, Barnes had to endure yet more racist taunts from opposition supporters, which he dealt with in characteristically disdainful fashion. During a match against Everton at Goodison Park, one of the Everton fans threw a banana at him, which Barnes casually flicked away with a back heel. In 2021, he wrote a book, *The Uncomfortable Truth About Racism*, in which he argued that racism was still embedded in all aspects of British society.

Barnes believes that Graham and Elton constituted the perfect partnership. 'Elton understood the nature of football. He knew if you wanted to be successful, the most important person has to be the manager. I remember there were times when Elton would be in the dressing room and very excited about something and Graham would say, "Right, you've been here for too long. Fuck off now, we're going to get serious." And Elton would just go, "Sorry, boss!" and get out. It was obvious that the two of them had this instinctive understanding and they brought out the very best in one another. But I think it went further than that; each one learned from the other in a way that had a hugely beneficial effect on both their lives.'

Having started out as a left-winger and then been reborn as a left-back, Wilf Rostron stayed at Watford until 1989, when he joined Sheffield Wednesday. The day after he retired, he went down to his local Job Centre in Sunderland to see what work was available – thereby following in the footsteps of generations of ex-footballers who faced an uncertain future with barely any savings to sustain them. Taken on by a company selling furniture, Rostron later set up his own furniture business and then worked for the North East Autism Society.

*

Nigel Callaghan left Watford in 1987 and went to Derby County for two seasons before being reunited with Graham at Aston Villa. At the age of thirty, Callaghan decided that he'd had enough of football and went to work as a DJ in Ibiza. 'From the age of eleven, I never smoked, I never drank and I never went out with girls. Suddenly no one was going to tell me what to do.' But Callaghan's plans to whoop it up in the sun were dealt a big blow when he was diagnosed with arthritis while he was still in his thirties. Then, in 2009, he learned that he had bowel cancer which had spread elsewhere. But after an operation to remove 70 per cent of his liver, Callaghan has remained cancer-free and now, aged sixty, is still spinning records in Ibiza.

Steve Sims missed out on the 1984 Cup Final after breaking his ankle. When he recovered, he was troubled by a recurrent knee injury. Feeling that Sims's playing days were drawing to a close, Graham put him on the transfer list. After Sims had spent two years at Notts County, Graham called him up and asked if he would come back to Watford. But once again, Sims was dogged by injuries, with a dislocated elbow effectively ending his career. 'I went in for a tackle, glanced down and saw that my arm was pointing the wrong way.'

Looking back, what sticks in Sims's mind most vividly is the attitude that Graham instilled in the players. 'He always said that he wanted the supporters to see us as normal people, not these specks on a football pitch. That we should never give ourselves airs and graces and remember we were the same as anyone else. And if we ever forgot how it felt to be like everyone else, then we'd find out soon enough because Graham would kick us out.'

Sims now works as a part-time monitor for the Premier League, visiting footballing academies and making sure that coaches are teaching youth players correctly.

★

Bertie Mee retired from Watford in 1991. His record of 241 victories at Arsenal would not be surpassed for almost twenty years. When Mee died in 2001, Graham gave the address at his funeral and paid tribute to how important he had been both to Watford's success, and to him personally. 'Football can make you one dimensional and lose focus,' Graham recalled, 'but Bertie was excellent at developing me as a person, not just as a manager.'

One of his former Arsenal colleagues, Joe Marshall, remembers seeing Mee at Highbury in 1994. After having a cup of tea with him and Mee's wife Doris, Marshall watched as the two of them walked off to the tube station. 'It struck me as poignant that this Highbury legend could just stroll down to Arsenal station and get on a train just like the rest of us, almost anonymous. It seemed to symbolize how humble this man was. No fuss, no muss. A gentleman of the first order.'

Having joined Watford at the age of twelve, Kenny Jackett spent his entire playing career at Vicarage Road. He played 428 games for the club – as well as being capped thirty-one times by Wales – and after he retired in 1990, joined the club's coaching staff. When Graham returned to Watford as general manager in 1996, he decided that Jackett and Luther Blissett should take over day-to-day running of the team. At the end of the season, Graham became director of football while Jackett was appointed manager.

Subsequently Jackett managed various clubs including Swansea City, Millwall and Portsmouth, and is currently director of football at Gillingham. When he first became a manager, Graham gave him what proved to be an invaluable piece of advice: however much a manager might be plagued by dark thoughts and self-doubt, he must never show it. 'I remember Graham saying to me, "This is my way of dealing with pressure: I go home, I sit in the bath, and that's where I do my worrying. Then I get out of the bath, dry myself off and decide not to worry any more."'

★

Steve Sherwood left Watford in 1987 and went to Grimsby Town FC. He continued playing until he was forty-four years old, and would have kept going even longer if he hadn't gashed open his knee on a brick that was half-buried in the goalmouth. After inspecting his wound and telling him he was lucky not to have contracted septicaemia, a doctor suggested that the time might have come for him to hang up his boots.

Now aged seventy and working as a financial adviser, Sherwood still wonders what would have happened if he had never met Graham Taylor. 'I guess I would have kept bumping along the bottom. But Graham had something you very seldom come across in life – an ability to make you exceed your own expectations of yourself. You would have this image in your mind of how good you were, and what your natural level was. And then Graham came along and said, "No, no, you're wrong, you're much better than that. All you need is faith in yourself – faith and hard work." And the extraordinary thing was, he was right.'

After being given a free transfer by Watford, Ross Jenkins moved for a while to Sheffield Wednesday – then to a club in Hong Kong. At first, he had hoped to become a coach, but the opportunities proved to be thin on the ground. Moving back to Watford, Jenkins went into business installing double-glazing. But it wasn't long before he realized that double-glazing was unlikely to offer him the fulfilment he was looking for.

In search of adventure, he and his wife, Evie, moved to the wilds of north Michigan in the USA. There, they bought a plot of land in the middle of a wood where they built a house from scratch. Once in a while, Ross would look in his mailbox – and there on the bottom would be an airmail letter from Graham.

The letters would be chatty and informative, and Ross always enjoyed reading what Graham had been up to. But he would also wonder why he was bothering to write. Was he just being friendly, or was something else going on? Although there was never anything apologetic about the tone of these letters, Ross felt that they were Graham's way of saying sorry. 'I believe he let me down, and he knew he had let me down, so that's why he wrote.'

After a couple of years in Michigan, Ross and Evie decided to move again – this time to the Costa Blanca in Spain, where they ran a bar during the week and escaped to a two-room shepherd's cottage in the mountains at the weekends. Then in 2010, Ross was asked if he would come back to Watford for a public reunion of players who had served under Graham – 'The Watford Legends', as they were billed.

Among the other players present was the former Watford left-back Neil Price. 'Before Ross arrived, it was clear that Graham was nervous,' Price recalls 'He kept asking, "Do you think he'll want to see me?"' In the event, Graham needn't have worried. When they met, the two men immediately hugged each another. A watching Neil Price noticed that neither of them spoke, not at first. 'There was a reason for that; I could see they were both in tears.'

Ross Jenkins is now seventy-one. While he has given up running a bar, he and Evie still live in southern Spain. But they spend several months each year in Africa where they load up an old taxi with camera equipment – Evie is a keen photographer – then head off into the bush, photographing wildlife and sleeping under the stars. Now and again, as he's lying in his sleeping bag, Ross finds himself thinking back to his time at Watford. Back to the triumphs and the setbacks and the sheer implausibility of it all.

But as the years go by, he feels increasingly distanced from what went on, rather as if he's looking through the wrong end of a telescope at these tiny figures scurrying about on a faraway rectangle of grass. And sometimes, gazing up at the night sky,

Ross has the strangest sensation of all. 'Just occasionally, I'll catch myself drifting back, except that now it doesn't even feel real, not any more. Instead, it's as if the whole thing happened to someone else, someone completely different, long ago and far away.'

# Acknowledgements

This book could never have been written without the support and participation of Elton John and David Furnish. Elton has been enormously generous with his time, as well as giving me access to his personal archives. David has been unwaveringly behind the project since we first discussed it back in the distant days before Covid took hold. As he told me when we first met, he and Elton wanted their two sons, Zachary and Elijah, to be able to learn more about a comparatively little-known side of Elton's life – and I hope they will enjoy reading this book as much as I have enjoyed writing it.

It was my friend Caroline Law who first drew my attention to the statement Elton issued after Graham's death in 2017 and suggested that the story of their friendship might form the basis of a book.

I'm very grateful to Patrick Woodroffe, a friend of more than fifty years' standing, for all his help.

I was extremely lucky to have been able to talk at length to Oli Phillips, the former football correspondent of the *Watford Observer*. As well as being a fine writer, Oli was a delightful man and his death last year leaves a large hole in the lives of everyone who knew him.

Many thanks also go to: Gerry Armstrong, John Barnes, Lionel Birnie, Luther Blissett, Ian Bolton, Dennis Booth, Nigel Callaghan, Karen Colley, George Crawford, Helen Crawford, Laura Croker, Liz Dexter, Sam Ellis, Ross Jenkins, Joanne Glover, Steve Harrison, Kenny Jackett, Mark Lawson, Gary Lineker, Alan Morgan, John Motson, Eddie Plumley, Neil Price, Wilf Rostron,

Steve Sherwood, Steve Sims, Rita Taylor, Mike Vince, Ian Wilson, Muff Winwood and everyone at Watford Museum.

My agent Natasha Fairweather has been a pillar of strength and support. At Penguin, I want to thank my original editor, Tom Killingbeck, his successor, Shyam Kumar, Amelia Fairney and everyone else who worked on the book.

Closer to home, my wife, Susanna, has, as always, offered unfailingly good editorial advice, while our teenage children, Joseph and Milly, have listened patiently and with a plausible semblance of interest as I have regaled them with stories of Watford's glory days. My love to them all.

# Sources

Watford FC has been unusually lucky, both in the devotion of its supporters and in their willingness to record their memories for posterity. I have found the following books invaluable: *Enjoy the Game* by Lionel Birnie; *From Father to Son* by Paul Bishop; *Beyond the Final Whistle* by John Boyers; *There to be Shot At* by Tony Coton; *Watford Season by Season* and *The Watford Football Club Illustrated Who's Who* by Trefor Jones; *The A–Z of Watford FC* by John Murray; *The Golden Boys* and *Watford Centenary* by Oliver Phillips; the Tales from the Vicarage series, in particular *Rocket Men* by Oliver Phillips and Mike Walters; *Watford FC: On This Day* by Matt Rowson; *Watford: A Tale of the Unexpected* by Geoff Sweet and Graham Burton; *In His Own Words* by Graham Taylor; the Hornet Heaven series by Olly Wicken as well as the *YBR!* and *Watford Treasury* magazines.

More generally, I have also benefitted greatly from: *Forever England* by Beryl Bainbridge; *John Barnes: The Autobiography* and *The Uncomfortable Truth about Racism* by John Barnes; *The Telegraph Complete History of British Football* by Norman Barrett; *When the Lights Went Out* by Andy Beckett; *Elton: The Biography* by David Buckley; *Watford through Time* by John Cooper; *Granddad, What Was Football Like in the 1970s?* by Richard Crooks; *Captain Fantastic* by Tom Doyle; *Watford: A History* by Mary Forsyth; *England's Managers* by Brian Glanville; *Provided You Don't Kiss Me* by Duncan Hamilton; *When Footballers Were Skint* by Jon Henderson; *Out of His Skin* by Dave Hill; *The Seventies Revisited* by Kevin Keegan; *Me* by Elton John; *Music and Maiden Overs* by Vic Lewis; *Sir Elton* by Philip Norman; *Seasons in the Sun* and

*Who Dares Wins* by Dominic Sandbrook; *The Mavericks* by Rob Steen; *When England Called* and *Football Training Can Be Fun* by Graham Taylor; *Do I Not Like That!* by Geoff Tibballs and *Bertie Mee* by David Tossell.

# Photo Credits

1, Evening Standard/Getty; 2, Colorsport/Shutterstock; 3, 4, Michael Putland/Getty; 5, 6, 9, 11, 19, 25, 26, Alan Cozzi Archive/ Watford FC; 7, 15, PA Images/Alamy; 8, Mike Hollist/Shutterstock; 10, 12, 21, Bob Thomas Sports Photography/Getty; 13, 14, 28, Paul Popper/Getty; 16, 17, Andrew Cowie/Colorsport; 18, Cairns/Mirrorpix/Getty; 20, Keith Hailey/Getty; 22, Harry Prosser/Mirrorpix/Getty; 23, Std/Daily Express/Getty; 24, David Graves/Mirropix/Getty; 27, 29, Mirrorpix/Getty; 30, Huew Evans/Shutterstock; 31, Steve Bardens/Getty; 32, Matthew Impey/Shutterstock; 33, 34, Ben Gibson/Rocket Entertainment; 35, Michael Zemanek/Shutterstock.

# Index

*'EJ' in the index indicates Elton John.*

'Abide With Me' 249
AC Milan 239, 266
Adelphi Hotel 230–31
Advocate Lutheran General
          (hospital) 254
Albino Bob 26, 28
Aldershot 124
Amis, Martin 239
Armstrong, Gerry 177–8, 215, 226,
          265
Arran, Earl of 33, 167
Arsenal 114–15
Ashen, John 18–19
Aston Villa 254, 260
Astroturf pitches 201
Atkins, Martha 206
Atkinson, Ron 216
'Auf Wiedersehen Sweetheart'
          (Lynn) 203

Baileys (nightclub) 112–13
Baldry, Long John 37, 38
Ball, Alan 183, 213, 226, 228
Bangor 177
Bangs, Lester 171
Barnes, Colonel Kenneth 181–2
Barnes, John 215, 244
     comments and views
          EJ and Taylor partnership 269
          racist abuse 211
          Taylor's influence 268–9

England (football team) 268
Liverpool 268
racist abuse towards 210, 211, 256,
          268, 269
Sudbury Court 181
Watford
     confidence 212
     debut 210, 211
     matches
          Chelsea (A, 1981) 211
     signs as a professional 182
     wins cross-country run 182
Barrymore, Michael 249
Benskins Brewery 32, 215, 247
Best, George 54, 114–15
'Better Off Dead' (John) 105–6
*Beyond the Final Whistle: A Life of
          Football and Faith* (Boyers)
          266
Blackpool 137
Blissett, Luther 156, 187, 199, 233, 261
     Mee's praise for 141
     playing for England 239
     racist abuse 119, 139, 144, 145, 266
     skull fracture 266
     transfer to AC Milan 239
     Watford
          confidence 110–11
          EJ's parties 202
          ever-present for Watford 235
          fined for dissent 141

Blissett, Luther (*continued*)
    honorary life president 267
    joins 7
    matches
        Manchester United (A, 1978)
            141 142, 143, 144, 145
        Newcastle (H, 1978) 138–9
    meeting with Taylor 92
    potential 91–2
    rejoins 266–7
    reserves 91
Bluesology 36–7
Bolton, Ian 99, 156, 177, 187, 261
    EJ's appearance 110
    jobs
        car salesman 264
        industrial doors company 264
    slipped disc 152, 264
    spine operation 264
    treasured possessions 264–5
    visiting patients in hospital 168–9
    Watford
        ever-present for 235
        signs for 98
Bolton, Tina 264
Bolton Wanderers 219
Bonetti, Peter 'The Cat' 94
Boney M 159
Bonser, Jim 29, 30, 58, 61, 63
    sale of Watford 65
Bonser, Pat 31, 131
Booth, Dennis 143, 144, 168, 177
Boyers, Reverend John
    article in *Watford Observer* 125
    assistant Baptist minister 124
    feelgood factor in Watford 168
    Graham Taylor
        invited to training 126–7
        letter to 125

    meeting with 125–6
    offers chaplaincy services 125–6
    official chaplaincy position 127
    unofficial chaplaincy position
        126–7
    joins Manchester United 266
    leaves Watford 266
    meeting with Alan West 124
    meeting with Aldershot's
        chaplain 124
    message from God 125
    prays to God 124–5
Brentford 111, 137, 163
    Reep's analysis 163
Brighton and Hove Albion 265
Bristol Rovers 161–2
Brixton 210–11
Buford, Bill 206
Burkinshaw, Keith 232

Café Royal 74
Callaghan, Nigel 226, 241, 243, 270
    car stereo system 217
    DJing in Ibiza 270
    dropped from team 218
    ill-discipline 216, 217
    restored to team 219
    scores against Southampton 188–9
    staying with the Taylors 217
    talent 188, 216, 217
    'Teacher's Pet' 217
Cambridge United 242
'Candle in the Wind' (John) 106
*Captain Fantastic and the Brown Dirt
    Cowboy* (John) 105
Cassiobury Park 102
Challis, Paul and Karen 219
Challis, Terry 265
Channon, Mick 183

Charlesworth, Chris 45
Charlton, Bobby 54, 256
Charlton, Jack 213
Chelsea 31, 172–3, 209–10, 211
China 239
China (backing band) 105, 106
Clough, Brian 198, 200, 237, 247–8
Colchester United 153
Coventry City 196–7
Crawley Town 265
Croker, Laura 68
Cronkite, Walter 69
Cruyff, Johann 201
Crystal Palace 53, 54

*Daily Mirror* 145, 232
Daniels, Paul 225
Darlington 3, 4–5, 6–7
Davies, Taffy 'Welsh Wizard' 140
Dean, Elton 38
Death, Steve 101
Dee, Kiki 251
DER Rental Televisions 166
Derby County 215
'Don't Go Breaking My Heart'
        (Dee and John) 251
Dove, Heneage 46–7, 49
Downes, Bobby 143
Durrants School 221
Dwight, Edna (née Clough) 24, 25,
        150
Dwight, Reggie *see* John, Elton
Dwight, Roy (cousin of EJ)
        18, 19, 36
Dwight, Sheila (mother of EJ,
        later Farebrother)
        8, 26, 76, 160
    divorce and remarriage 24
    EJ's loneliness 148, 193

    marital strife 8, 16, 24
    record collection 17–18
    worries about EJ 193
Dwight, Stanley (father of EJ) ix, 8
    attending Anfield with EJ 231
    disapproval of EJ's ambitions
        25, 36
    divorce and remarriage 24, 25
    illness
        get-well card from EJ 150
        heart attacks/troubles 149–50,
            229, 230
        NHS operation 229
        rejects EJ's offer 229, 231
    job at Unilever 150
    lunch with EJ 229–31
    marital strife 8, 16, 24
    mood changes 10–11, 16
    musical skills 17
    silence and distance from EJ 50,
        66, 230–31
    takes EJ to Watford 8, 9–11

Edwards, C. F. 191
Elliott, Paul 245
Ellis, Sam 47–9, 98, 98–9, 104, 111,
        113, 265–6
*Elton John* (John) 44, 50
*Empty Sky* (John) 38–9
England (football team)
    European Championship (1980)
        205–6
    European Championship (1992)
        256
    World Cup (1994) 256–7
European Championships
    Italy (1980) 205–6
    Sweden (1992) 256
Everton 226, 244, 249, 269

FA Cup Final (1984) 247–52
  'Abide With Me' 249
  Royal Box 249
Fabergé eggs 108
Fairport Convention 44
Farebrother, Fred (stepfather of EJ) 24
  collection for EJ 27–8
  encourages EJ 25–6
  Portakabin 133
Farebrother, Sheila *see* Dwight,
    Sheila (mother of EJ, later
    Farebrother)
Fleet Street 213
football agents 237
football grounds
  facilities 134
  fencing 134, 207
  women 134
football hooliganism 5, 64, 134,
    205–7
  England fans rioting 205–6
*The Football Man* (Hopcraft) 22, 34
*Football Training Can Be Fun* (Taylor)
    102
Foreign Office 159
Francis, Trevor 237
Frost, David 4–5
Furnish, David 262

Gaelic football 177
Garland, Judy 108
George, Charlie 183, 187
Gillies, Caroline 207
Gillingham 141
Glanville, Brian 213–14, 255
Goldsmith, Harvey 159
*Goodbye Yellow Brick Road* (John) 60
Grand Union Canal 127
Gray, Andy 250, 251

Grimsby Town 20, 120
Grumbleweeds 113
Gurney, P. R. 58, 59
gym (Tottenham Court Road) 243

Harrison, David 104, 183–4, 184,
    184–5, 188, 190
Harrison, Steve 135, 145, 155
Harrowell, Jim 154
Hartley, Simon 165
'Heartbreak Hotel' (Presley) 17–18
'He'll Have To Go' (John's version)
    27, 160
Hilburn, Robert 51
Hill, George 26
Hillier, Roger 167
*In His Own Words* (Taylor) 93
Holiday Inn 176
Holland (football team) 256–7
Hollywood Bowl 60
homosexuality 119
'Honky Tonk Women' (John's
    version) 45
Hopcraft, Arthur 22, 34
Huddersfield Town 6, 55–6
Hull City 154, 156

*An Impossible Job* 257
inflation 64
Irwin, Colin 171
Isle of Wight 219

Jackett, Kenny 186–7, 199, 271
Jahr, Cliff 68–9
Jamaica
  Arsenal vs. Jamaican national
    team 181
  bobsleigh team 181
  football team 181

Jenkins, Evie 272–3
Jenkins, Mrs 221
Jenkins, Ross 111, 142, 144, 156, 186,
        187, 215, 219, 226
    background 53
    Brentford 54
    cash dispenser opening event 225
    change in behaviour 209
    comments and views
        bluntness of Taylor 238
        childhood dreams 189
        despair 55
        Graham Taylor 112
        Luther Blissett 138–9
        new beginning 56
        Southampton players'
            overconfidence 185
        Vicarage Road 55
        Watford's stagnation 201
    Costa Blanca 273
    critical point in career 94
    criticisms of 55, 93
    Crystal Palace 54
    double-glazing business 272
    football apprenticeship 54
    injuries 101, 197–8, 221, 238
    Michigan, USA 272
    non-football interests 94
    physique 93–4
    plain speaking 54, 200
    plaster cast 221–2
    praise from Oli Phillips 55, 137
    reinvigoration 211
    rejected by Arsenal 53–4
    rejects move to Huddersfield 55–6
    reminiscing 272–3
    retirement 273
    school teams 53
    skills 93

Taylor's funeral 263
wallpapering 199–200
Washington Diplomats
    loan 200–201
    return from loan 205
Watford
    ever-present for 235
    hat-trick vs. Nottingham
        Forest (H, 1980) 199
    instructions from Taylor 103–4
    objects to substitute decision
        183
    players' reunion 273
    returns to team 185, 209–10
    scoring against Southampton
        (A, 1980) 188
    signs for 53, 54–5
    standing up to Taylor 138
    transfer fee 53
    transfer listed 198, 200, 238,
        272
    wanting to impress Taylor 138
Watford fans
    disparaging comments from
        5–6, 55
    greeted by 137–8
    ignored by 137
    praise from 104
John, Elton
    albums see individual albums
    alcohol and cocaine 105, 108, 147,
        193, 194
        hospital treatment 254–5
        recovery 195, 255
        therapy treatment 255
    appearance 51, 60, 63, 100, 101, 105,
        110, 118, 146, 192
    audition 37
    bedroom sanctuary 16–17, 107

John, Elton (*continued*)
   Bernie Taupin 37, 38, 77, 192
   chairman of Watford
     anonymity opportunities
      174
     board meetings 128–9
     celebrating promotion to
      Division One 219–20
     European ambitions 78–9
     feeling of belonging 130
     fulfilling dream 85
     Royal Box at Wembley 249
     scouting 174
     sitting in directors' box 101
     sitting on managerial bench
      100, 101
     telephone broadcast of
      matches 149, 190,
      219, 244
   change of name 37
   comics 16–17
   comments and views
     attending matches 11
     bluntness of Taylor 97
     celebrating promotion
      219–20
     commitment 66–7
     conduct 146
     council opposition to new
      stadium 168
     dealing with homosexual
      abuse xii, 119, 120
     death of Taylor 262
     desire for affair 68–9
     disappointment to father 25
     entertainer ambitions 25
     faith in Taylor 173
     fantasy world 19
     father's mood changes 10–11

     at home at Watford 107
     magical feeling 36
     managerial credentials 70–71
     Manchester United directors
      146
     meeting with Watford
      board 62
     misses Taylor 254
     nervousness 51
     nervousness meeting
      Taylor 76
     ordinary people and normality
      107
     parents' arguments 16
     passion of footballers 10
     performing 27
     players' choking 251
     playing piano in public 27
     retirement 106
     rituals 67
     scouting at small clubs 174
     sense of shame 194–5
     smaller clubs 120
     songwriting ambitions 36
     in sync with Taylor 129
     Taylors' normal life 122
     Taylor's spending 129
     trust issues 107
     Watford's style of football
      232–3
   cousins as heroes 18–19
   diary entries 43
   dinners at the Taylors' 121–3
     cards 122–3
     happy times 123
     non-football discussions 122
     relaxed atmosphere 122
   exhaustion 147, 148
   fame 50

father
    attending Anfield with 231–2
    attending Watford with 8, 9–11,
       230
    disappointment to 25, 50, 230
    fear of 8, 24–5
    lunch at the Adelphi Hotel
       229–31
    notices mood changes of 10–11
    seeking approval from 229–30,
       231
    severance from 38
    silence and distance from 50,
       66, 230–31
flamboyance 51, 60
Fred (stepfather), support from
    25–6
friends 107
Graham Taylor
    chemistry between 132
    craves respect from 195
    criticized by 194–5
    deference to 109
    differences in lifestyles 108–9
    discussing players with 129–30,
       174
    embraces 234
    friendship 121–3
    interviewing and appointing
       75–9, 84–6
    offers new five-year contract
       173
    regular phone calls with 260–61
    seeks approval from 109
    speech for funeral 263
    trust 109
homes
    Northwood 24
    Pinner Hill Road 8

Windsor 75–6, 202
Woodside 107
illness 147
    get-well card from father 150
impressed by John Barnes 210
loneliness 107–8, 148, 192
material possessions 108
moods 105–6
mother
    buys car for 50
    fear of 8
music
    ambitions 36
    early prowess for 17
    escapism 27
    forms Bluesology 36–7
    passion for 18, 229
    Radio Luxembourg 19
    record collection 18
    Saturday-morning classes 24
passions
    football 11, 18, 61, 77, 229
    music 18, 229
performances 160
    Empire Pool Wembley 105–6
    first-night nerves 149
    Hollywood Bowl 60
    Leningrad 160
    Madison Square Garden 64, 65
    Northwood Hills Hotel 26–8,
       160
    Stockholm 148–9
    Troubadour 50–51
    Yorkshire Folk, Blues and Jazz
       Festival 44–5
personality
    confidence 50
    introversion 17
    shyness 9, 27

John, Elton (*continued*)
  pianist entertainer ambitions 25
  pre-season parties for Watford
    staff 202
  private helicopter 230
  private jet 60
  retirement 106
    reverses decision 148
  school 24, 36
  sexuality 38, 68–70, 108, 119
    abuse from fans 119
    abuse from Rotherham
      directors 121
    showbusiness and 148
  solitude 192–3
  songs *see individual songs*
  talking to footballers 129–30
  tours
    America 50–52
    Australia and New Zealand 60
    Europe 148–9
    Soviet Union 159–60
  warehouse job 36
  Watford
    ambition for 169–70
    appointed vice-chairman 63–4
    appointed vice-president 62–3
    attends without father 24
    cheerleading 110
    expenditure 254
    first match attended 8, 9–11
    heads consortium in takeover
      bid 259
    joining the board, ambition
      61–2
    joy of promotion (1978) 112
    match-day rituals 67
    match programmes 9, 11
    meeting with Bonser 62
  purchase of 65–6
  sale to Jack Petchey 254
  worldwide album sales 65
Johnston, Maurice 'Mo' 242–3, 248
Johnstone, Davey 105
Jordan, H. 172
Jordan, Joe 142
Joslyn, Roger 143, 156

Kaiserslautern 240–41
Katalinić, Ivan 185, 186, 187, 188,
  189
Keegan, Kevin 183, 185
Keen, Mike 3, 7, 55, 69–70
Kelly, Graham 254
Kent, Duchess of 251
King, Billie-Jean 147–8
Koeman, Ronald 257

Ladbroke Hotel 248
Last Night of the Proms 234–6
Law, Denis 54
Leicester City 152
Lennon, John 64, 196
Levski Spartak 241–2
Lewis, Vic 61
Liberty Talent Agency 37
Lincoln City 21, 34–5, 152
  attendances 42
  Division Four champions 49
  downturn 174
  *see also* Taylor, Graham
Lineker, Gary 255, 256, 260
Liverpool 116, 231–2, 234, 238
  fans 5
London Clinic 147, 150
*Los Angeles Times* 51
Luton Town 5, 124, 234, 244, 245
Lynn, Vera 203

Madison Square Garden 64, 65
Manchester City 233–4
Manchester United 140–41, 142–5,
    216, 233–4, 238
  directors 146
  fans 5, 145
  *see also* Old Trafford
Marshall, Joe 271
Mayes, Alan 111
McBain, Neil 29–30
McCracken, Bill 87
McGill, Ken 257
McIlvanney, Hugh 206
McMenemy, Lawrie 189–90, 226
McQueen, Gordon 144–5
Mee, Bertie 234
  appearance 114, 117
  Arsenal
    friendly vs. Jamaican national
      team 181
    manager 114
    physiotherapist 114, 115
    training regime 115
  death 271
  diplomacy 118
  discipline 114
  football philosophy 116–17
  Graham Taylor
    high-handed approach to 116
    meeting with 116, 117
    rejects loan request from
      115–16
    writes to 114
  John Barnes
    offers to supervise 181–2
    scouting mission 180–81
  military career 181
  protocol 180
  as a romantic 132

Royal Army Medical Corps 181
  scouting 174–5, 180–81
Watford
  assistant manager 117
  invites Plumley to Watford
    131
  meeting with Plumley 130–31
  retirement 271
  watches reserves at Coventry
    130
Mee, Doris 117, 234, 271
*Melody Maker* 44, 45, 171
Mercer, Keith 6, 58
Millichip, Bert 74–5
Mills Music 36
'Mockin' Bird Hill' 26
Moore, Bobby 70
Morgan, Alan 40
Moss Side 211
Motson, John 255, 263
Mundy, Mrs 83

*New Musical Express* 37, 44
Newcastle United 138–9
North East Autism Society 269
Northwood Hills Hotel 26–8, 36–7,
    160
Norway 226–7, 267
Nottingham Forest 198–200, 237

Old Trafford 140
  Directors' Lounge 140
  North Stand 142
  Stretford End 142
Oldham Athletic 209
Olsen, Egil 267
Orange Tree 26
Osborne, Gary 192
own goals 187

Palmer, Charlie 240
'Part Time Love' (John) 148
Partick Thistle 242
Patching, Martin 187
Pegg, Dave 44
Penfold, Gary 221–2
Petchey, Jack 254
Phillips, Oli
  call from Vic Lewis 61–2
  EJ's tears of joy 112
  Graham Taylor
    funeral 262–3
    interview with 103, 125
  Jim Bonser
    arranges meeting with EJ 62
    presents cheque to 63
  Sam Ellis 265–6
  Watford match reports
    Blackpool (H, 1978) 137
    Derby County (H, 1982) 215
    Levski Spartak (A, 1983) 241–2
    Southampton (A, 1980)
      187, 191
Pink Floyd 44
Pinner County Grammar School
  24, 36
  skiing holiday (1972) 57
Platt, David 257
Plumley, Eddie 130–31, 237, 239, 254
  appointed executive manager at
    Watford 132
  enormity of task 133
  Graham Taylor
    impressed by 131
    meeting with 131
    receives thanks from 248
  meeting prospective players 135–6
  meeting with Bertie Mee 130–31
  meetings with EJ 131–2

  observes chemistry between EJ
    and Taylor 132
  resignation from Coventry 132
  as a romantic 132
Plumley, Fran 131
Plymouth Argyll 244
Pollard, Brian 143, 144
Poole, Ian 141–2, 143, 145
Poskett, Malcolm 186, 189
Powell, Jeff 213
Pownall, Ron 68
Pravda 160
prefabricated houses 12
Presley, Elvis 17–18
Price, Neil 273
professional footballers
  agents 237
  apprenticeships 268
  house prices 176
  living in hotels 176
  money 253
  mortgage applications 176
  on strike 242
  transfer fees 237
  wages 237
property prices 176

race riots 210–11
racist abuse
  John Barnes 210, 211, 256, 268,
    269
  Luther Blissett 119, 139, 144, 145,
    266
Radio Luxembourg 19
Rankin, Andy 95–6, 142, 144–5, 152
Reading 100–101, 110
Record Retailer 43–4
Reep, Wing-Commander Charles
  232

death 267
Graham Taylor
 letter to 161, 164
 meeting with 164–5
 research for 165
outsider 267
research, friend's gambling
 winnings on 165
statistical adviser
 Brentford 163
 Sheffield Wednesday 164
 Wolves 163
statistical analysis 161–3, 267
Reid, John 52, 61, 66, 106, 251
Reilly, George 242, 244, 251
Revie, Don 71, 72
Rice, Pat 177
Richard, Cliff 159
Richardson, Ian 240
Rigby Taylor, T. 29
Robertson, John 198–9
Rochdale 174
Roche, Paddy 143, 144
Rocket Records 68
Rolling Stone 68, 69, 119
Rollitt, Ron 84
Rostron, Wilf 176, 186, 207, 241, 245,
 269
Rotherham United 120–21
Rous, Sir Stanley 189
Royal Academy of Music 24
Royal Statistical Society 163
Royal Variety Club 105
Russian Ministry of Culture 159

Scunthorpe Evening Telegraph
 12, 13, 112
Scunthorpe Grammar School 13, 14
Scunthorpe Star 13

Scunthorpe United 12–13, 112
Sexton, Dave 140
Shankly, Bill 116, 246
Sharp, Graeme 250, 251
Sheffield Wednesday 47, 154, 164
Sherwood, Steve
 change in fortunes of 209
 ever-present for Watford 235
 FA Cup Final (1984) 248, 249–51
  memory of goal conceded 251
 nerves 249, 251
 financial adviser 272
 Graham Taylor
  first meeting 89–90
  guard of honour for 261
  influence of 272
 injuries 247, 272
 joins Grimsby Town 272
 lack of sleep 240
 matches
  Coventry (H, 1980) 196–7
 personality and character 196
 substitutes' bench 179, 196
 training 95–6
 turning point 197
Shilton, Peter 237
Shrewsbury Town 153–4
Shrodells Hospital 149
Simmons, Les 93, 266
Sims, Steve 152–3, 185–6, 187, 189,
 198, 241, 270
A Single Man (John) 148, 159, 264
Sochaux 154–5
'Song For Guy' (John) 148
'Sorry Seems To Be The Hardest
 Word' (John) 148
Southampton 183–91, 226, 244
Sparta Prague 243
Speke Airport 230

Sports Chaplaincy UK 266
sports science 243
St James Road Baptist Church 124
St Mary's (church) 262
Stamford Bridge 172
Stapleton's Tyre Depot 166
Starr, Freddie 249
Steele, Eric 196
*Steptoe and Son* 38
Stewart, Rod 63
Stockport County 103–4, 110
Stratford, Muir 64, 71, 128
Studio 54 170–71
Sudbury Court 180
    compensation 182
    John Barnes 180–82
Swarbrick, Dave 44–5
Sweden (football team) 256
Swindon Town 161–2

Taupin, Bernard 37, 38, 77, 192
Taylor, Dorothy 12
Taylor, Graham
    ambition 14–15
    Aston Villa
        appointed manager 253
        fan's fury 260
        promotion to Division One
            254
        resignation 260
        returns as manager 260
    attending Scunthorpe fixtures
        12–13
    attitude to homosexuality 119, 120
        Rotherham incident 121
    Bertie Mee
        appoints as assistant manager 117
        establishes authority over 117
        letter from 114
        meeting 116, 117
        shared beliefs with 116–17
    birthdays
        Last Night of the Proms 234–6
        present from EJ 202–3
        signed Vera Lynn album 203
    buys house in Watford 97–8
    caravanning holidays 73–4, 114,
        134, 161
    Charles Reep
        dossier 164
        letter from 161
        meeting with 164–5
    coaching
        common purpose 22
        FA qualifications 21
        learning lessons 21–2
        reads *The Football Man* 22
    comments and views
        anger at referee 245
        announces FA Cup Final team
            246
        background research on
            players 176
        calming influence of Mee 117
        criticisms of England job 257
        difference between supporters
            and fans 34–5
        disappointment at FA Cup
            Final defeat 251–2
        Division Four players 95
        eavesdropping 175
        EJ's cheerleading 110
        fines 41
        football for the
            supporters 261
        football supporters 34–5
        footballers and local
            community 34, 77

freedom (programme notes) 233

homosexual abuse 120

identifying players' strengths and weaknesses 88

injury crisis 242

losing Luther Blissett 240

manners and etiquette 116

message to Lincoln supporters 40

milking a pig 46

personality of Mee 117

players' anxiety 172–3

players' wages 129

praising players 21

reminiscing 123

revisiting Watford 253–4

self-confidence of players 111–12

signing players 129

style of football 232–3

talking football with EJ 123

watching World Cup (1994) 258

Watford supporters 261–2

dealing with criticism 214, 257

death 262–3

depression 258

diary entries 87, 89, 92–3, 97

distraction tactics 154–6

EJ

attitude to homosexuality 119, 121

brotherly feelings towards 195

chemistry with 132

concerns about 193–4

criticizes and threatens to leave 194–5

declines managerial offer 73

embraces 234

impressed by 73

meetings with 75–9, 84–5

receives gold discs from 159

regular phone calls with 73, 260–61

England (football team)

allows cameras and microphone 256

appointed manager 254, 255

bullishness 255–6

criticisms of appointment 255

criticisms of performances 256

criticisms of tactics 256

European Championship (1992) 256

mockery 257

promising start 255–6

sacking 257

scarring 257–8

World Cup (1994) 256–7

football commentary career 260

funeral 262–3

Grimsby Town

apprenticeship 20

captain 20

debut 20

shocked by players' behaviour 20

special training session 20–21

wages 21

homes

Mandeville Close 97, 113, 121–2, 202–3

Scunthorpe 12

interest from WBA 74–5

interview with Oli Phillips 103

John Barnes, impressed by 210

Lincoln City (manager)

appointment 35

bet with Dove 46–7, 49

Taylor, Graham (*continued*)
    disciplinarian 41
    dreadful mistake 40–41
    fans' call for sacking 42
    fines 41
    initial team talk 35
    interview with directors 34–5
    losing run 40–41
    meeting with Dove 46
    methods 41
    purple patch 46
    requests loan of Arsenal player
        115–16
    requests loan of Liverpool
        player 116
    signing uglies 47, 98, 177
    stress 42
    success 49
    tactics 41
    training 42
    visits Sam Ellis at home
        48–9
  Lincoln City (player) 40
    captain 21
    injury 21, 22–3
    transfer from Grimsby 21
  man-management skills
    186–7
  meetings with
    Bert Millichip 74–5
    Muir Stratford 64
  musical tastes 72–3
  non-football interests 122
  opposed to barriers at Vicarage
    Road 207
  parents
    influence on 13
    pride of father's match reports
        13, 112

  personality and character 13–14
    chatterbox reputation 175
    temper 13, 122–3, 143, 203
  recommendation from taxi driver
    180
  recommendations for Watford
    post 71, 72–3
  Rita
    dating 13–14
    marriage 20
  school 13, 14–15
  Shakespeare play 245
  telephone call from Revie 72–3
  watches World Cup (1994) 258
  Watford 88
    announces team for FA Cup
        Final 246
    assessment of facilities 87–8,
        92–3
    assessment of playing staff 84
    celebrating promotion to
        Division One 219–20
    collecting and studying
        statistics 102, 165, 232
    disguises 174–5
    fact-finding visit 84
    feelings of guilt 173–4
    lingering doubts 179
    list of staff 88
    losing mentality of team 89
    motivational talk 110
    party 113
    physio room 96–7
    players
      angry with 173, 184
      background research on 89,
        176
      fines 113
      ignoring injured players 198

imparting self-confidence in 111–12

interviewing 89–92, 94

letters to players 88

new signings 177–9

off-field rules 95

on-field rules 95

pre-match talk 185

transfers 98–9

programme notes 184

reappointed manager 259

resignation 253

resignation threat 173

retirement 260

returns for ceremony 261

scouting at small clubs 174, 175–6

sharing bench with EJ 100, 101

signs contract 85–6

spending restraints 129

supporters

apology to 218

learning from 175

meeting and engaging with 169

replying to letters 169

tactics 99, 141, 214

£10 note picture frame 253

training regime 95–6, 101–2, 111, 127, 151, 227, 243

troubled thoughts 151–3

videos of matches 164

visits pub landlords 88

watching play behind the goal 175

Wolverhampton Wanderers

appointed manager 258

resignation 259

Taylor, Joanne 97–8, 141

Taylor, Karen 141

Taylor, Les 233

Taylor, Rita (née Cowling) 141, 193, 235, 236, 257–8

dinner at Café Royal 74–5

Graham

admires confidence of 14

dating 13–14

marriage 20

Graham's interview with EJ 78

invites EJ to dinner 121–2

personality 14

Shakespeare play 245

telephone call from Revie 72

Taylor, Tom 12–13

Thatcher, Margaret 205

*The Tiger* 16–17, 19

*The Times* 242

Tottenham Hotspur 232

Toxteth 211

Train, Ray 186, 188

transfer fees 237

Triple A beer 32

Troubadour 50–51

Twyndle, Jack 83

*The Uncomfortable Truth About Racism* (Barnes) 269

unemployment 64

Unilever 150

US football (soccer) league 200–201

Vancouver Whitecaps 135

Venables, Terry 213

Verna, R. K. 70

Vicarage Road
  changing room 103
  community spirit 235
  comparison to other grounds 235,
      239
  disrepair, state of 9–10, 55, 74
  EJ concert 63
  electronic scoreboard 133–4
  Elton John Stand 262
  engineers and safety 133
  falling attendances 215, 216, 218
  family enclosure
    adults with children 208
    birthday presents for children
        208
    code of conduct 207–8
    introduction 207
    presents for children 208
    seats named after
        children 208
    success 208, 215
  food provision 140
  football hooliganism 206–7
  full-time maintenance
        man 103
  funding for repairs 63
  Graham Taylor Stand 261
  greyhound track 31, 58, 96–7
  improvements 215–16
  The Kremlin 31, 64, 67, 84–5, 117
  Ladies Room 31, 131
  Portakabin 133
  relocation, opposition to 168
  Rookery End ('The Bend') 9
  Rookery Stand 259
  Shrodells Stand 259
  Sir Stanley Rous Stand 259, 261
  uncovered manager's bench
      216

Vicarage Road stand 259
Victim of Love (John) 170–71
Village Voice 171
Vince, Mike 149, 190, 244

wages, footballers' 237
Walker, Graham 211
Walley, Tom 90–91, 186, 188, 239,
      267–8
Ward, John 199, 241
Washington Diplomats 200–201
Watford fans 6
  affection for Graham Taylor 261,
      263
  attendances
    returning 111
    staying away 111, 215, 216, 218
  blackberrying 31
  celebration at Baileys 112–13
  displeasure 172
  FA Cup Final (1984)
    applause for Everton 251
    support for team 249
  hooligan problem 5
  matches
    Darlington (A, 1975)
        3, 4–5, 6
    Manchester United (A, 1978)
        142–5
    Southampton (A, 1980) 183–4
    Stockport (A, 1977) 104
  optimism of 4, 104
  pessimism of 59
  plastic horns vs. Kaiserslautern 240
  resignation of 4
  revolt against Bonser 58
Watford Football Club
  attendances 10
  board meetings 128–9

broadcasting of matches
  Shrodells Hospital 149
  telephone line to EJ 149, 190,
    219, 244
European qualification (1983) 237
FA Cup
  Chelsea (SF, 1970) 31
  Luton (A, 1984) 244
  Luton (H, 1984) 244
  Manchester United (H, 1950)
    140
  Manchester United (H, 1982)
    215–16
  Plymouth (SF, 1984) 244
  West Ham (H, 1982) 217
FA Cup Final vs. Everton (1984)
    247–52
  coach journey 249
  defeat 251–2
  EJ rejects request for cup song
    247
  embroidered team shirts for
    staff 249
  party at Reid's house 251
  quiet location for squad 248
  Sherwood injury 247–8
  tickets 247
  TV coverage 248, 249
financial problems 31, 58
football ground see Vicarage
    Road
friendlies
  Sochaux (1979) 154–5
  Weymouth (1975) 3
leading scorer transfer listed 31
League Cup
  Coventry (H, 1980) 196–7
  Manchester United (A, 1978)
    140–41, 142–5

Newcastle (H, 1978) 138–9
Nottingham Forest (H, 1980)
    198–200
Reading (H, 1977) 100–101
Southampton (A, 1980) 183–91
message from the Chairman
    (programme) 169–70
meteoric rise 235–6
Minority Shareholders
    Association 58
new badge 133
1950s culture 31
1958/59 (Division Four) 29–30
1960s and early 1970s history 30
1975/76 (Division Four)
  Darlington (A) 3, 4–5, 6–7
  early defeats 3–4
  pre-season training 3
1977/78 (Division Four)
  champions 112
  consecutive victories 110
  matches
    Brentford (A) 111
    Reading (A) 110
    Scunthorpe (A) 112
    Stockport (A) 103–4, 110
    York City (H) 110
  winning streak 112
1978/79 (Division Three)
  matches
    Blackpool (H) 137
    Brentford (H) 137
    Colchester United (H) 153
    Gillingham (A) 141
    Hull (H) 154, 156
    Rotherham (A) 120–21
    Sheffield Wednesday (A) 154
    Shrewsbury Town (A) 153–4
  self-doubt 151–3

Watford Football Club (*continued*)
  1979/80 (Division Two)
    Chelsea (A) 172–3
    predictability of performances
      173
    results 172–3
    Taylor's public broadside 173
  1980/81 (Division Two)
    stagnation 201
  1981/82 (Division Two)
    matches
      Bolton (H) 218
      Chelsea (A) 209–10, 211
      Derby (H) 215
      Oldham (A) 209
      Wrexham (H) 219
    winning runs 214–15
  1982/83 (Division One)
    fish and chips in boardroom
      237
    fitness 227
    matches
      Everton (H) 226
      Liverpool (A) 231–2
      Liverpool (H) 237
      Southampton (A) 226
      Tottenham (A) 232
      West Brom (H) 233
    new signings 227–8
    public announcement
      233–4
    silencing of critics 238
    success 238
    top of the table 234
    tour to China 239
  1983/84 (Division One)
    injury crisis 240, 242
    Luton (A) 245
    new signings 242
  players mingling with local
    community 168–9
  promotions
    Division One 219–20
    Division Two 4, 156
    Division Three 30, 112
  Premier League 259
  reducing travelling expenses 7
  relegations
    Division Two 4
    Division Three 3, 4, 29, 63
  'rocketmen' 253
  scouting 87, 92
  signing of Ross Jenkins 53, 54–5
  staff resignations 4
  style of football
    criticisms of 213–14, 226, 232
    'hit and hope' 213
    'kick and rush' 214
    'proper football' taunt 226
    support for 213
    Taylor's defence of 214, 232
    'wholesalers' 232
  training facilities 87–8, 93
  training kit 88, 92
  transformation 235
  trips
    Isle of Wight 219
    Norway 226–7
  UEFA Cup (1983/84)
    Kaiserslautern 240–41
    Levski Spartak 241–2
    Sparta Prague 243
  Under-15 team 268
  *Z Cars* theme music 30
  *see also* Taylor, Graham
Watford Football Club Supporters
  Club 31
  repairs to tea bar 205

Watford Football Supporters Club
30–31
Watford Hospital Radio 219, 244
Watford Mercury Motor Hotel 32
*Watford Observer* 55, 58, 112, 124,
147
collapse of EJ 147
destruction of historic buildings
in Watford 32
friendliness of Watford 225
letter from Mr Verna 70
medieval merchants' houses 166
overexcited Watford fans 156
redevelopment in Watford 83
Ross Jenkins 205, 225
Taylor's announcement 169
vandalism in Watford 225
Watford town 83
*see also* Phillips, Oli
Watford (town)
civic enthusiasm 167
decline 32
destruction of historic buildings
32–3
estate agents 167
exhibitions 167
FA Cup Final (1984) celebration
247
friendliness 225

lack of facilities 32
'laughing stock' 167
'a living hell' 33, 167
medieval merchants' houses 166
pride 235
printing industry 32
unemployment 167
untidy and dirty reputation 83
vandalism 225
Wembley Stadium 249
West, Alan 124
West Bromwich Albion 74–5, 232
West Ham 217
fans 205
Weymouth 3
White Hart Lane 206
Wilkins, Ray 216
Williams, Ray 37
Wolverhampton Wanderers 163,
258, 259
Workington AFC 75, 120
World Cup (1994) 256–7
Wrexham 219
Wright, Billy 213

York City 110, 120
Yorkshire Folk, Blues and Jazz
Festival (1970) 44–5
'Your Song' (John) 43